Nick Thorpe was born in 1970, and studied English at Oxford University. An award-winning journalist and travel writer, he began his career as a reporter on the *Edinburgh Evening News* and the *Scotsman*, and has since worked for a range of media including the *Guardian, Independent, Daily Telegraph, The Times, Sunday Times, Scotland on Sunday,* and the BBC World Service. His travels have taken in such destinations as El Salvador, Zanzibar, Oman and the wilds of Drumcree, with assignments ranging from Russian presidential elections to the coca wars in Bolivia, for which he was shortlisted for the Martha Gellhorn Prize for Journalism. In 2001 he won the Travel Story of the Year Award from the Foreign Press Association, and a Travelex Travel Writer's Award. He was previously BT Scotland Feature Writer of the Year. *Eight Men and a Duck* is his first book. He lives in Edinburgh with his wife Ali.

Eight Men
and a Duck

*An Improbable Voyage
by Reed Boat to Easter Island*

NICK THORPE

LITTLE, BROWN

A *Little, Brown* Book

First published in Great Britain in 2002 as a paperback original by Little, Brown

Copyright © Nick Thorpe, 2002

The moral right of the author has been asserted.

A CIP catalogue record for this book is available
from the British Library.

ISBN 0 316 85801 3

Typeset in Centaur by M Rules
Printed and bound in Great Britain by
Clays Ltd, St Ives plc

Little, Brown
An imprint of
Time Warner Books UK
Brettenham House
Lancaster Place
London WC2E 7EN

www.TimeWarnerBooks.co.uk

For Ali

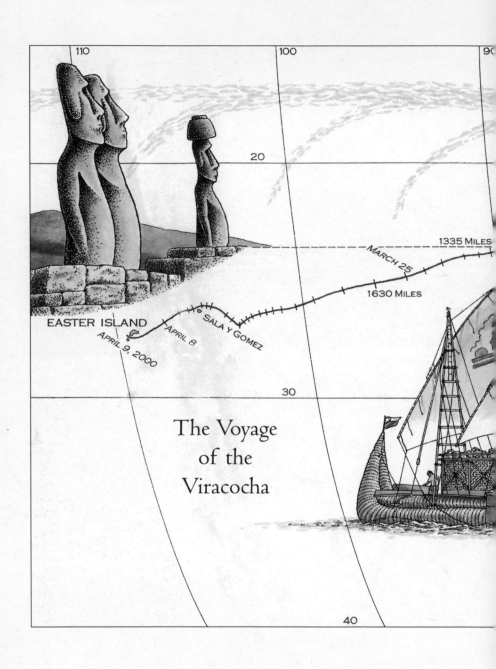

110
100
90

20

1335 MILES
MARCH 25
1630 MILES

EASTER ISLAND
SALA Y GOMEZ
APRIL 8
APRIL 9, 2000

30

The Voyage
of the
Viracocha

40

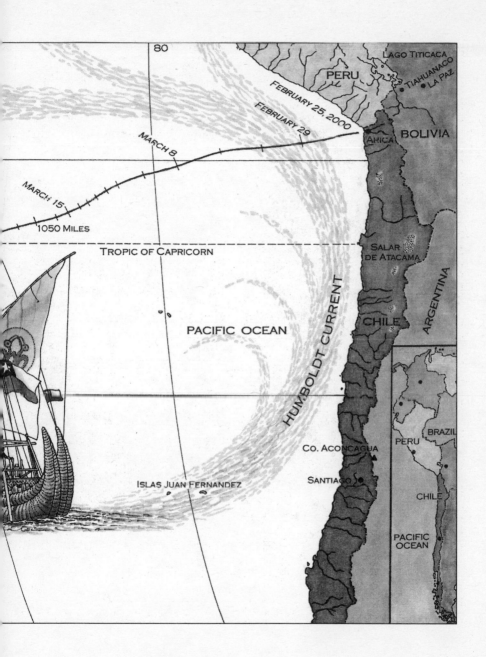

80

Lago Titicaca

PERU

FEBRUARY 25, 2000

FEBRUARY 29

TIAHUANACO
LA PAZ

ARICA

BOLIVIA

MARCH 8

MARCH 15

1050 MILES

TROPIC OF CAPRICORN

SALAR
DE ATACAMA

ARGENTINA

PACIFIC OCEAN

CHILE

HUMBOLDT CURRENT

Co. ACONCAGUA

ISLAS JUAN FERNANDEZ

SANTIAGO

BRAZIL

PERU

CHILE

PACIFIC
OCEAN

Contents

Journey from a land-locked country: how the Viracocha reached the ocean.

Prologue

Can I Borrow Your Safety Harness?

I woke in the darkness, groggy yet anxious, to a sound I couldn't place. The usual cacophony of the bamboo cabin, flexing and creaking like a rabble of ancient rocking chairs, had ceased. Instead came a kind of muffled roaring.

Holding back a swill of fear, I groped for the few familiar reference points: the rounded bamboo roof beams; my spectacles hanging from a string; my life-jacket used as a pillow; my harness hanging at the end of my bunk. Good: all there. It was 1.30 a.m. I lay there feeling the shift of my body against the safety rope, waiting to remember.

The noise was constant like radio static, yet swelling too, all around me, as if I were inside it. Familiar yet . . .

Something snatched at the canvas flap of the cabin door, flung it wetly open.

Rain. Torrential rain. A wall of rain so dense that the head which appeared, sleek and seal-like in the magnesium glare of a hurricane lamp, seemed to be suspended behind the glazed panel of an aquarium.

'Everybody up! We have an emergency!' shouted Phil, spitting raindrops into the cabin. Our captain sounded different, his voice stretched tauter than usual. At the other end of the cabin, Marco's buzz-saw snoring had conspicuously ceased. None of us spoke as we pulled on waterproofs. Was this . . . *it*? I wriggled into my harness, checked its built-in strobe rescue light, fastened my life-jacket, and stepped outside.

The *Viracocha* was a mess. Both her sails were blown taut against the wrong side of the masts, hollowed out and hugging the shrouds and spars like skin across the ribs of a carcass. We were sliding sideways before the wind, two wooden leeboards hanging splintered in the water at a strange angle. The bundled reed hull rode the swell uncertainly, and the windward foot of the A-shaped foremast was lifting six inches from its rope binding at every wave. A strong gust might topple it.

'The wind just changed again,' shouted Phil, straining vainly on a rope pulled tight as a crowbar. 'We need to haul the sails round the mast or pull them down completely before it gets any worse.'

Peering out into the darkness I could make out only the glittering curtains of falling rain, the outer circumference of the pool of light around our hurricane lamp. The wind had swung round to a northeasterly, the waves fractious, confused, jostling up against each other, occasionally spraying upwards over the plump gunwales. Even with the wind on our side and all eight of us pulling, we had never yet managed to change the complex sails in less than half an hour. Now we had to pull against the full force of the wind, in a storm, in the middle of the night.

'Are you sure it wouldn't be safer to wait till morning?' I asked Phil, trying to sound thoughtful rather than terrified.

'Maybe. But if the wind strengthens any more it'll be too late to do anything. Except maybe cut the sails off to save the mast.' He looked haggard. 'It's a tough call.'

Another fear gnawed, unspoken. Somewhere ahead of us lay a rocky island with a submerged reef. In our 2500-mile voyage from northern Chile to Easter Island, the uninhabited territory of Sala y Gómez was to have been our first and last Pacific landing before our destination. Now we needed to avoid it at all costs.

I wiped my rain-mottled spectacles and looked around at my crewmates. Lined up in differently coloured raingear, Marco, Jorge and Greg looked like damp garden gnomes. Marco grinned nervously and began drumming on the lid of a water vat, steeling us for a decision. As Phil's Chilean brother-in-law, he often assumed the role of right-hand man, though his only prior maritime experience was a summer spent towing tourists round a beach resort on a large inflatable banana. Carlos, on his own atop the rickety bamboo steering platform at the back of the boat, was yelling something that sounded like 'What course?' as he struggled to control rudder shafts the size of telegraph poles. Phil appeared not to hear him, as he craned his neck up into the torrent, scrutinising the reversed sails as if looking for operating instructions.

I clambered sodden and squelching astern in search of Erik, our Bolivian Aymara boatbuilder and the man to whom I often turned when I was having difficulty remembering what the hell I was doing on a bundle of reeds in the middle of the Pacific.

I found him hanging off the windward side of the boat, up to his waist in the boiling seas, struggling to pull a broken leeboard up before we lost it altogether. As I edged along the side of the boat to help him, sheet lightning flashed soundlessly around us, briefly illuminating a wilderness of angry, rain-pocked water.

'*No es bueno* – not good,' murmured Erik, with characteristic understatement. He threw a sodden rope up to me and together we pulled out the leeboard. The upper layers of *totora* reeds were for the first time beginning to feel spongy underfoot. 'The boat's already sunk a foot lower than it was when we left Arica,' he said gravely, plastering his black hair across his forehead. 'But now the rain will soak the reeds from above as well as below. If it buckets down like this for much longer we may be too low in the water to continue.'

Meaning what exactly? We would sink? I looked at the water line, now barely two feet from the deck, and decided not to enquire any further.

Through the flimsy woven bamboo of the cabin walls, Marco's voice was clearly audible, radioing urgently for a weather report on the VHF. '*Viracocha* calling all shipping. Do you copy?' Nobody did. We had had no radio contact for days.

The only other source of weather information, a Trimble Navigation system with satellite link, had never actually worked in the first place. Its egg-shaped aerial hung pointlessly upside down from the crossbar of the steering platform, a monument to our technical ineptitude. Whatever weather lay ahead of us, we weren't going to know about it until we sailed into it.

As we edged our way back along the side planking towards the foredeck, I clipped my harness onto the safety line. Ever since we had left Chile's northernmost port of Arica a month earlier, a single nightmare had haunted me. I knew it like an old enemy, could reach into my mind for it and feel its familiar shape like a cold pebble in a coat pocket. It was always the same:

Alone on night watch, I lose my footing and tumble into dark waters. I surface coughing and mute with shock to find the rounded stern of the boat already 10 metres away, out of reach and retreating by the second, my shipmates asleep. I scramble to locate the safety buoy, trailing on 30 metres of nylon rope. Too late I see its tiny wake, rippling past, moving quickly. I thrash out for it, catch it momentarily in my palm like a rugby ball, and then a surge tugs it from my grasp. I swim in abject panic to catch up, gasping and swallowing water, but my clothes hold me back and it retreats into the darkness before me. And then, after my yelling, my cracked and feeble cries, the silence in response, comes a strange icy calm, a terrible, rational weighing up of my situation as the ocean gently tugs at my boots.

Even if someone saw me fall, the ship will be a mile away by the time they get the sails down. And if nobody saw me, it could be dawn — 30 miles of sailing — before anyone notices my absence. I am alone on this black ocean, 1000 miles from land in any direction, and 3 miles of unknown beneath me. Nobody will ever find me.

I pull down on my life jacket to relieve the growing tension under my arms, and in doing so remember my one last hope of rescue. The strobe safety light on my harness. I am fumbling with it when something makes me stop. If I switch it on, I raise the stakes, perhaps speed my own death. Even if my crewmates use it to home in on me, so too will other, more predatory life forms in the infinite waters below me, attracted by the light. And that is the decision that leaves my nightmare jammed and flickering. Which is it to be? A long, slow draining of hope, a death from thirst or worse, with nothing to guide a rescuer? Or the Russian roulette of my strobe light, every second promising either a cry of a friend from the darkness or the shock of a shark's razored teeth closing around my legs . . .

I shivered and wrenched myself back to the present. The rain on my hood sounded like ripping fabric, and a thin stream of water was trickling down my spine.

Whatever happens I'll stay with the boat. As long as I clip onto the safety line.

Stephane appeared, grinning and wet, swinging round a mast stay. 'Excellent!' he shouted, yelping happily at the rain. 'Now we see how this boat *really* performs!'

This was typical of Stephane. If I was the ship's Woody Allen, neurotically rehearsing the risks, he was its stunt-driving James Dean, always ready to leap before he looked. As for a harness, he would sooner be seen wearing women's underwear. Only four of us had brought professional harnesses in any case, but he had constantly brushed off suggestions that he splice his own makeshift one from spare rope. 'I feel more alive without one!' he told me early in the trip, hanging from the masthead with one arm while trying to thread a shackle. The day Stephane resorted to wearing a harness, ran the joke, we would know we were *really* screwed. What would it take? A typhoon?

Phil, an experienced mountaineer but a novice captain, had an altogether more complicated approach to risk. Standing tired and drenched on the foredeck now after a solid five hours on watch, he was still weighing up the danger to his crew of manhandling two heavy sails in pitch darkness with no safety equipment.

'We'll change the sails at first light,' he pronounced finally. 'It's too dangerous to attempt at night, in case someone goes overboard. As long as the wind doesn't get any stronger, we can afford to drift for a while. I've got to get some sleep. Keep an eye on the GPS and wake me if there are problems.'

I swung myself wetly up to the steering platform to help Carlos. 'Hey Neeky!' wailed the Chilean, his curly beard dangling like a wet mop as he struggled with the huge tiller. 'I can't hold the course! What is happening to us?'

'Everything's OK,' I lied. 'Just let her go with the wind for now.'

We stood in silence together, watching the compass swing, grunting as the twin tillers nudged us in the chest like truculent oxen. Hours merged. Occasionally I checked the small handheld GPS in the cabin, the satellite-linked Global Positioning System. We were still 20 miles from Sala y Gómez, but closing at about 3 knots on a course which should take us a few miles to the north of the island . . . give or take a few miles. The rain eased to a drizzle and the wind seemed to relent, with sheet lightning still flickering sporadically.

At about 6 a.m. I tried to snatch some sleep, contorting my body into an S shape to avoid various drips now coming through the ceiling. Maybe we had seen the worst of it.

What woke me, an hour and a half later, was the sensation of being thrown against the side of my bunk. I swung myself down to the cabin floor only to find it awash with water spattering through the roof in dozens of places. The boat tipped and lurched again, pitching me against Phil's bunk.

'Holy shit, what was that?' groaned the captain. We listened, hanging on to any available upright. The roaring of torrential rain was back again, but accompanied this time by a new noise, the noise no sailor wants to hear: the rising moan of a gale in the shrouds.

'We're going to lose the sails,' muttered Phil. 'Everybody out on deck!' A wave broke heavily on the side of the boat and the GPS tumbled to the floor. I cursed as I was thrown against the bunk again and felt the rising of fear and anger in my stomach. I thought suddenly of my wife Ali, my family, and experienced an odd pang of guilt, guilt that I might be about to leave them for this foolishness. *Man dies on floating haystack.* What kind of legacy was that?

I pulled aside the canvas door flap and stepped into horizontal rain. In a malign grey half light, enormous waves were rolling in from the south, their whitish windblown peaks level with the cabin roof before they heaved our pitching bulk aloft, giving brief glimpses of deep valleys of water striped with trails of white foam. Rain and swirling clouds cut off the view after 20 metres. Up aloft, the eucalyptus yardarms were bowed in huge arcs round the masts, the taut sails quivering under the strain. It was a miracle they had not already been torn off. We were sailing into the centre of the storm only miles from dangerous rocks. Could the omens get any worse?

A moment later they did. Stephane staggered through the doorway and grabbed my shoulder. 'I'm going up the mast to try and free the sails,' he said, avoiding my gaze. 'Can I borrow your safety harness?'

1

The Bus of Destiny

The day Stephane Guerin materialised like an unshaven ghost from the exhaust fumes and clambered on to my bus, I had no reason to expect that he would alter my life. Four months on Bolivian public transport had taught me not to expect anything very much, and certainly not from a backpacker.

I could tell he was a backpacker, though he had done his best to disguise it. He had a natural tan, studied casualness, filterless Bolivian cigarette dangling listlessly from the corner of his mouth. The usual gargantuan rucksack had been craftily replaced by an anonymous-looking shoulder bag, and his Spanish even extended to local slang, I noticed, as he greeted a passenger. He could almost have passed as a Latino, had he not ruined it all with his striped llama-wool jumper of the authentic home-knitted type only ever worn by tourists.

Like me, he was also permanently handicapped by being well over six feet tall — a good foot taller than most Bolivians. An Australian couple were already muttering in discomfort a few cramped seats in front of me, their legs folded up level with their shoulders like huge grasshoppers.

'No legroom left I'm afraid,' I grinned, as his eyes flicked up and down the crowded bus, and met mine. Despite arriving early I had failed to bag the one good seat near the door, and was now wedged in behind an Aymara woman and her enormous multicoloured bundle. I was damned if this interloper thought he was going to recline comfortably all the way to Lake Titicaca.

He registered my presence with a smile, waved his smouldering cigarette between two fingers and said: 'OK brother . . .' Then, to my outrage, he got off the bus, strolled up to its front door, and clambered brazenly into the spacious seat next to the driver, whom he greeted like an old friend. As he spread out his long legs under the dashboard, he turned briefly and winked at me.

Utter *bastard*.

I turned rigidly to the window, ripped off a piece of yellowing sticky tape that seemed to be holding it shut, and gazed out, defeated. We were still sitting outside La Paz municipal cemetery, point of departure for disembodied souls and, apparently, buses to Copacabana. Teenage alcoholics with bloated faces were drinking something from plastic bags, their eyes dull and empty, heading for makeshift shelters among the tombstones. Aymara women hawked coca leaves from giant bundles, chewing slowly, and the taxi drivers read the tabloids through the bluish haze of their idling engines. The smell of stale urine lingered, mingling with rotten fruit.

I've been here too long, I thought.

I had arrived with my wife Ali in Southern Chile nearly eight months previously on a year-long travel-writing contract with the *Scotsman* newspaper. We had intended, a little naively, to backpack all the way up the Americas to Alaska, passing through eighteen countries. So far we'd managed three.

This had been a slow-moving weekend, even by Bolivian standards. I had only meant to be in La Paz long enough to email an article home, leaving Ali to take photos in Copacabana for the day. But I had found myself stranded in the capital overnight by a municipal election. Such is the enthusiasm for local democracy in Bolivia, that the only way to persuade anyone to bother voting is to ban all transport and trading on polling day, thus making it almost impossible to do anything else.

So I had spent polling day walking the empty streets, killing time. I had watched a solitary child skateboard down the deserted main city thoroughfare, then wandered to the only café that was open and found it packed full of fleece-jacketed British backpackers sipping cappuccino. I might as well be in Hampstead, I thought, blankly.

I was escaping to phone Ali when a notice in the entrance hall caught my eye. It advertised a 'Ritual Moondance' on a nearby mountain. Perhaps here, at last, was something authentically Bolivian which might make a good article. I decided to enquire.

A man named Angelo answered the phone. 'What is a moondance, exactly?' I asked, slightly thrown by his flawless American English.

'OK, basically, we climb a sacred mountain, abstain from all food and drink for three days and dance ourselves into a trance in celebration of the solstice,' said Angelo. There was a pause. 'It's an ancient indigenous ceremony. There are some preparatory saunas here in the city if you're interested.'

Preparatory saunas? I frowned. 'Could I come up the mountain to interview the indigenous dancers?'

Angelo cleared his throat. 'Actually most of the dancers are backpackers from New Zealand,' he said. 'And I'm not sure an interview would really work. The whole point is that we'll all be in a state of altered consciousness.'

I thanked him and hung up.

It was ironic, I thought now, as I sat on this idling bus. I had come to the other side of the world to work in a different culture, to make contact with another way of life only to find myself dogged by people I could as easily have met on a London tube train. Even with Aymara passengers all around me, I felt no shared experience, no sense of connection with their lives. They seemed a quiet, shy people, who watched gringos only out of the corner of their eyes. I needed a project, I mused, something to immerse me in this place.

'So, where are you from, mate?' It was one of the Australians, opening another tired old conversation with someone further up the bus. 'France.' It was the backpacker in disguise, blowing his cover from the driver's seat. 'Ah, right. Nice one. Where are ya headed?'

Here we go again. The gringo trail was well worn.

The Frenchman settled back against the window, ready to begin his travelogue.

Please, I thought, *just for once, surprise me.*

'I am going to see some Aymara boat builders at Huatajota,' he said, with a spreading grin. 'And then I'm going to sail to Easter Island on a boat made out of reeds.'

Had I misheard him? Evidently the Aussie backpacker wasn't too sure either. He blinked and stared at the Frenchman as if waiting for the end of a sentence. 'Reeds?' he repeated. 'Right! You mean like whatsisname, *Kon-Tiki* man . . .'

'Thor Heyerdahl, yes,' said the Frenchman. 'Except that the *Kon-Tiki* never sailed to Easter Island. And also, this expedition will continue right around the world in five different reed boats. It will be a new record. Look, I'll show you . . .'

He pulled a well-fingered map out of his daypack. I caught a glimpse of large blotches of deep blue dissected by a fat red dotted line running roughly east to west. The bus was moving now, beginning its coughing, spiralling ascent inside the fume-filled basin of La Paz. But my mind was already scanning wider horizons.

What little I knew of the Norwegian explorer Thor Heyerdahl was centred on a grainy newsreel image of his 1947 balsa raft, the *Kon-Tiki*, resembling a garden shed lashed to some logs and set adrift on mountainous seas. I remembered the wild, bearded men seen waving from it, their eyes strange and sun-blasted like old-testament prophets. I could not have told you their purpose, but it hardly mattered to me. What inspired me was their sheer unorthodoxy, their pioneering spirit, so different from the sheep-like existence of modern travellers. And yet here on my bus was a present-day pioneer! How wrong could you be about someone? I swallowed my pride, squeezed out past my neighbour and edged up the aisle.

'Ten years?' the Aussie was saying. 'Blimey, I hope you get on with your crew mates. All it'll take is a couple of irritating little habits, and you'll end up feeding each other to the sharks! How many of you are there?'

The Frenchman frowned. 'Eight. Two Chileans, two Bolivians, three North Americans and one European. I think it will be OK. This first voyage is the test. I have not met them all yet, but the captain is a good man.'

At that point he saw me approaching and grinned widely. 'Ah, I think I got the best seat in the end, no?' he crowed. 'You have to know the local ways to travel in comfort. I think you are angry with me, no?'

Yes, I thought, resisting the impulse to poke his Gallic lights out.

'No,' I grinned. 'Just interested in your mad trip.' I shuffled one buttock on to the corner of a seat occupied by an enormous man. 'Sorry for eavesdropping. I'm a journalist.'

And that was how it started. A possible lead for a possible news story, just to keep the money coming in. At least that was as much as I would admit to myself, as our bus laboured through the flat wastes and thin air of the Altiplano towards Lake Titicaca.

'I'm sure the captain would be interested in showing you the boat,' said Stephane. 'His name is Phil Buck. But come soon. We leave for Chile on Friday.'

The village of Huatajata was easy to miss. I had barely noticed it before except as a two-minute interlude of adobe houses scrolling past the bus window on trips between La Paz and Copacabana. 'Are you sure this is the right place?' asked Ali, squinting sceptically, when we got off the bus there two days later. The only residents immediately apparent were a few dogs lying asleep, or possibly dead, at the side of the road. A mile or so away, a woman looked up from a field, then turned away, a flash of colour among the corn. There was no sign of a large reed boat.

Since pointing out the village from the bus window two days ago, Stephane had journeyed on to Peru to buy fishing gear and was not due back until tomorrow. We wandered into a small shop apparently managed by a small boy whose head was barely visible over the counter.

'I'm looking for a very big boat made out of reeds,' I began, my broken Spanish sounding thin and ridiculous above the quacking of a lunchtime soap opera on a small black and white television. 'Do you know where it is?'

The boy stared at us, and wrinkled his nose as if a very bad smell had just entered his shop. A single car whined past on the road behind us. Seconds passed. We left.

Further up the road an Indian woman was hanging out washing. 'This might sound a little strange,' I began again, 'but we're looking for a big reed boat.' The woman flashed us a row of brown teeth and yelled something in Aymara. Instantly, three other women peered over the fence behind her.

'*Mas locos!* More mad gringos for Hostal Inti Karka!' she said, and all four cackled with laughter. Presently, she collected herself long enough to jab a finger over her shoulder. 'A mile down the road, Señor Catari's place.' They were still cackling as we walked away.

You could see the funny side. Why would a man hoping to sail round the world in a reed boat choose to set up his base camp in one of the two landlocked countries in South America? As we turned down a narrow lane towards the lakeside hostel, I was imagining an eccentric old sea dog of a character. Even the name seemed to hint at it. Phil Buck. Buckshot. Buccaneer. A beard big enough to support nesting birds.

As it turned out, Buck Rogers would have been closer to the mark.

Standing at the foot of the track was a tall, muscular American about my age wearing an expensive fleece jacket and wrap-around sunglasses propped on top of his head. A well-clipped goatee softened his angular Hollywood jaw, while behind him something monstrous lurked beneath luminous tarpaulins. On the tarpaulins were taped skulls and crossbones printed with the words: 'Danger, Toxic'. There was a noticeable absence of swagger about the man, no sign of the American need to shout. He was speaking quietly to an Aymara man in a tentlike poncho.

'What do you need for the ceremony?' he was asking the man, who wore the traditional knitted *gorro* hat with earflaps and pom-poms, and was a good foot shorter than him. 'I want the proper rites, a symbolic blessing for the boat. From the village shaman. That's you, right?'

The man nodded sagely. 'Many things are necessary for a *cha 'lla*. Beer, firewood, a llama foetus for sacrifice . . .'. He rummaged inside his poncho and brought out a crumpled shopping list to show the gringo.

'Right,' said Phil Buck. 'Sure. How much do you think it will cost?'

The shaman looked thoughtful, allowing the ghost of a smile to flicker across his face as he sized up the captain. Then he ran down his list with a stub of pencil, making little mutterings and nodding movements with his head, before looking up.

'Two hundred dollars,' he said, firmly.

'Ah,' breathed Phil. 'Look, um, wait a second . . .' He glanced round the yard. 'ELI!' he yelled.

A beautiful Latina woman appeared from the door of the hostel. 'What?' she said bluntly. At a guess, his Chilean wife.

'Can you sweet-talk this guy?' Phil asked her quietly in English. 'He wants two hundred bucks to bless the boat. Seems a lot to me, but we need it for the video. Can you see if you can get him down a little? You're better than me at this kind of thing.'

'That's way too much,' agreed Eli, shaking her head. 'It should be a hundred maximum.' They both turned back to the shaman. It was at that point that Phil glanced over his shoulder and noticed us watching. He excused himself and came over.

'Hi there,' he said, offering his hand. 'Can I help you?'

'We're looking for the captain of the *Viracocha*,' I said.

'That's me,' he replied with a cautious smile. 'Phil Buck. Who's asking?'

Some people clam up when they hear you're a journalist. Others tell you their life stories. Phil Buck grinned with the easy confidence of a man who knows from experience that publicity almost always equals funding.

'You've come just in time,' he said warmly. 'We leave for Chile by road tomorrow. Do you want to look up on the boat? The guys are just about to take the tarps off. Just don't breathe in too deeply — we've been fumigating her for bugs. A Chilean customs thing.'

I watched, fascinated, as several Aymara untied the orange tarpaulins and the *Viracocha* began to show herself. There was a first glimpse of reeds showing like bunched muscle through a gap, then her coverings crumpled downwards to reveal a sandy-coloured curved hull of almost disturbing beauty, vulnerable like the soft interior of some crustacean, removed from its shell. Propped on eucalyptus logs, her huge reed haunches stood several feet above our heads, and the tapered bow and stern curved up to pointed ends like a crescent moon, a good 60 feet from tip to tip. I crept into the cleavage beneath her bow, patted the surface gingerly, and to my surprise found it not soft and spongy but taut as a drum. The thick, hairy ropes that held her together spiralled around the two vast intersecting barrels as rigid and evenly spaced as ribs. Awestruck, I could almost believe she was alive.

'Beautiful isn't she?' said Phil, smiling. 'Come on up.'

We scaled a home-made ladder and found ourselves on the bare back of the *Viracocha*, where smaller reed cylinders as thick as tree trunks formed protecting gunwales. Down the centre ran the V-shaped furrow where the twin hulls met — the only place you could say you were *in* a boat rather than simply *on* one. She was the very antithesis of modern sea-going vessels, with their blade-like hulls, clanking innards and hard, blank walls of fibreglass or steel. I looked out over the silver blue of the lake, and imagined instead this stately prow breasting a Pacific swell, the reeds firm beneath my feet. Centuries, perhaps millennia ago, ancient mariners had ventured out in just such a boat. I envied them their simpler age, their simpler faith.

Something in me was lifted like a flag in a breeze. Ali caught my expression and gave me a knowing smile.

'You're sure she'll float?' I asked Phil, trying to stay hard-headed about the thing.

'For a while at least,' he replied, poking at a rope with his designer hiking boot. '*Totora* reeds float pretty well for a while, but Easter Island is 2500 miles away, which could mean up to three months at sea. If it takes much longer than that we could get a little wet. The best man to tell you about that is Erik.'

He introduced me to the Cataris, one of the last remaining reed boatbuilding families in the world who, in a colourful cluster of red ponchos and leathery faces were trimming reeds together at the upturned bow. Erik, the youngest, had taken a break from his engineering degree in La Paz to join the expedition. He showed me a little reed model with a cut-away cross section.

'The *Viracocha* is a very good boat,' he told me earnestly. 'The best thing about her is that she has two boats inside her, one bundle inside another for extra firmness.' He pointed out the two parts on the model.* 'We kept on tightening the ropes, day after day, until our whole bodies ached. That means it will take much longer for the water to penetrate the reeds. But there could still be problems.' He paused and looked at Phil, who nodded for him to continue. 'As each reed is soaked with water and loses buoyancy, the boat sinks lower in the water, a little each day. We should have enough time to reach land, but if a storm comes and soaks the reeds from above and below . . .' He trailed off and shrugged. 'We will see.'

I laughed nervously. 'Any other nagging doubts, Phil?'

'Sharks,' said the captain without hesitation. 'Sharks like slow-moving boats because of the smaller fish that shelter underneath. And we'll be pretty slow moving — about walking pace. So we'll need to keep a close eye on each other whenever we're making repairs.'

* For more technical information on full construction. see pp. 294–301.

I wanted to find it ludicrous, I really did: the slowly sinking boat, surrounded by sharks; eight men with eight sets of irritating little habits squashed into 18 metres of deck space. But as I stood there grinning and shaking my head in the dying afternoon light, I knew I loved everything about it.

'So you've chosen your crew, then,' I said, hoping to shut the door on my growing hope, an outrageous hope. *What if there were vacancies?*

'Pretty much,' said Phil. 'You've met Stephane and Erik and me. Then there's Erik's Uncle Ramón and Craig the navigator — they're both around here somewhere — and my Chilean brother-in-law Marco, and a US cinematographer friend who's flying down next month. The only doubtful one is a Chilean TV cameraman who hasn't called us in a while. I must give him a call tomorrow.'

Ali raised her eyebrows and shot me a strange, inscrutable smile, which Phil noticed.

'It wasn't supposed to be an all-male ship,' he explained, misinterpreting her. 'I asked a couple of very good women friends but both dropped out for work reasons. And my wife Eli would love to go, but someone needs to stay home and look after our son Mark.'

Eli poked her head over the side of the boat and grinned. Down below, the shaman called a farewell and wandered off with his ceremonial shopping list. 'Ninety dollars,' whispered Eli, looking pleased with herself. 'And I've told him we want to do it tomorrow before it gets dark.' She lifted their little four-year-old up on to the bundles. He grinned impishly and hugged his dad.

'It must be great having a dad who makes Superman look dull,' I joked.

'It has its drawbacks,' said Eli, sitting down by her husband. 'When I went into labour seven weeks early, Phil was climbing a mountain. It wasn't easy, but I knew the deal when I married him. It's certainly never boring.' She smiled playfully and slid her arm round him.

'Eli is an integral part of the expedition in any case,' put in Phil, quickly. 'She'll be running it with me from Arica while we build the cabin and masts and sail system over the next month or so, and then she'll be the land-based co-ordinator while we're at sea, typing up our satellite reports for the website, handling the media. We couldn't do it without her.'

We had a two-hour trip back to our hostel in Copacabana, so we thanked them, wished them all luck with loading the boat on to the lorry tomorrow, and promised to send on the resulting article. As we walked back up to the main road I sensed the hiss of a retreating dream.

'Fancy it?' I said to Ali jokingly.

'No, but it's right up *your* street,' she said, giving my hand a significant squeeze. 'You'd absolutely love it.' I didn't argue.

'I bet he'd let you come,' she persisted. There was a playful tone in her voice, but I sensed she was serious. 'You should at least ask him about it.'

'What about you?' I asked, trying to keep my voice calm.

'I'd find something else to do. It's only for a few months. Why don't you ask him?' She looked up at me, scrutinising my eyes. 'Nick, you've spent the last month telling me you want a new challenge. When are you ever going to get an opportunity like this again?'

My heart was beating very fast. 'We don't even know there *is* an opportunity,' I said, weakly. 'He just said the eighth guy hadn't been in touch. It may not mean anything.'

'Yes, but it could mean a lot. And if you get on a bus and leave now you could spend years wondering what if. You should at least make sure. We could stay here tonight.'

I stood there in the darkness weighing up the situation, shivering slightly. Ali knew she only had to say the word and I would cast the whole mad idea out of my mind like any responsible husband. But she was deliberately holding the door open.

A minibus roared past in the darkness, its headlights sweeping our white faces. Another followed, crammed with passengers. Neither stopped for us.

But the next one might, and we might climb aboard and leave behind this moment, this crossroads crackling with possibilities.

'I think we've missed the bus,' I said slowly. 'Let's stay here tonight.'

2

The Missing Voyage

'Phil, have you got a minute?' I asked, around mid-morning the following day.

The crane was coughing blue exhaust, and huge canvas lifting slings were about to rumple the wide buttocks of the *Viracocha* for the first time. The crane driver was steeling himself with a quick cigarette break.

'Sure,' said Phil. 'What's up?'

'I've been thinking,' I began, trying hard not to sound like a man delivering a line he had been mentally rehearsing all morning. 'If your Chilean TV man doesn't turn up – and I know he still might, so this is only hypothetical . . .' I swallowed. 'Could I come instead?'

Phil rubbed his beard and looked at me in a new and interested way.

'Hypothetically, I think the answer is . . . maybe. I think you'd fit right in. But it could be a few weeks before I know what the full crew situation is. Have you done much sailing before?' he added, a little too casually.

'Oh, loads,' I answered, a little too quickly. I trawled for every more-or-less maritime experience I had ever had, and threw them at him in roughly chronological order. There were the weeks spent messing about in dinghies on family holidays in the west of Scotland, and a youth holiday in a 30-footer on Lake Windermere. Later I joined a sailing club on the river Thames in London, where I capsized near a sewage outlet and contracted a bout of rats' syphilis (I did not mention this part to Phil). Moving north to Scotland for my first reporting job, I had been assigned on a trip across the North Sea on the schooner *Sir Winston Churchill* to cover the Tall Ships Race. 'That's when I really fell in love with bigger sailing boats,' I said, as enthusiastically as I could. 'In between filing reports over the VHF radio, I got my competent crew certificate and learned some basics of navigation . . . port, starboard . . .' I was struggling. 'Pulling lots of ropes . . .'

None of this seemed to have quite the desired effect on Phil. He was nodding in that automatic way that people do when they're still waiting for you to deliver the punchline.

'I almost forgot,' I concluded desperately. 'I used to row for Oxford.'

This wasn't a lie exactly, just creatively misleading. In fact I had spent two terms rowing in a reserve college squad so miserably inept that our boat was known as *Eeyore*. One of the few memories I still retained was the day we almost rowed over a weir.

Still, I felt, it wasn't a bad haul of experience. I was gratified to see that Phil's well-groomed eyebrows had risen about half an inch. 'Great,' he said, with a slight grin. 'If we can't work out how to operate the sails, you could row us to Easter Island.'

We were prevented from discussing the matter further by the crane driver finishing his cigarette and revving the engine. Not that this necessarily heralded anything very much. We seemed to have been stuck all morning in a small convoy of slow-moving problems, each presenting a new obstacle to the central task of hoisting the *Viracocha* from her cradle of eucalyptus logs on to the large flatbed lorry waiting alongside.

The first headache had been the crane itself, which arrived promptly but in several pieces, requiring us to assemble its 60-foot arm in grunting groups of twenty. The high wall of the Cataris' boatyard then proved to be blocking the way between the cradle and the lorry, but the family had obligingly solved this one by demolishing the mud and stone barrier with sledgehammers.

Now attention turned to a tangle of electricity lines passing only metres above the boat. We were, it seemed, in danger of lifting the *Viracocha* through the village power supply. A local official had been summoned for advice, and his solution was dangerously simple. As the crane now winched the hull slowly upwards, he balanced himself on its swaying prow and poked at the electricity lines with a long stick. About half the village stood watching with folded arms, genuinely interested to see if their expert would be electrocuted.

'Isn't that a bit dangerous?' queried Ali, appearing behind me, as the splayed reeds of the prow nudged the crane arm with a loud rustle, the wires sprung back, and the man tottered like a high wire performer to excited shouts from the crowd.

'I'm sure Phil knows what he's doing,' I muttered. Phil was checking the reinforcement planks, placed at strategic points under the slings to protect the *totora*.

'He seems a good man,' said Ali presently, as the boat touched down on the flatbed truck to a chorus of cheers. 'But are you sure he's a good sailor?'

My already well-thumbed copy of the *Viracocha* expedition

brochure was, admittedly, ambiguous on this point. It listed awe-inspiring mountaineering adventures he had undertaken, but didn't quite explain the sudden change of direction into seafaring.

'I'd say I've been gearing up for this trip for nearly twenty-five years,' said Phil, a touch defensively, when I asked him at sunset that same day what his qualifications were for it. 'This is the expedition that all the others led up to.'

At age eleven, I learned, Phil Buck was already rather overactive. A bored fifth-grader in a small New England town, he had tried out most things before deciding to be heroic for a living. From what I could gather, there was a time when he could have gone either way: a reed boat or state penitentiary. The act which had really set him on the road to clean-living was breaking into his own school.

'It was an eleven-year-old's dream, running through the empty corridors, playing soccer, that buzz of knowing you could be caught at any moment. But I pushed it too far. I stole five meal tickets from the canteen, and gave them to a friend. I just forgot about it, but I hadn't realised each one had a number, and our lunch ladies were waiting for the numbers to come up.'

The lunch ladies got their man. 'There were terrible scenes in the principal's office, police questioning, even a trip to juvenile court. My parents were devastated. They grounded me completely for several months – some kind of last ditch effort to save me from the beckoning finger of crime.

'And I guess it worked, because that's when I went rummaging in my dad's bookcase. I'd been too busy to even notice it before, but now there was no TV, no ping-pong, no baseball, it was all I had. And the first book I picked up was *The Kon-Tiki Expedition*.'

He looked out over the lake, where the clouds were lit like yellow loft insulation by a low sun. 'It changed my life, swallowed me whole. I still remember being awestruck at this amazing, crazy guy setting sail from Peru on a balsa raft and actually making it to Polynesia. I still am.'

The 1947 expedition was a controversial affair. For years anthropologists had held that the South Sea islands of Polynesia were settled from Asia. Polynesians had a strong seafaring tradition, it was argued, while South Americans were known only for their coastal trading on balsa rafts or reed boats. Few experts had even countenanced the possibility of migration from the west, because it was assumed that South American craft were unsuited to open-sea voyages. Thor Heyerdahl, biologist by training and anthropologist only by enthusiasm, blew this assumption out of the water in a way that armchair academics found intensely irritating.

From the moment his authentic Peruvian balsa raft crash-landed on a Polynesian reef at Raroia after 101 days at sea, Heyerdahl and his five crewmates became instant folk heroes.

By the time the young Phil came across him in the mid-seventies, Heyerdahl had made several other strange journeys, including the *Ra* expeditions in boats made of papyrus reeds from Egypt. In 1969, *Ra I* had foundered in the Atlantic 500 miles from Barbados in its journey from Morocco, and its crew had to be picked off by yacht; but *Ra II* had made it all the way the following year, despite being virtually submerged by the time it arrived. Within a few years would come the *Tigris* expedition, another reed boat attempt, this time navigating from Iraq down the Persian Gulf and across to Djibouti in a replica of a 5000-year-old Sumerian boat.

'I couldn't get enough of it,' said Phil. 'I raided the local library for everything he had written. It was a very long summer, but by the end of it I knew I was going to be an explorer.' He looked up at the *Viracocha*, now silhouetted above us. 'And here I am.'

At moments like this, I find even my most curmudgeonly English recesses warmed by the power of the American dream. Which eleven-year-old boy has not dreamed of becoming an adventurer, or an astronaut, football player or film star? Most of the world watches its dreams gently erode into something more manageable, yet so many Americans seem uniquely and doggedly literal about seeing them through. As an inveterate Brit, expert in the art of being realistic about things, my own yearnings to be an explorer probably lasted until the end of my first damp, scout camp.

Phil, by contrast was stubbornly determined, low on fuss, high on adrenalin – from the moment he read *Kon-Tiki*. Before he'd even left high school, he cycled 4000 miles across the USA one summer with a friend. Then at the next available slot on the calendar – shortly before finishing his Wildlife Biology degree at the University of Massachusetts – he had embarked on a seven-month canoe trek from coast to coast with a girlfriend, covering 5000 miles from Oregon to Washington DC and following, in reverse, the route of the pioneers Lewis and Clark.

'Exploring became a kind of compulsion,' he explained. 'If I was not on an expedition or at least planning the next one, it was like there was a huge hole in my life. I wanted to go faster, higher, better all the time.' He decided to try something a little more long-term, turning his mountaineering hobby into a quest to climb the highest peaks in all thirteen South American countries. When he ran out of mountains in 1993, he extended the challenge to the whole of the Americas, giving him another ten to conquer. If anything was going to put him off adventuring, this should have been it. By 1998 he had lost his best friend in a skiing accident, and encountered avalanches, land-mines, quick-sand, frostbite, snipers and a particularly nasty flesh-eating parasite, *leishmaniasis*, which left him disfigured by translucent sores.

'I had a few narrow escapes,' he admitted. 'Mountaineering was beginning to feel a little dangerous, and I had Eli and little Mark to think about. So I thought: Why not pick up where Thor Heyerdahl left off? Why not sail round the world in a reed boat?'

It was the kind of logic that would have had Plato enrolling for therapy. Phil's own maritime experience, it was emerging, consisted of a few months crewing on a small yacht during the 23 Peaks Challenge, and a stint as a filleter on board a factory fishing boat off Alaska. But once born, the new idea was hard to resist. Heyerdahl had based his migration theory on the possibility of South Americans voyaging to Easter Island, but his own ancient craft had passed well to the north. Phil decided to begin his circumnavigation with the missing voyage that would rekindle that debate, perhaps rejuvenate Heyerdahl's now largely discredited claim.

He set to work immediately with Eli, costing the dream, trying to find someone to build the strange craft. 'Lake Titicaca was the obvious place to start,' said Phil. 'It's just about the last remaining place on earth where you still see reed boats, and these guys are just about the last reed boatbuilders. José Limache here actually worked with Thor Heyerdahl building the *Tigris* in the 1970s.'

A middle-aged Aymara man was inspecting a tear in the weave of reeds where it had scuffed the side of the lorry. He turned at the mention of his name, and nodded, moon-faced and sage-like, offering his hand. Phil introduced us and I complimented his workmanship.

'I learned from my father and he learned from his,' he said with a smile and a shrug. 'We used to build these boats to survive, to fish, until wooden boats took over. Now it's about preserving an art more than anything. The only market for reed boats these days is for tourist trips and expeditions. But we must make sure there will always be some people who can build them.' The Catari family, relative newcomers to the art, were José's first apprentices, now considered experts in their own right. It was Erik who accompanied Phil on a first, experimental voyage round Lake Titicaca in a smaller prototype reed boat. 'It was amazingly stable, and it got better as the reeds absorbed more water,' said Phil. 'It was pretty clear from the outset that we'd need more than one boat to get round the world. Even in fresh water these things only last a year, max. In salt water, with bigger waves, more turbulence, it's going to be a lot less.'

There was only one way to know for sure, and that was to make the first sea trip. *This* trip. The previous year, the Cataris and Limaches had begun to harvest one and a half million reeds from around the shores of the lake, cutting well below the waterline. *Scirpus Riparius* was a hardy, adaptable plant. Over on the Peruvian side, the Uros people literally lived on it, thatching the famous floating islands that still sustained small villages. Here in Huatajata, Phil's Aymara friends had spread out the harvested reeds to dry for weeks in the sun. Then they wove them into *chorizos*, long sausages the thickness of tree trunks, ready for binding together to form the hull. It had been arduous work, much of it overseen by Phil between return trips to the US to seek sponsorship and funding. There had been delays, let-downs. Phil recruited among his friends and colleagues for crew members. Two women climbers signed up, but dropped out as the launch date was pushed back.

One crew member, however, stayed committed from the very beginning. Craig Homan, a Seattle-based oceanographer, had met Phil through a mutual friend. A seasoned mariner with twenty-five years' experience of sailing and navigation around the treacherous west coat, he lived and worked on boats and couldn't resist the opportunity to try out sailing as it was done more than a millennium ago.

I had met Craig the previous night over a trout supper, and found his presence reassuring. A stocky and jovial man with a goatee beard and a booming chuckle, he seemed to complement Phil's determination with a sizeable chunk of technical know-how. Today he seemed more nervous, and had so far hovered on the edge of things, lending muscle where required, but otherwise saying little. I learned later this was because he spoke no Spanish, which seemed to be the main language of the expedition.

'So you're the man who knows how to sail this thing!' I said, as Craig edged in on our group, silhouetted against the sunset. He gave a short laugh. 'Actually, I'm used to something a little faster, with sails you can change with a winch. This is going to be . . . an education.' He guffawed again, and I wished I could see his eyes behind his sunglasses.

'Craig and I are going to share the navigation,' said Phil, quickly. 'Craig's going to read the stars like the ancients would have done, while I read the satellites on the GPS, just to check we're not way off-course. Easter Island is a small target in a big ocean. If we miss her, it's another few thousand miles to the next island. So, better not to miss.'

Tomorrow the team would drive down the long, winding desert road, descending nearly 4000 metres to sea level in Arica where work on the superstructure – the cabin, masts, rigging, sail system, steering mechanism – would begin. The projected launch date was 18 January 2000 – less than two months away.

From above us came a sudden whoop of joy and an exuberant sexual expletive: '*Concha tu madre!*' It could only be Stephane, who had returned that afternoon laden with fishing gear, and was now perched on the highest tip of the crane with his camera pointing down at us. Phil shook his head and grinned. 'Hey, monkey boy!' he yelled. 'Come down here – I want to ask you something!'

Monkey boy swung himself down into the group. 'Would you sleep on the boat tonight?' Phil asked him. 'Someone needs to keep watch.' Stephane agreed immediately, his cheeky grin disappearing in an almost reverential nod to his captain. But it seemed to me an odd, overanxious request. The boat, weighing 16 tonnes, was not the most obvious target for theft. What exactly was Phil afraid of?

'Unfortunately, there are people who would very much like to see the *Viracocha* expedition fail,' said Phil, cryptically, to knowing nods from the Cataris. 'And one lit match or severed rope could be enough to destroy the entire boat. We don't want to take that risk.' I was intrigued. Who were these mysterious enemies?

Phil didn't elaborate, and I was distracted from further questioning by the arrival of the village shaman, carrying a plastic shopping bag that was clinking with the weight of its beer bottles. It was almost time for the $90 ritual blessing, and time for me to go – Ali had taken an earlier bus and was now waiting for me in Copacabana. 'You'll be in touch then, Phil?' I said, failing to hide the desperation in my voice, as I thrust a note of my email and hostel address into his palm. 'Sure,' said Phil, shaking my hand. 'I'll let you know by Christmas.'

Stephane winked at me. 'Good luck, brother!'

Craig shook my hand. 'Hope we see you again!'

Word had obviously got round that I was looking for a place on the crew. I hoped that was a good sign.

The shaman bent down by the trailer and began kindling a small fire of sticks, paper and what looked like sweets (the dried llama foetus seemed to have fallen victim to cost cuts). A circle of crew members, workmen and local residents gathered round him to watch. His lips moved silently in prayer as he squirted pure alcohol from a plastic bottle, and the flames rose momentarily higher. Then in a curiously tender movement, he kissed the flank of the *Viracocha*, both hands placed flat against her, before picking up a bottle of beer, shaking it up, and spraying it along the sides of the boat. Everyone cheered and clapped, their faces lit from within the circle by an orange glow of fire.

But I was not in the circle. Sitting up front next to the bus driver (I had learned at least one thing since my first encounter with Stephane), I watched the black hills loom against the cold steel of fading sky and imagined that in all probability, I would never see these eccentric dreamers again.

In the following weeks I found it almost impossible to concentrate on my work. I was supposed to be writing features on Che Guevara and on the cocaine trade, but Ali would frequently return from her photographic forays into Copacabana to find me staring absently from our hostel balcony, the cursor on my palmtop computer once again winking on an almost empty screen.

In the absence of any news from Phil, I decided to turn my attention to some useful research. What, for example, was the relevance of the name *Viracocha*? I had heard that Viracocha was the Andean creator god, adopted by the Incas from their predecessors, but I couldn't quite see what that had to do with Easter Island. I took a day trip to the remains of the ruined city of Tiahuanaco to find out.

According to my guidebook, its architect was said to be the creator god himself.

Viracocha sounded like a hands-on kind of deity. Originally, he'd made a race of giants out of stone, but found them so evil and disobedient that he'd turned some back into stone and washed the rest away in a great flood. He started again using a different medium — clay — and formed human beings and animals instead. And this time, to help them not to become like the giants, he wandered the earth himself, a tall, pale, bearded man-god with his own entourage, busy teaching his people and founding great civilisations. The greatest of these was Tiahuanaco, a huge complex of temples, pyramids, homes and monoliths founded in around 600 BC on the shores of Lake Titicaca at the very place he had first created humans. Once a thriving city of 20,000 people governing vast areas of what are now Bolivia, Peru, Chile and Argentina, it was completely abandoned by AD 1200 following a mysterious cataclysm.

Now the lake was twelve miles away, shrinking as if from a

haunted place, and even the stones themselves were mostly gone, thanks to the Spaniards. Arriving in the 1500s, the conquistadores prised off all the gold facing and dragged off every movable stone to build churches in La Paz. A strange, otherworldly atmosphere remained.

Wandering across wind-raked, grassy plazas on a grey December afternoon, I found myself face to face with two Viracochas. One, carved into the huge sun gate in the ceremonial compound of Kalasasaya, was a stylised, hollow-eyed mask face, with rays of light standing up around the head, and thunderbolts in each hand. The creator god, supreme deity, able to call down floods and lightning. The other, carved on a tall, thin obelisk, in a subterranean temple compound, was an altogether more human god, a tall figure carved on a single piece of stone. Beneath his feet were two pumas, symbols of earth, while at his side a long, curving snake, representative of the lowest realms, took the place of a sceptre. This was an incarnated god, with a triangle of beard, who shed stone tears. He also looked vaguely familiar.

'Kon-Tiki or Viracocha — two names for the same god,' said Eduardo, my guide, as we looked up at him. 'His face was painted on Thor Heyerdahl's sail when the *Kon-Tiki* raft sailed to Polynesia.'

Heyerdahl was honeymooning on Fatuhiva, a small island in the Marquesas group of Eastern Polynesia, when the deity first aroused his curiosity. An ancient elder told him of a chief-god called Tiki who brought his ancestors from a land far beyond the sea. Could this be Kon-Tiki Viracocha, the god-man whose image stood at Tiahuanaco? If so, bearing in mind the more or less constant trade winds from the east, was it possible that South American navigators peopled Polynesia before the wave of Asian navigators even thought of setting sail from the west?

Returning to Tiahuanaco after the violent interruption of the Second World War, Heyerdahl found other legends that seemed to back up his theory. When the Spanish conquistadores arrived here to find this high plateau dotted with monolithic statues, pyramids and gold-plated sungates, the Incas could only tell them it had been built by a race of tall, bearded white gods who had come before them. These architects had disappeared after an attack from a neighbouring tribe, which slaughtered many on an island on Lake Titicaca. Kon-Tiki Viracocha was among those who escaped, and he had later retreated with his surviving followers to the South American coast, where he disappeared westward across the sea.

Doubly intrigued, Heyerdahl visited Easter Island and found that one myth there spoke of the first island forefathers arriving from the east. Add to this the reports of the first European visitors to the island, who were astonished to see many islanders with pale skins and beards, and his thesis began to seem plausible.

In Copacabana, it was to be some weeks before I could get my hands on a copy of the *Kon-Tiki Expedition,* let alone any reference to wider academic opinion, but Phil had set out a précis of the evidence in his expedition brochure, and the apparent parallels between Easter Island and Tiahuanaco fascinated me. In both, the white teachers were distinguished by their elongated earlobes – a ceremonial feature which also found its way on to the *moai,* the famous statues of Easter Island. Digging on the island subsequently, Heyerdahl had also unearthed similarities with the statuary and architecture of Tiahuanaco, which suggested that the pale-skinned architects brought with them their highly developed craft of stone-masonry.

He also pointed to several plant species found in both Polynesia and South America – tomato, sweet potato, the bottle gourd, and perhaps most significantly for our purposes, the *totora* reed, which grew both in Lake Titicaca and in the crater lakes of Easter Island.

Wandering around the deserted plazas, I asked Eduardo what he thought of Thor Heyerdahl.

'Nobody believes him,' he replied, with a dismissive wave of his hand. 'Everybody knows the Polynesians came from the west.' It was a response that has greeted Heyerdahl all his life. But in fact, as I was to discover later, Heyerdahl has never disputed that Polynesia was populated from Asia, only that an earlier wave of migration may also have taken place from the east. In the case of Easter Island, he suggests, those early white migrants, perhaps led by Kon-Tiki Viracocha, were later massacred by Polynesian settlers. The story is given some credence by local legends of a great battle in which the 'long ears' were vanquished by the 'short ears', and according to Heyerdahl, it helps explain the almost exclusively Polynesian genetics of the present-day islanders.

I was agnostic on such matters at this stage. What seemed more compelling was Heyerdahl's simple argument that the Humboldt and Southern Equatorial Currents and the prevailing trade winds made east–west migration comparatively easy – indeed much easier than journeying in the opposite direction. His opponents had argued that even such a natural conveyor belt still could not compensate for the state of South American navigation – they claimed that neither the balsa log rafts commonly used for trading, nor the small reed boats like those used on Lake Titicaca, were suitable for making long, open sea voyages. Which is why Heyerdahl proved them wrong in the only way he could – by doing it himself in a balsa raft.

The one thing I found strange was that, despite decades of controversy focused on his Easter Island theory, he had never actually attempted a raft or reed boat trip to the island itself. *Kon-Tiki* washed up hundreds of miles to the northwest. I couldn't help wondering why the *Viracocha* was apparently the first modern reed boat ever to test precisely the link that had stirred up the controversy in the first place. It made me a little uneasy.

'Telephone for Nick Torpe!'

It was the morning after Christmas Day and Manuel the hostel manager was on the balcony, smirking down at us in the garden at Copacabana. The cleaning lady stifled a titter, as was entirely normal when my surname was pronounced in Spanish. In South America I was 'Nick Clumsy'.

I gave a self-deprecating grin to show I was in on the joke, but I was already half-way up the stairs. There was only one person I knew who had the hostel telephone number.

'Nick?' It was Phil, on a crackly line.

'Yeah, it's me.' My hand was trembling slightly. 'So what's the story?'

'Well . . . congratulations. You're on the boat.'

I had spent so long insuring myself against disappointment, that this blunt statement rather took my breath away. For a moment I could only grin, bug-eyed, at Ali. She gave a brave smile back.

'Nick? Hello?'

'Fantastic!' I spluttered. 'The TV man dropped out?'

'No, actually it was Rambo, Erik's uncle. He decided someone had to stay behind to help run the family business. But Erik's still coming. So when can you get here?'

Suddenly, everything seemed to be moving very fast. I felt a pang for Ali.

'How does two weeks' time sound? I've got a few jobs to tie up, and we're supposed to be spending New Year with friends on Isla del Sol.'

The Island of the Sun was a barren speck of land, clearly visible from the crags above our hostel. It marked the sacred place where the Creator Viracocha had once conjured the sun and moon from the deep waters of the lake. Now it seemed doubly fitting as our venue for the birth of a new millennium.

'I guess I could be down in Arica by, say, January the eighth,' I concluded.

Ten days before the projected launch date.
'Great,' said Phil. 'See you then.'

'How can you be so sure that everything is going to be all right?'
said Ali, sighing. 'You're going on a raft made of reeds that's sinking from the moment you step on it.'

It was New Year's Eve, and we were sitting on a rocky hillside on
Isla del Sol, waiting for the millennium's last sunset. Since the
phone call, we had both found our moods swinging violently
between nervous excitement and a kind of gibbering terror.
Tonight was a gibbering terror night, and I was trying to hide it.

'It'll only be sinking slowly,' I said, lamely.

Ali laughed and swept a stray Irish curl out of her face. 'Look,
I'm not trying to stop you going,' she said, patiently. 'I know you'll
love it, and I think you've got a good chance of making it to Easter
Island – or at least of being rescued safely. But I think it's important
we talk about . . . the other possibility.'

I gazed out over the lake in silence for a moment. A tiny boat
with a red sail was moving slowly across the mouth of the bay hundreds of feet below us. It moved through a shimmering patch of
reflected sun, suddenly a silhouette. At the far end of the lake,
clouds were gathering.

I took a long breath. 'OK, let's be completely honest about this,'
I began, trying to keep my voice as level as possible. 'Yes, it's possible I could die.'

I let the words hang in the air in front of us for a moment for
consideration. I felt somehow relieved that they were out in the
open. I also felt like I might howl if I left them there too long. Ali
clenched my fingers.

'But,' I said, hurriedly, 'it's also true that we could die at any
moment of our lives. I honestly don't believe this trip is any more
dangerous that living in your average city.' I paused to see if Ali

agreed with what I was saying, but I couldn't see her eyes. Did *I* agree with what I was saying? I was pleasantly surprised to find I did.

'In some ways we're at an advantage,' I continued. 'The only difference between us here and us back in Edinburgh is that here we *know* life is fragile, that any moment could be our last. Back home we could just as easily be killed by a heart attack or a train crash, or hit by a bus on the way to the newsagent – but we would never have had the chance to talk about it first.'

'Right,' said Ali quietly. 'So let's talk about it.'

So we did. For more than an hour we looked unflinchingly at possible death. We found ourselves weeping, laughing and, for the first time in a while, praying.

Once upon a time as a passionate teenager, I had firmly believed God was a sort of personal bodyguard, a cosmic airbag, there for my own protection. Since then, however, the armoured limo of my faith had been over some pretty rough terrain. Over the years I'd watched a lot of bits drop off. In fact, so many of my old certainties had clattered into the road behind me that these days I found myself riding something resembling one of Laurel and Hardy's collapsing jalopies, not much more than a chassis with a steering wheel.

But, as we each discovered that afternoon, the old banger was still going, and the engine was good. We remembered what we *did* believe: that God himself was a risk-taker and became participant as well as creator, an incarnate being who at some stage walked – like Kon-Tiki Viracocha – through the world he had made. He wouldn't necessarily intervene to stop you drowning, we decided, but he'd be there alongside you, whether in this life or the next. God was love, and love was stronger than fear.

'If you have to die some time,' said Ali, butting my shoulder gently with her head, 'I think I would prefer to know that you died doing something you loved. Better that than being so afraid of taking risks that you wake up aged sixty and realise that you've never really lived.'

This was the reason we had both left Scotland in the first place, taken the risk of packing in our staff jobs in journalism and social work, to wake up and be closer to the fertile, dangerous edges of our lives. It all felt quite stirring and heroic in theory. From a sodden raft in the middle of the Pacific, I realised, it might feel a little different.

'Do me a favour,' said Ali, finally getting up. 'Try not to die, eh?'

Walking back towards our hostel on the peak of the hill, we were overtaken by a little girl pulling a llama on a rope, and a man who looked nervously skyward carrying twigs like a human porcupine. Looking down on the lake it was now impossible to see the far shore. Instead, a sky the colour of gunmetal seemed to be dissolving the view, its shadow spreading like an oil slick across the water towards us. Occasionally a shard of brilliant lightning split the looming wall of darkness. As we climbed a dry stone wall, and jogged across a field towards our hostel, the first hailstones began to fall.

'Maybe tonight is the end of the world after all,' joked the landlord with his characteristic mournful smile, meeting us in the entrance hall as marbles of ice crashed on the plastic skylight. Later, over a millennial trout supper and plenty of wine, we sat with other guests and watched the ice become rain, staring through the window of the little hostel, as lightning flashed brief images of tormented trees.

It was a peculiarly unsettling omen as I prepared to trace the path of the bearded man-god over the lake towards Tiahuanaco, and away across the sea.

But Viracocha, I was later to discover, was both Creator and Storm God.

'What is the purpose of your visit?' asked the bored Chilean immigration official. I toyed briefly with the idea of telling him, but the queue behind me stretched out of the building. 'Tourism,' I said. He brought down the visa stamp with a sudden violence and handed my British passport back with silent contempt. It was difficult to know whether my crime was being a scruffy backpacker or simply being British at the time of General Pinochet's imprisonment. Ali, with her Irish passport, got a faint smile.

The usual posters, done up in cartoon colours, showed that Chile prohibited the importation of firearms, drugs, animals, semen and agricultural products. I tried to imagine the look on the bureaucrats' faces when the *Viracocha* had pulled up outside, made entirely of Bolivian reeds. According to Phil, it had taken five days and a sheaf of paperwork to complete the 350-mile trip.

Our own bus journey was proving a little smoother, though no less strange at a height of 4700 metres. We gazed through wheedling altitude headaches at green lakes studded with pink flamingos, all dwarfed by the overbearing alien crags of the 6300-metre Parincota volcano.

After our discordant New Year's celebrations on Isla del Sol — involving, at one point, a kind of millennial head-to-head between thudding techno and indigenous wind instruments — we had spent a frantic final week making last-minute plans in La Paz. Ali had arranged to join an expedition with the British youth development charity Raleigh International in Southern Chile, where she would be responsible for providing food for 120 young adventurers. 'I don't want to have any spare time to think about what might be happening to you,' she explained, succinctly. It seemed an excellent idea to me, though it had the disadvantage that she had to leave within days for the long journey south, and therefore would not see the boat launched.

Outside the dusty glass of the coach, vast walls of sand were rearing up on either side, as we wound our way down from the Lauca National Park and into the desert regions of Northern

Chile. We watched in silence as the dusk closed in, draining the sky of its remaining blue or coppery hues, leaving the world in grainy sepia, and then darkness. Even the coastal lights of Arica, when they came, were not welcoming but otherworldly, seeming to rise towards us like some vast, extra-terrestrial mothership as we descended from among the black dunes.

We had planned to treat ourselves to a final night in a hotel before going to find the boat the following day, but as we flashed along garish bypasses, past filling stations, we both knew things already felt too intense, too weird. We wanted distraction from our impending separation, a few beers with people who, if not quite friends yet, were at least familiar faces. By the time the coach swung into the station with a grunt and hiss of airbrakes, we knew we were going to the beach.

'Where do you want to go?' asked a taxi driver, as he humped our bags into the back of a battered Datsun and got in. 'I'm not exactly sure,' I said. 'It's near to Hotel Chinchorro, on the beach.'

The driver pulled one of those expressions reserved for foreign tourists. 'What is it you're looking for? Is it Hotel Chinchorro or not?'

'We're going to the *balsa de totora*,' I said. 'You've probably seen it. It's near the hotel.'

'The big boat on the beach?' he said, drumming his fingers on the steering wheel. We were turning down a slip road, towards the sea.

'*Exacto!*' I smiled. 'So you *have* seen it?'

The driver pulled in at the side of the road, hooked his arm over the back of the seat, and looked me in the eye.

'Didn't you hear, friend?' he said gently. 'The reed boat has already gone.'

3

A Bag of Flies

'It can't have gone,' I insisted. 'I'm in the crew. It must be here somewhere.'

We drove down a slip road, over a railway track, past a cluster of box-like holiday villas. Jolting onwards across rocky waste ground, the driver raised an empty hand ironically: 'That was the Hotel Chinchorro. Where now, *señor?*' A terrible doubt thrummed suddenly in my stomach. I opened the window to see if I could hear voices, but there was only the overheating engine, and surf. Our sceptical chauffeur was just turning the wheel to go back, when the headlights flashed across something in the darkness. Two fat horns of *totora* protruding above the walls of a small rectangular compound, barely 50 metres away. The driver grunted in surprise, scrunched the car to a halt, and stopped the engine.

A familiar American voice sounded close by in the darkness. 'Welcome!' shouted Phil, appearing above us, presumably standing on the deck. I paid the taxi driver gratefully and liberally. He drove off shaking his head and chuckling.

Groping through a hessian flap, we found ourselves in a dimly lit enclosure. It was about the size of a tennis court, but had the cluttered ambience of a squatter settlement. Bamboo walls, strewn with bits of clothing, were surmounted with a strip of woven bamboo roofing along one side, giving shelter to a row of dusty-looking tents. In the centre of the compound, Phil's little son Mark was scrambling after a yapping Dalmatian puppy, dodging around eucalyptus logs the size of telegraph poles, which had been lashed into A-shaped double masts and lay propped on huge coils of rope. The *Viracocha* herself, installed on a new log cradle, brooded over the camp like a mother hen, while 50 metres beyond her the Pacific boomed and hissed on a pebbly shore.

Over in the corner several people got up from an improvised chipboard table to greet us – Stephane, Craig, Eli, and some others I didn't recognise. Someone handed me a beer. Phil clambered down from the boat to join us, and in the midst of the backslapping, I realised I was no longer an outsider.

'Well it was good of you to wait,' I said to Phil, wryly. 'The taxi driver told us the reed boat had already left.'

Phil looked blank for a moment. 'Oh right,' he said presently, cracking open his beer. 'I guess he meant the *other* reed boat.'

The *Viracocha* was, it emerged, the *second* modern replica of a pre-historic reed boat to squat on the beaches of Arica. The first had indeed already left – more than eight months ago. Captained by a Spanish adventurer, Kitin Muñoz, the *Mata Rangi II* had been more than twice the size of the *Viracocha*. Muñoz's eventual aim, like Phil's, was to show the prowess of ancient vessels by circumnavigating the globe, but his first intended destination was somewhat more ambitious: Japan. In a lather of media coverage, corporate sponsorship and local excitement, he had set sail on a voyage of more than 10,000 miles.

Everything went well for three months. Then it all began to unravel, quite literally. In high seas, some of the ropes binding the hull broke, reeds were washed away and the two ends of the boat began to part. Muñoz was forced into a drastic decision: he downsized. Hacking through ropes and reeds, he jettisoned the entire front half of the boat, losing two masts in the process. By re-rigging the one remaining mast in reverse, he was then able to limp to the Marquesa island of Nuku Hiva, 5000 miles from Chile, on the still-buoyant back end.

The defiant captain had no doubt where to lay the blame. His ship had been attacked, he said, by a voracious breed of rope-chewing mollusc. The *Teredo Navalis*, he believed, had latched on to the hull in Arica and gorged itself on his boat ever since.

It wasn't his first stroke of bad luck, however. The similarly sized *Mata Rangi I*, launched in 1997 from Easter Island on a westward course, had rotted so extensively in the rain during construction that it lasted less than three weeks at sea before it disintegrated, necessitating a dramatic rescue by a passing yacht. As if jinxed by association, that yacht was subsequently dashed to pieces back on Easter Island when it broke free of its moorings.

A bus whined past in the distance. I looked around the table. 'Maybe I'm missing something,' I said. 'But if two out of two reed boats have fallen apart, what makes you think the same thing won't happen to the *Viracocha*?'

'Two very good reasons,' said Phil quickly. 'First, we're half the size of the *Mata Rangi*, which means we have half the flexing. The longer the boat, the more it bends with the shape of the waves and works itself loose. Shorter is stronger.' He got up and ushered me over to the *Viracocha*. 'Second, we're tighter and firmer than the

Mata Rangi. Try and get your hand under that.' He slapped one of the ropes encircling the barrel-like flank. The rope was as tight as a bar, unmovable. 'We've spent weeks hauling on them. There's no way this boat's going to fall apart. That's what I've said to every journalist who's been down here.

'Unfortunately,' he added, 'Kitin Muñoz has taken it all kind of personally.'

He tossed a Chilean newspaper on to the table, where a Spanish headline caught my eye. Roughly translated, its salient points read as follows:

KITIN ACCUSES US ADVENTURER OF FRAUD

Kitin Muñoz, the Spanish director of the *Mata Rangi* expedition, has launched a direct attack from Madrid against the US adventurer Phil Buck, accusing him of using plastic materials in his reed boat.

'Personally I consider this project a fraud, a shameless insult, not only to the *Mata Rangi* but to all the expeditions which, maintaining authenticity, have built replicas correctly with natural materials,' said Muñoz. 'The ship was built in Bolivia with plastic cord in its interior and natural fibre on its exterior, and who knows what other tricks. It is a contemptible joke. The most logical thing would be for the builder to cancel this farce, build a new boat with original materials, and try crossing the ocean with clean hands instead.'

'Ouch,' I said. 'He's lying, right?'

'No, just exaggerating,' said Phil with a sigh. 'We did use a few metres of nylon twine to bind the long centre bundles, way back at the start. It was a mistake and I've never denied it. We were behind schedule and didn't have time to take it out again without delaying the expedition. It didn't seem like a big deal from the point of view of the whole experiment, because the structural strength of the boat is in the thick, outer ropes, which hold it all together – and all of those are natural.'

The others were studying their beer. I was silent for a moment, fighting a twinge of disappointment towards Phil. It seemed a clumsy decision to have made for the sake of a few weeks. When every other part of the boat was to be constructed from wood, rope, glue or canvas, this was a tiny but ugly detail asking to be pointed out, like a piece of toilet paper stuck to the sole of your foot.

On the other hand, Muñoz's high-minded invocation of a community of offended reed boatbuilders was laughable. Was there any activity in the world so obscure that it didn't have a little club of cranks bickering about it? Here were two men engaging in the exceptionally odd activity of recreating 1500-year-old pre-Inca voyages, both happy enough to use power tools, cranes, VHF radio, GPS navigation systems, compasses, wrist-watches and inflatable rescue boats – yet squabbling over *bits of plastic string*.

'Maybe the media will lose interest,' I said, without conviction. As a cub reporter I had personally spun weeks of copy out of far less.

'Are you kidding?' said Phil. 'I've spent all day today being interviewed – TV, radio, newspapers – everybody wants in on it. Your taxi driver will have to be living on Mars if he hasn't heard of the *Viracocha* by the end of this week.'

I felt suddenly exhausted. Ali had already retired to a vacant tent, and I badly needed to join her. But something was still niggling me.

'What about the rope-eating molluscs?' I said.

Phil laughed and swigged his beer.

'I don't believe in the rope-eating molluscs.'

✻

Two things became obvious in the week that followed. First, a steady stream of journalists from the Chilean press, international news agencies and an obscure Japanese magazine confirmed Phil's fears that the controversy over the plastic string was not going to go away. Second, neither were we – at least for the time being. The official launch date was only a week off, yet the *Viracocha* was still little more than a hull despite the passage of more than a month since I had last seen her. She lacked masts, a sail system, a cabin, and a rudder. Apart from the masts, lying in the yard, there was no sign of any of this in preparation. 'We're a little behind schedule,' admitted Phil, sprucing himself up for another TV cross-examination. 'Two weeks, maybe.' I mentally adjusted my calendar.

More worryingly, there wasn't much sign of a crew. Erik had gone back to Bolivia to attend to family business almost as soon as I arrived, which left Phil, Stephane, Craig and me. Four out of eight. Various others would arrive soon, Phil insisted, but in the mean time the *Viracocha* took shape slowly and steadily with the help of a miscellaneous assortment of workers and guests. Jorge and Ernesto, two out-of-work local fishermen, were taken on as night watchmen, then rapidly promoted to resident rigging experts. An amiable older man with silver stubble and a limp, who turned out to be Phil's dad, Charlie, knocked up a simple wooden *Viracocha* figurehead, while Steiny, a Buck family friend who was a graphic designer, painstakingly painted it. Steiny's partner, Ann, an Appalachian Trail ranger, made herself useful hosing down the fine white dust which blew through the camp each afternoon on a warm desert wind. Ann was a kind woman with a throaty, uproarious guffaw, and I liked her instantly. Sometimes, though, when she was lost in a cigarette or staring out to sea, you sensed a deep sadness about her. Her son Mark, I was later to discover, had been Phil's best friend right through high school, until he had died, early in 1991, in a skiing accident while the pair were climbing together.

Phil's own son had been named after his lost friend. What little I knew intrigued and disturbed me, but it was to be some time before I felt able to ask for the full, tragic story. For now, we all worked wordlessly together, sanding down rudder boards, cutting wooden cradles for the mast feet, and taking it in turns to operate three wheezing power tools from a single extension cable.

We were camped on a promontory of hard-packed sand and rock. It was an oddly isolated spot, an apron of no-man's land which neither sea nor tourism had quite got round to claiming. On one side of us the rubble subsided into a long stretch of sandy beach, spiked with occasional piers and dotted with sunbathers. On the other side, a small stream and a lonelier stretch of rocks and sand separated us from a derelict pier cluttered with pelicans, which dived noisily for fish with all the grace of collapsing umbrellas. And before us, a few short metres beyond our fence, lay the Pacific, steely blue, seemingly infinite, waiting to be claimed. Gazing out over its mirrored, benevolent surface, watching turtles bobbing their heads lazily at us, I found it hard to envisage the kind of power that could tear a boat in half on a whim.

At such moments of complacency, however, I had only to turn to Craig for an injection of reality. 'There are basically a couple of major dangers in this trip,' he told me affably, during the first week, as we stood waiting for Stephane to finish using the electric sander. 'Number one is someone falling overboard – we've got no motorised rescue boat, and I sure as hell don't know how to stop a reed boat in a hurry, so if you lose your footing you lose your life. Number two is being hit by another ship. Because we're made of reeds, our radar profile is almost nil, and most tankers run on auto-radar alarm systems. So if we're really unlucky, they might not even notice they've hit us.' He gave a humourless chuckle.

'But we've got a covered life raft, right?' I asked, aghast. 'So if the worst came to the worst . . .'

'We're *supposed* to be getting one,' he said. 'But you're assuming we'll even have enough warning to get into it. And the trouble with rubber life rafts is that sharks like to rub their backs on them. So you're doing almost constant maintenance on them to stay afloat. A life raft is only a last resort, and we want to make damn sure we're not in there longer than absolutely necessary.'

I decided not to pass on any of this information in my emails to Ali. I had waved her off tearfully on a long-distance bus to Santiago the previous day, and knew she would be needing encouragement as she began her own expedition in Patagonia. I was also selective in what I told my parents, who were already in shock. My mother emailed me to confess she was feeling 'negative and frightened' and seemed to think a newspaper editor must be coercing me into taking the trip. My father, meanwhile, had dug up an internet story about Muñoz's ill-fated ship, which he sent to me with the typically understated comment: 'Thought you might be interested in this.' I wrote back breezily from a local internet café to argue that any boat which still floated after being ripped in half must be extremely safe – a bold mixture of positive thinking and journalistic spin which seemed to convince everyone apart from me. In all my reassurances I emphasised Craig's decades of maritime experience, and carefully left out his reservations.

If Craig's was the sonorous voice of grim realism in the camp, Stephane could always be relied upon for an unbridled optimism that was refreshingly free of facts. His loyalty and trust towards Phil never wavered, and I would go to him for reassurance as he sawed with a happy, furious intensity at whichever chunk of wood had been set before him.

'You worry too much,' he would say, grinning at me, as I relayed the latest nightmare scenario. 'Phil is a good captain. Soon we'll be out there, working as a team, on our way to Easter Island. You'll see. *Una gran aventura.*' He would pat me on the shoulder and make a reassuring clicking noise, as if calming a horse.

I might have found this more helpful had Stephane's maritime experience not been even more lacking than mine. As far as I could gather, the sum total of his seamanship was a three-week stint as a crew member on a Mediterranean yacht, and an even shorter but more recent trip across Lake Titicaca as a passenger on a small reed boat – though much of this was hazy in his memory due to extreme cold and the ready availability of mind-altering herbs. On the plus side, however, he had at least a rudimentary knowledge of the principles of sailing.

This was more than could be said for our fifth crew member, Marco Rodriguez, who arrived a few days after me, and launched himself into the work like a custard pie on a spring. Eli's brother seemed to have been recruited primarily as ship's jester. A 33-year-old jewellery salesman on unpaid leave from his job in Santiago, he had no recognised maritime qualifications, unless you counted the summer he spent in a Zodiac boat, towing holidaymakers round a beach resort on an inflatable banana. But he had a seemingly endless source of nicknames, impersonations and jokes – most of which could usefully have been accompanied by a clown-horn to signal the laugh-line. 'This expedition is a fraud!' he exclaimed angrily one day, striding up to Phil. 'How can you possibly claim to be mounting an authentic pre-Inca voyage? Not a single member of your crew is more than 1000 years old!' His brother-in-law looked at him blankly for a moment, until Marco's grin flashed into view. The two of them snorted with laughter and slapped each other on the back.

Unfortunately, Kitin Muñoz's slurs were not so easily banished. The vestiges of his influence in the city were easy to see. Fading posters in shop windows showed the conquering hero tanned, muscled and posing in swimwear in front of his enormous boat and a phalanx of company sponsorship logos. His taut, ex-commando body exuded discipline, while his confident eyes and mane of sandy hair seemed to embody an airbrushed spirit of adventure. Along the bottom of the poster, the most handsome of his crewmembers were individually named and profiled like members of a rock band. Market vendors were still flogging off the last *Mata Rangi* souvenir duffle bags, and down at Chinchorro beach, sunbathers peered up at an enormous billboard on which hundreds of local people could be seen wading into the surf to touch the reed boat, like the climax of some Hollywood epic.

By contrast, Phil's efforts to gain official support from the city government seemed fruitless. Much of this, we surmised, was a direct result of Muñoz's failure. The city mayor, Ivan Paredes Fierro, had poured several million pesos of public money into his friend's expedition, and even flew out to greet the ravaged half-boat as it arrived in the Marquesa Islands. Since then, however, opposition councillors had turned on him for squandering taxpayers' money, and it was obvious he was not going to risk attracting the same criticism again. Now Muñoz's accusations of fraud gave the mayor a perfect excuse to avoid any involvement with the *Viracocha* project. Despite its obvious potential as a temporary tourist attraction, the only reference he made to the existence of our boat was a brief, curt television statement in which he wished us well but repeated Muñoz's assertion that the experiment was 'unscientific' and therefore unworthy of municipal support. There was no official welcome, just as there would be no official farewell.

Phil and Eli, trying to arrange meetings with port officials and potential food sponsors, found a knock-on effect. Initial promises of free building materials were downgraded to small discounts, phone calls were not returned, and an air of scepticism prevailed. Journalists continued to visit, spurred on by regular updates from Kitin or his boatbuilders, the Esteban family, who faxed press releases to all media whenever the controversy looked like it might finally lose its momentum. The Estebans operated scarcely a mile from the Cataris on Lake Titicaca, and Paulino, the head of the family, had been involved with two of Thor Heyerdahl's expeditions. Originally he had agreed to build the *Viracocha* too, but had suddenly pulled out on instruction from Kitin Muñoz, which was when Phil contracted the Cataris and Limachis living further down the road. Now, the Estebans drafted a 'declaration', from something called the Communidad Indigena de la Isla Suriqui and signed mainly by people with the same surname, claiming that the *Viracocha* brought shame on the whole Aymara people. Muñoz, meanwhile, had gone as far as to claim our few metres of plastic string were an insult to the whole of Chile.

One afternoon, I asked the local barber if he found our boat a personal insult. He laughed thinly. 'It's nothing to do with your plastic string or whatever it is you're arguing about,' he said, casually wielding the razor around the nape of my neck. 'It's just that nobody really believes you're going anywhere. The Spanish guy already tried it twice, and look what happened to him. It's obvious that reed boats don't work.'

Not everyone shared this view. Aricans, separated from the populous bulk of their fellow countrymen by several thousand miles of desert, seemed an earthy, independent breed, determined to make up their own minds. Once part of Peru, the nitrate port had been the focus of a fierce battle between Chile, Bolivia and Peru in the War of the Pacific in the late nineteenth century, when Chile finally annexed a sizeable portion of the coast, and turned Bolivia into a landlocked country. Passed around like a child between divorcing parents, the self-styled Independent Republic of Arica was slow to take sides. Its people, predominantly working class, took their time to weigh us up.

Little by little we won friends. At the camp, Marco gave enthusiastic tours for those who came to look at this new oddity parked on their beach, and we got used to downing our tools for snap shots with grinning visitors. The slightly chaotic atmosphere of the camp seemed to appeal to them, contrasting markedly with Muñoz's much tighter operation, in which armed guards had apparently kept sightseers permanently outside the fence. Phil's mother-in-law, Gloria, arrived to take on the cooking arrangements, bringing an assortment of three grandchildren to stay for their summer holidays, and there was a resulting sense of family that grew as we built up a small and slightly eccentric retinue of supporters. Among them was Victor Burgos, a placid, curly-haired driver who proudly put his dusty black taxi at our disposal, and who was instantly recognisable by the small solar-powered fan mounted on his baseball cap. Miriam, a buxom and beaming community pharmacist, was another who hung around the camp on her days off, earning the affectionate title 'The Fan Club' because of her endless photos of the boat and habit of asking crew members to sign things – anything, in fact. Even the most casually discarded off-cut or fraying rope-end could become a souvenir for our keenest admirer, often before it had hit the ground. Meanwhile a jovial, barrel-chested craftsman called Roberto set out to produce a rather higher class of souvenir by creating miniature reed boats with leftover *totora* and mounting them in bottles. He had soon cornered an insatiable market in *Viracocha*s-in-bottles, and could probably have made a reasonable income from his models, had he not insisted on giving them away to delighted crew members.

His generosity was characteristic of a growing sense of goodwill, which Phil did his best to sustain among the now familiar journalists visiting the camp. When the issue of plastic string arose, as it invariably did like a bad smell at the end of each interview, he simply reiterated that he had used a small amount of it, denied that it had any effect on the durability of the ship, and extended a cordial invitation to Kitin Muñoz to come and inspect the *Viracocha* on

Easter Island, where he would be happy to cut her open to show exactly how she was constructed. Muñoz, launching his faxed salvos from Madrid, never made any response to these invitations. As far as we know, he never so much as set eyes on the *Viracocha*. Our local friends seemed disappointed at the apparent friction — all of them had helped Kitin, just as they were helping us, and could not understand the fuss. Jorge and Ernesto had actually worked for Muñoz and found him decent enough. But they loved the *Viracocha* for the same reason they had loved the *Mata Rangi II* — as a symbol of a simpler, more heroic age which summoned almost forgotten yearnings in them.

Phil had admired the *Mata Rangi II* while researching in Arica the previous summer. 'She was one of the most beautiful things I had ever seen,' he confessed. He had introduced himself to Kitin Muñoz, who had been cordial and proud as he showed Phil around the enormous ship — though Eli had been asked to wait at ground level due to Muñoz's firm conviction that women brought bad luck. When Phil told him he was planning to sail his own reed boat to Easter Island, Muñoz had simply shaken his head. 'Almost impossible,' he had said. 'The winds are all wrong.' All the same, when Phil called back a few days later, he found his reception markedly cooler, and the Spaniard too busy to talk properly. Phil wished him luck and left. It was, to date, the only face-to-face contact the two men had had.

However much we tried to ignore the steady drip of denigration, we found ourselves resenting this unknown enemy. Muñoz became for us a shadowy, Machiavellian figure, forever lurking in the background, waiting to spoil our fun.

One bizarre incident took us to the brink of paranoia. It was about 8 a.m. and we were all slumped around the table clutching coffees, waiting for our eyes to open fully. Young Mark was contentedly drawing extra spots on his long-suffering Dalmatian puppy with a felt-tipped pen, and Gloria was serving porridge oats. In other words, an ordinary breakfast scene — except that we slowly became aware of the distant buzz of a light aircraft. It approached from the south, low in the cloudless sky, and turned towards us.

'TV crew?' I suggested.

We watched as the plane banked close to the camp, and suddenly Fernie, one of Gloria's assorted grandchildren, aged nine, pointed and yelled excitedly.

'They're dropping us a present!'

A brown paper bag was pirouetting down through the still air. It disappeared from view about 10 metres outside the camp walls. Fernie sprinted off to investigate, determined to be the first to open the present, but Phil's eyes were narrow and suspicious. By the time we arrived at the door of the camp, Fernie was already bending over it with the look of a child on Christmas morning. He lifted a flap of torn paper, gingerly, and suddenly recoiled, slapping his legs. He backed away, looking frightened and confused.

'It's a lot of *bugs!*' he shouted.

The bag buzzed like a broken loudspeaker as I approached with Phil. Using a piece of driftwood, he eased back the torn flap. A black mass of flies covered the inside of the bag. There was nothing else. We backed away as an angry cloud of them escaped.

'What kind of a sick bastard . . . ?' muttered Phil, striding back towards the camp in search of insecticide.

My imagination was in overdrive. It was like some dark plot from an industrial espionage thriller. Were the flies bred to lay parasitic larvae on *totora* reed? Or perhaps even worse, were they carrying a debilitating human virus? Who could hate us openly enough to hire a plane to drop live insects in broad daylight on a camp where young children played? Only one name suggested itself. I pictured our arch enemy hunched over a bell jar full of young larvae, cackling like a maniac. I could see cash-stuffed envelopes changing hands in back alleys, a sealed, buzzing brown bag given wordlessly to the pilot of an unmarked aircraft at a private runway. I pictured the headlines: 'Tragic mystery virus halts *Viracocha* expedition . . .'

Phil walked past me shaking up a canister of Raid, a determined look on his face. At the camp entrance he met Jorge, arriving for work.

'Did you see that, Jorge? A bag of bugs!'

'Yes *capitán*,' said Jorge, looking at the canister in Phil's hand. 'The municipal government drops them as part of its pest control scheme. And if you kill the flies it won't work properly.'

Phil sagged slightly. A pest control scheme that *released* live insects?

'They're special fruit flies,' explained Jorge. 'They're bred in laboratories and sterilised – some kind of genetic engineering. Then they mate with the other flies, so in one generation – no more flies. It was in the newspaper.'

He shrugged.

'Oh,' muttered Phil. 'Neat.'

Apart from marking us out as a bunch of paranoid conspiracy theorists, the incident showed just how distracted we were becoming from our real goal. Every week that we were delayed made our ultimate success less likely. As Muñoz had hinted to Phil, the turbulent weather system around Easter Island was difficult enough to negotiate at any time of year, but in April the winds would begin to shift to a prevailing west wind. In other words, if we didn't get underway soon, we could sail to within 500 miles of our target, only to be blown back the way we had come.

One rather large obstacle to our onward journey was that we hadn't yet got round to making any sails. Six rolls of virgin canvas lay untouched in cardboard boxes beneath the *Viracocha*, and Phil had so far been rather vague about how they would convert themselves into our sole means of propulsion across 2500 miles of open sea. I got the feeling he was avoiding the issue, and one morning I told him so.

'You're absolutely right,' said Phil, nodding thoughtfully. 'So you know what? I'm gonna put *you* in charge of making the sails. You can take a break from everything else – just keep me posted on how the sails are going. And try not to spend too much money.'

I was speechless. This was not the result I had anticipated. I barely knew how to darn a sock, let alone design and stitch a pair of sails. 'Me neither,' sympathised Phil. 'I've got a book if you want to read up on it, but don't take too long over it. We'll need them in a couple of weeks.' He winked at me and walked off, adding: 'Remember, Nickers, if you screw this one up, the whole expedition fails.'

It took me a couple of days to come to terms with the enormity of the task before me. It was like blagging a last-minute seat on a long-haul flight only to have the pilot tap you on the shoulder in the boarding queue and say: 'Excuse me, mate, we seem to have forgotten to fit an engine. Could you possibly knock us one up?' I was terrified. As well as the six rolls of canvas, Phil had given me a bag full of extra-strong thread, some leather sewing palms, a box of round metal eyelets, and a tome as thick as two phone directories called *The Sailmaker's Apprentice*. I opened it at random: 'The length of the seam taper is determined by the desired draft position. That is, the seam begins to widen at the intended point of maximum draft, and widens progressively further as it approaches the luff.'

I shut it again, feeling dizzy.

I had one lifeline. Phil gave me a sheaf of printouts from a website connected to something called the *Manteño* expedition. A few years previously, it seemed, a Texan businessman and a few others had set out to reconstruct a balsa raft of the type ancient traders might have used as they plied the coast of South and Central America. Unlike the *Kon-Tiki*, they had used triangular 'lateen' sails, on the basis of research that seemed to show that square European-style drift sails of the type used by Heyerdahl had only become widely used after the arrival of the Spaniards. Phil favoured the lateen sails not only on grounds of authenticity, but because they would enable us to sail closer to the wind, and if necessary to tack into it, while square drift sails were more or less reliant on a following breeze. The best part of all this was that the *Manteño* team, apparently a meticulous and big-hearted bunch, had left detailed sail plans on the internet, presumably for anyone else who might feel like knocking up a pre-Colombian balsa-wood raft in his spare time. Feeling extremely lucky, I began to follow the instructions.

It was laborious and frustrating work. Stephane and I spent three mornings cutting and laying out long strips of fabric on the beach outside the camp, tacking them together with safety pins, and then putting rocks on top before the afternoon wind blew them to Peru.

Lateen sails seemed superficially more or less the same shape as those I had used on yachts and dinghies, with the exception that instead of being attached to the mast, with a boom along the bottom, their only stiff edge would be a long supporting beam known as a yard, lashed along the diagonal, and suspended from the top of the mast. I couldn't quite visualise how it would work, but Phil assured me I didn't need to worry about rigging it – that was Craig's job.

Craig looked dubious about this prospect. In fact Craig had been looking a little stressed for some time. One day he returned from the internet café looking even more stony than usual. 'I've just had an email from my boss,' he said. 'If I'm not back at my desk by 20 March, they're going to start advertising for a replacement. That means we need to be on our way by 1 February at the latest, or I'm in deep shit. I might have to think about pulling out.'

Ordinarily, I would have taken this with a pinch of salt. I couldn't believe anyone who had invested as much time and energy in an expedition as Craig would jeopardise the experience for the sake of a mere job. Wasn't that the whole point of this thing? We were leaving all that behind, free of the usual ties and constraints and boxes, making rude gestures in the face of convention. Weren't we? Yet I got the impression that the decision, if it were to come to it, would not be so easy for Craig. There were other considerations. Something else was eating him, and that something was Phil.

The friction between the two men was becoming impossible to ignore. One day I wandered into the camp after a particularly frustrating morning of sail-pinning, to find Craig hunched glowering at the table, while the rest of the crew worked at the frame of the cabin, up on the boat. In front of him was a scale plan of his suggested cabin design, immaculately plotted on graph paper and complete with exact measurements and materials. It had taken him several hours.

Yet when he finally completed it, he had discovered that Phil was already well-advanced with corner posts from a design of his own, scrawled on the back of an old receipt. 'Craig got really pissed with me for not waiting,' said Phil, when I climbed up to find out what had happened. 'His plan may be excellent, but we can't really afford to sit around waiting for it. *He's* the one with the deadline.'

I clambered wearily back to earth, preparing myself for the role of peace ambassador. I liked Craig, and had developed a trusting friendship with him that the others seemed to lack, but I was beginning to tire of shuttling between what felt like two different planets. He had retreated to his tent, where he was rummaging noisily for something. 'Well it looks like you're pretty much on the same track,' I said, with breezy and entirely forced cheerfulness. 'It turns out your plan is more or less the same as Phil's.'

Craig turned and stared at me. 'Phil actually *has* a plan?' he said, his voice creaking with sarcasm. 'You surprise me.' He wandered off into town and came back only late that night.

It was easy to see where the problem lay. Craig, something of an introvert, was used to running a tight ship, oiling his tools, plotting his course. He liked precise planning, achievable goals, and unambiguous orders. Phil, meanwhile, did not so much give orders as ask favours. He liked to try things out, and was emphatic that the *Viracocha* was an experiment, not a perfectly finished product. Thus it was that Craig found himself in a chaos of improvisation, his tools spread around the camp, children under his feet, and unable to communicate to the Spanish-speaking people who might carry out his suggestions except through a man who was rapidly becoming his antithesis. Increasingly he grew angry and distant. While other crew members sat around the table chatting or drinking beer at night, he could often be found sitting on his toolbox among the tents, reading *101 Useful Knots*.

The rift grew steadily wider as Craig's 1 February deadline approached. It all came to a head one afternoon in the last week of January. Phil, Craig and Jorge were drilling and dowelling planks on the deck at the back of the boat. Stephane and I had sent our ragged triangles of sails to a local jeans factory for primary stitching, and were back at work on the foredeck, from where we could hear the sparse conversation drifting through the cabin.

'What the hell is this?' It was Craig, his voice crackling with tension.

'It's a new power cable, Craig — I thought we could use both tools at once that way.'

'No way are you gonna use my electric saw with that flimsy thing – you'll fry the insides or blow the power.'

'OK, Craig,' said Phil, in the kind of voice you might use on a particularly crotchety mother-in-law. I heard him explaining the new rule in Spanish to Jorge.

A tense five minutes of silence ensued. Then the sound of the drill.

'Goddamit, Phil!' The drill ceased.

'What?' Phil sounded exasperated.

'I've just told you not to use my tools with that fucking cable!'

'Actually you told me not to use the saw. You never mentioned the drill. And I'd really appreciate it if you wouldn't talk to me with that tone.'

'Right, I've had it. That's *it*.'

From the aft deck came tinkles, clanks, the sound of plugs being disconnected, muttered curses. Craig was collecting up his tools, lifting them from the hands of his crewmates. Stephane and I exchanged glances, and then carried on sawing and chiselling. Craig stomped through the cabin and stepped over us without a word. We listened as he descended the ladder, dragged out his enormous toolbox and began throwing things into it. Finally, he locked it with a padlock.

Jorge, audibly puzzled, asked Phil if he could have the hammer back to carry on with his job.

'I guess we're finished working for today,' answered Phil, quietly.

The real implications were soon unavoidable even to me. Pointedly refusing to have lunch with the rest of the crew, Craig continued to drag plastic trunks out to the centre of the yard all that afternoon. In them were the various nautical gadgets and safety equipment which Craig had purchased for the expedition: the VHF radio, the compass, the sea anchor, reference books, immersion suits, waterproofs, harnesses. Clearly, he was moving out, jumping ship, refusing to play the game any more. Would he take all his toys with him? Later that afternoon, I confronted him.

'I've got to get home,' he said, heavily, avoiding eye contact. 'I've wasted enough time here.'

'But what about all the equipment?'

'Phil can keep whatever he can pay for.'

The next three days had the awful hollowness of a final divorce settlement. There were terse, level exchanges between the dividing parties as they negotiated for the furniture they had once shared. There were tactful silences from everyone around them. Phil, it emerged, was already heavily in debt and could only afford to buy the absolute essentials. Crew members were invited to buy their own safety equipment. I bought some dry-bags, a harness with a strobe, a few books about navigation. The immersion suits disappeared for good. Craig, staying in a nearby hotel, came back now and again to finalise things. I spent an hour or so with him trying to glean every last fragment of knowledge about the sail system. Once he left, it would all be my responsibility. 'I'm not exactly sure how the sails will work,' he admitted. 'You're using a lateen rig like on a dhow sailing boat, but you've got bipod masts. I don't know if anyone has ever done that before.'

You, not we. I was acutely aware of Craig's sudden detachment, his distance. He was no longer coiled and tense, but flat and placid. Overwhelmingly, he seemed relieved to have made his decision. We stood in the yard and looked up at the boat together. The camp was deserted.

'You must be glad to be free of all this,' I said bitterly, trying to provoke at least some acknowledgement of the relationships he was leaving behind.

'It was tough – I've been working on this project for more than a year. But it's time to go home. I've got a good job and I don't want to throw it away . . .' There was a pause.

'What about you?' he asked.

'I'm still thinking about it. Obviously I'm worried, but I'm not sure I can drop out that easily.'

He forced a wry grin.

'Well, good luck!' he said, shouldering his bag. We shook hands formally, and he turned to walk out of the camp for the last time. He looked intently into my face for a moment.

'Do yourself a favour, Nick,' he said gently. 'Don't get on that thing without a life raft.'

And with that, we lost our navigator.

4

The Longest Launch

Craig's departure hit me hard and square, like the side of a bus. I twitched with nervous indecision for days. My crisis of confidence was, however, a source of puzzlement to others in the crew, who went about their work with a new freedom and a rather inferior selection of cheap or borrowed hand tools.

'We're better off without him,' insisted Stephane, clambering up on to the boat one evening to find me still agonising about whether to come or not. 'Do you think Craig would have taken orders from Phil? Before long it would have come to blows — maybe in the middle of the ocean, in the middle of an emergency. That's a bad vibe, *hermano*.' He shook his head and made his clicking noise.

'But at least Craig would know what to *do* in an emergency,' I argued, keeping my voice low. 'None of us are competent navigators, including Phil. Don't you realise how complicated it is sailing a boat?'

The trouble was, I had flirted just enough with sailing boats to know how much there was to go wrong, but not enough to put it right. While Stephane and Phil, I imagined, had gained false confidence from the exhilaration of sailing under another's captaincy, I had helmed my own dinghies a few times, and recalled vivid failures. There was the memory of being tipped unceremoniously overboard after taking my eye off the wind direction for five seconds; or being smacked across the forehead for no apparent reason by a swinging boom. If the wind could be so unforgiving of ineptitude in the Thames, what would it do in mid-Pacific, when every move was complicated by the mysterious arithmetic of navigation?

The darkening expanse around me offered a familiar undertow of conflicting emotions. I had always both loved and feared the sea, perhaps loved it *because* I feared it. Unlike the ordered, hedged-in commuter suburb where I grew up, it was impossible to pretend that the ocean was tame. I remembered the delicious wildness of the small Scottish island where I had holidayed as a child. Late at night, I would lie awake in my bunk, listening to the howl of the wind, the boom and hiss of surf and the strange incantation of the shipping forecast, thinking of lonely fishermen tossed on gigantic seas. Even in good weather, sailing across an outwardly placid surface, you knew the ocean was tolerating you, and no more. A few miles from our island, the infamous Gulf of Corryvreckan had been known to swallow ships whole. We had sailed through the treacherous gap at slack tide once, and even then the surface was disfigured by strange muscular boilings and streakings, upflows which sent bladderwrack and jellyfish writhing. A whirlpool surfaced abruptly only metres from our boat, yanking at the rowing boat we towed, spinning it round. I knew then that we were tiptoeing across the surface of something huge and dangerous and indifferent. Fathoms below us, I imagined, were the bones of the unlucky, tumbling back and forth.

The one crucial insurance against a terrifying death – the thing that had enabled me to enjoy these bold excursions rather than cling, whimpering to the mast – was the firm hand of Uncle Chris on the tiller. He wasn't really an uncle, but my brothers and I called him that because he had a reassuring quality of someone to whom you might trust your life. A towering Anglican minister with unfeasibly large feet, he exuded a patrician confidence as he charted courses, barked orders to us in the bow, scrutinised the skies for changing cloud formations, let us know when it was time to head for shore. He was indisputably *in charge*. Every expedition should have an Uncle Chris. He was an essential item, like a compass or a lifeboat, I thought, as I gazed at the Pacific now. And the trouble with this expedition was that Uncle Chris had just walked out.

Stephane had no time for my romantic reminiscences. 'On this boat nobody is an expert, not even Craig, because it's a reed boat and nobody has ever done what we are going to do! That's the whole point – it's an experiment! We don't rely on experts, we rely on each other.' It was one of Phil's lines, and it simply made me more nervous. Stephane gave up and climbed back down the wooden ladder.

Craig's immediate replacement was Jorge, which was comforting. I instinctively liked Jorge, though I occasionally had trouble understanding his heavy accent. A native of the region, he was a youthful forty, with a round, friendly face and the quiet wisdom of an experienced fisherman. His expertise in knot work was also invaluable. Knots were, after all, what held the boat together. Yet he admitted that while he could operate a ship's radio, he had no navigational expertise, and had only ever worked on engine-powered boats. How much would he know about sailing?

In the end, it was Erik who won back my trust in the expedition. He had returned to the camp only a few days before Craig's departure, seen the angry outbursts, and now broke his tactful silence for the first time. 'You cannot have two captains!' he said, wagging his finger at me as we shared a beer later that night. 'And what use is an expert if he doesn't speak the same language as his crew? In the end, sailing a reed boat comes down to instinct, not technical knowledge.' You needed, apparently, a feel for the slow turning of the reed hull in the water, an instinct for how best to set the sails when the wind was changing. 'Craig knew a lot about western yachts, but he did not understand *balsas de totora*. He did not have the patience.'

Erik, on the other hand, had spent years learning the technology of the ancients. He had been on no fewer than three expeditions using reed boats he had built with his own hands: a circumnavigation of Lake Titicaca in 1993, and two river navigations with the British explorer Colonel John Blashford Snell in 1998 and 1999. It seemed an impressive C.V. and there was a confidence about Erik that I had not really appreciated until now.

'Don't be afraid, Nick,' he said, fixing me intently. 'I have a good feeling about this expedition.'

And that was what clinched it. A good feeling, a sort of intuition. In carefully worded emails home I glossed over Craig's departure, enthused about Jorge's 'extensive maritime experience', and began to refer to Erik as 'our Aymara navigator'. It seemed churlish to point out, even to myself, that for all his lake and river navigation, Erik had never been to sea in his life.

Phil, meanwhile, seemed a little hurt by my lack of confidence in his own maritime skills. We had not spoken properly for days, and he was understandably annoyed to hear about my doubts indirectly, through others. When I announced to him that I was going to stay in the crew after all, he raised his eyebrows. 'Whatever you think,' he shrugged. 'Don't feel pressured from my point of view. We're perfectly capable of getting to Easter Island without you.'

In fact, the whole Craig crisis had blown up at a bad time for Phil. For weeks now, he had been promised the use of a crane and a submersible trailer, which could drive the boat a few hundred yards on to the sandy public beach, back her down to the waterline at low tide and then withdraw when the rising tide floated her off. The promise, however, had come via a friend of a friend in a haulage company, and it now emerged there had been some mis-understanding. Peering at the *Viracocha* and listening to Phil's planned route, the friend of a friend had suddenly announced that his trailer was not submersible after all.

This left us with a problem of an embarrassingly fundamental nature: we had almost completed a boat that we had no way of launching. The boat was positioned barely 50 metres from the sea, yet in the intervening space lay a rocky incline and a beach whose shallows were studded with boulders. Even if we were to find a way of getting the now 20-tonne *Viracocha* down the rocky incline, the act of dragging her into the shallows would be like applying a large cheese grater to her fragile hull, inflicting perhaps irreversible damage. The obvious remedies — some kind of wheeled undercar-riage beneath the existing cradle, for example — were ruled out on basis of the construction time needed.

While wrestling with this problem, Phil was also directing the rest of us in putting the finishing touches to the cabin. After var-ious extravagant plans, it had evolved into a simple, windowless box with a double layer of split bamboo walls, a roof of 4-inch thick bamboo canes laid side by side, and a doorway at each end. Lashed on top of beams laid across the bundled reed gunwales, it had stor-age space underneath and a planked walkway along the outside of each wall. Inside, spread along both sides of a central passageway, we had built a large map table and six bunks using pine, dowelling, glue and rope. Six was a compromise figure. At this stage, potentially a few days before launching, there was still some debate over exactly how many people would be in the crew. We were still two down on the original eight planned, due to the unexplained withdrawal of both cinematographers, and for weeks now, Phil had favoured keeping it that way. After all, it meant we would have to bring less food and water. Hadn't the *Kon-Tiki* sailed with five men? On the other hand, *Kon-Tiki* had only had one mast and one sail. It was doubtful that six of us would be sufficient to change both sails and man the tiller at the same time. As a result, Phil now seemed to be inclining back towards a full complement of eight. This would not disrupt sleeping arrangements, he stressed, as two men would be on watch at any given hour of the day or night, leaving six bunks for the rest.

But where would we get two new crew members at this late stage? I strongly favoured a public appeal for a navigator and a doctor. Phil, on the other hand, was desperate to include a film-maker who could help him recoup his enormous debts with a documentary.

We ended up with a tree surgeon.

Greg Dobbs was an old friend of Phil's who had been staying with Eli's sister, Fernanda, while backpacking through Chile. A stocky Texan with reddish-blond hair and a wide, good-natured grin, 'Dobbers' was an even-tempered man who seemed to ponder his words before he spoke them. He arrived looking slightly shell-shocked from the attentions of Fernanda and her friend Lorena, two fanatical party animals who had driven him several thousand miles across the desert from Santiago to see the launch. With their chic, stylish and inappropriate outfits, Fernanda and Lorena had a slightly stranded air while in the camp, as if they had inadvertently walked on to the set of the wrong sitcom. They certainly had no discernable interest in shipbuilding. They would emerge from their tent at lunchtime already wearing sunglasses, complaining in stage whispers that they had heard a mouse during the night, and then mooch around the camp taking calls on their mobile phones until it was time to go dancing again. Their most memorable contribution to the launching of the *Viracocha* was to pose coquettishly on the cabin roof in bikinis for a press photographer, thus getting on to the front page of the local newspaper.

Greg, meanwhile, clearly yearned for the open sea. 'Ain't it awesome?' he would murmur. 'This is one hell of an opportunity!' Yet for all his enthusiasm, Greg was not quite the expert I had hoped for. He had sailed to Cuba with Phil, both of them as crew members on a small modern yacht, but he knew nothing about navigation. Phil acknowledged this, but said Greg's gentle temperament would be a stabilising influence on board. So we welcomed our seventh crew member and left the eighth place vacant in the hope that our dream candidate would walk into the camp and announce himself to be a one-time solo yachtsman who had just left his job as a top-grade paramedic to make Oscar-winning documentaries.

In the meantime the work was boosted considerably by the arrival of a contingent of four determined helpers from Erik's family and village. Maximo, Justino and 'Rambo' Catari and José Limache all arrived one evening on the bus from Bolivia, and demanded to be set to work even before they had pitched their tent. Their faces were dark and weather-beaten and stern, their bodies lean and muscular, and they were angry – angry at the slur on their workmanship by Muñoz and the Estebans, more determined than ever that the *Viracocha* would succeed. Each morning all four would emerge from the same small two-man tent as if through a time portal, eat whatever Gloria set before them in polite silence, and leave the camp with Erik for a kind of team huddle. Ten minutes later, Erik would explain to Phil whatever it was that they had decided for that day – 'My father would like to work on the steering system today' – and Phil would gratefully usher them to the right part of the boat where they would work grimly, their mouths set in determined lines, until the job was done. In a matter of days they built wooden wave-shields at the prow of the boat, decked the stern, fitted the huge steering oars with tillers chopped from eucalyptus trunks, and helped me sew more than 200 feet of tough bolt-rope round the perimeter of the sails. The only thing that would deter them from their work was the arrival of a TV crew or newspaper photographer. At this point they would all scramble for their tent, swap their T-shirts for native Aymara ponchos and reassemble in front of the boat for the waiting cameras, scowling proudly from beneath colourful bobbled Alpaca hats in the merciless desert heat.

Stress levels grew steadily as February wore on, and most of us found ways to avoid the camp when we weren't working. I disappeared into town to file reports for the *Scotsman* when necessary, and took the sails up to a vacant tennis court to work on them in peace. Once on board, all solitude would evaporate, and in these last few days it became a priceless commodity. Stephane, meanwhile, found other ways to escape. Having already wooed a not insignificant section of the female population of Arica since his arrival, he became besotted by one raven-haired beauty in particular as our departure became more imminent. After a day of near-frenetic carpentry, he would slink off into the night and only return around breakfast time with baggy eyes, a sly grin, and the pronounced limp of a man whose nocturnal occupations had demanded hitherto unknown levels of athleticism. 'I have a problem with women,' he told me gravely, one afternoon. 'They can't get enough of me! Everywhere I go I am pursued by them! I must get away!' I wondered if spending three months cooped up on an all-male raft was quite the solution he was looking for.

Marco continued to work as watchman by night, and camp comedian by day, but even he seemed wearied by the delays. Gloria was clearly worried about her son. 'Do you think Marco will make a good sailor?' she asked me one night, quietly. 'You know he has a wife and three children back in Santiago – I keep worrying that something will happen to him. He gets excited about things, and doesn't always take care.' I liked Gloria. There weren't many grand-mothers who would camp on a beach for weeks on end simply to cook, but Gloria did it with gusto and gave enormous portions. Once, sensing Phil was flagging, she had presented him proudly with a birthday present of two live ducks, which, she explained, would keep us company on the long voyage as mascots. The idea had come from Thor Heyerdahl himself, who always took a pet of some kind with him on voyages. 'If Heyerdahl has a mascot, then so will my son-in-law!' she laughed. Pedro and Pablo – named after the Spanish *Flintstones* characters for Fred and Barney – settled into an energetic daily routine of furious quacking as they ran round and round the camp, stopping only to aim vicious pecks at the Dalmatian in excited pursuit.

On this night, however, even Gloria seemed to have lost her sparkle. I patted her shoulder. 'Don't worry, we will all look after each other,' I said, wishing I believed it a little more. She brightened suddenly: 'And God will look after you! My whole church will pray for you.' This was no easy promise – Gloria's church famously had 3000 members.

Erik too seemed confident that we would have some kind of divine protection – albeit from different divinities. 'My father consulted the shaman before he came here, asked him to foretell our fate,' he whispered solemnly one day. 'The answer was good. We will succeed, but not without many trials along the way.' How could I argue with such pleasingly vague fortune telling? But what was 'trials along the way' supposed to mean? Crew bickering? Or being forced to eat our mascots? Or each other? On the other hand, 'success' seemed nicely unequivocal.

Our luck did indeed seem to turn, in a way none of us had envisaged. One day, somewhere high in the Bolivian Altiplano, it began to rain. We saw no rain in Arica, of course – some adults here had *never* seen rain. But 50 metres along the beach, the little brook began to swell, fed from the mountains and plateaus high above the city. We had barely noticed it before, a sad, rubbish-choked gully coming down through the shanty neighbourhoods, bringing little more than a trickle. Now plastic bags began to lift from rocks like colourful jellyfish, the gurgling deepened to a roar, and our usual taxi route into town, fording the brook where it flowed under a fly-over, became impassable. It continued for days. Along the beach, holidaymakers stopped swimming, complaining of the silted red colour of the sea, and the newspapers ran stories about the damage to the tourist industry. None of it seemed to have much relevance to us until, one morning, Phil wandered back into camp grinning.

'Come and look,' he said. 'Seems like Mother Nature's helping us out.'

The tide was low, and directly below the camp, where once the beach was studded with rocks, it was now a smooth, wet expanse of reddish sand. Four days of rain, direct from the Bolivian Altiplano where we began our journey, had rearranged the beach by sweeping tonnes of sand on to the rocks, leaving them buried beneath a perfect natural causeway. 'Now,' said Phil, looking thoughtful, 'All we've got to do is get her to the waterline and we can float her without any danger of shredding her hull. As long as we can do it before the sea currents uncover the rocks again.'

Reinvigorated, he took three crew members and disappeared into town. When they returned, two hours later, it was on a flatbed lorry piled with iron railway girders and huge wooden sleepers. 'I borrowed them from the national railway company,' explained Phil. 'We're going to build a ramp, grease the rails, and slide the *Viracocha* into the sea.'

It took six of us to carry each rail, watched by three incredulous rail workers who had been sent to assist us. The high-pitched clinking of steel hammers against 10-inch nails, the smell of oil, seemed to bring a soiled, industrial aspect to the camp. People barked their shins on rails on the way to the toilet, and the yard suddenly became harder, more dangerous for the children. But slowly, amid hissing volleys of welding sparks, a simple iron cradle took shape beneath the eucalyptus logs like an enormous noughts-and-crosses grid. At the same time, Erik's family put the finishing touches to the rudders and decking, and Stephane climbed the mast to install the radio aerial. I reinforced the corners of the sails, my fingers raw with stitching, and worked on some rope ladders and pulley blocks with Jorge and Ernesto. And so the word went out: the *Viracocha* was almost ready for launching.

I'd seen ship launches many times on television, so I knew what was supposed to happen. Normally, the white-gloved visiting dignitary said something worthy, swung a bottle of something expensive at the bow, and off went the boat. If they were unlucky, the bottle didn't break and the dignitary had to do it again. I even saw one launch when the bottle had to be broken with a hammer after the fifth unsuccessful attempt. But that was as far as the problems went. Even if you didn't happen to have a dignitary, any reasonable and fair-minded boat would begin to move, accelerate down its ramp, and thunder into the water with a rush of foam, taking all of five seconds.

Not five *days*.

It all began so well. It was a Monday afternoon when the welders moved out, and perhaps 200 people gathered round the camp to help. There were local families, visiting tourists, all of our friends. Men stood with folded arms, holding in their paunches and talking loudly about how best to move the boat. Children ran around in the shallows squealing. Everyone relished the sense of something actually happening at last. Erik's family had successfully sawn away the vertical logs so that the *Viracocha* was now resting entirely on her new metal base, and a rope was being attached to it to help pull her into position for the slide down to the water. Marco was delightedly shouting orders to anyone who would listen, while Stephane and the others dismantled the seaward fence of the camp. Erik was using a stick wrapped in bundled rags to daub engine oil on to the tracks.

A JCB digger, driven by a teenager in shades, roared into the camp to apply the main forward push from behind, while Marco organised the chattering locals along two pulling ropes, one at either side of the boat. Then at 7 p.m. there was a hush, a shout of 'Ready, PULL!' the roar of the digger engine, and all at once the boat was moving, turning slowly into position on the main track with a mournful moan of metal. People whistled and cheered and had to be reminded to keep pulling, and I found myself laughing with surprise that such an enormous weight could be moved with a little bit of grease.

We had pulled her two boat lengths from the camp, stern first, and were preparing for the final slide, when Phil called a halt, just above the meandering line of seaweed and junk that marked high tide. 'OK, that's all for today!' yelled Marco. 'Thank you, and please come back tomorrow morning!' The boat stopped. It was a little disappointing.

There were two reasons for the delay. Firstly, the sun was going down, and secondly we had run out of track. Due to a shortage of available spares, and the fact that we were laying three parallel rails rather than two, the rails ended 20 metres from the surf. We were going to have to advance in stages, by dismantling the track behind the boat as it passed over, and bolting it on in front. Tomorrow, we assured everyone, we would span the final portion to the sea, and let the rising tide float our ancient craft as it had done more than a millennium ago.

We woke in the chilly half-light, our senses dulled by sleep, to the distant sound of Phil cursing. I found him kneeling below the curved stern, digging frantically with his hands in the place where the rails were supposed to be. 'There's been some kind of freak tide overnight,' he muttered. 'The sand has buried the rails.' By the time the JCB arrived to help us uncover them, we were slopping in water-filled pits of our own making and the new tide was advancing. It was too late to extend the track, and our only option was to retreat back beyond the reach of the surf. The returning public were puzzled to be told they would be pulling *up* the beach, not down it.

'But tomorrow's the big day, for sure!' yelled Phil, grinning apologetically, when the boat halted back where it had started the day before. I was beginning to wonder if it might not be quicker to swim to Easter Island.

The next morning should have been a textbook launch, if only there had been a textbook. By 7 a.m. we were staggering down to the sea with railway sleepers, and the engineer had stripped down to his shorts to nail rails on to them. Soon the track was in place, and the crowds were assembling excitedly.

'Now,' said Phil, straining his eyes looking out towards the harbour. 'Where the hell is that tow boat?'

The tow boat had been hired to pull the *Viracocha* out to her moorings, where she would stay temporarily while we spent a few days fitting her rudders and sail system and loading her with equipment and provisions. Jorge, up in the cabin, radioed her to find out what was happening, and emerged looking grave.

'They're having engine trouble, *capitán*,' he said. Phil looked incredulous, then suddenly determined. 'Give me half an hour!' he yelled, and sprinted off towards the port. It was 10 a.m. when he returned, panting. 'I got a replacement tug,' he said. 'She should be here any time. We can still make it.'

At 11 a.m. a small black silhouette chugged slowly from the harbour entrance and across the bay. It was an open, rectangular tub of a vessel, which from this distance looked slightly larger than a rowing boat. 'Are you sure that's going to be big enough?' I asked Phil, frowning.

'Yup. The guy told me these little boats called *pangas* are strong enough to shift fishing boats – very powerful engines.' He brushed away the doubt. 'Now – let's launch!'

After a further delay in which it emerged that the little boat had not brought a tow rope and we were obliged to swim out with a huge length of sisal, the *panga* crew of two secured the rope.

'Positions!' yelled Marco, and the gathered masses picked up their own ropes, while the JCB prepared to push from behind. There was a spurt of exhaust and a distant farting noise as the *panga* revved its engine and Marco raised his hand, waiting for the tow rope to tauten so he could give the signal to pull.

Unfortunately, the tow rope didn't tauten. No matter how furiously the *panga* strained at it, the rope stayed in a lazy arc across the water's surface, dragged by the running tide. The painful truth insinuated itself gradually like the onset of a migraine. If the *panga* had insufficient power to straighten a wet rope in a gentle tide, how would it pull a 25-tonne boat? If we were to push the *Viracocha* into the sea at this stage, we would most likely watch both boats drift helplessly up towards the coast of Peru. As if to confirm this, the distant straining of the engine ceased in a splutter. Jorge confirmed by radio that the *panga* had now burnt out its motor, and was itself in need of emergency assistance.

Phil cursed violently under his breath and looked at his watch. It was noon, high tide. Marco lowered his arm gently and told us all we could drop the rope. A general murmur of sympathy rippled round for the third time. It was obviously not going to happen. Someone, at a loss to know what else to do for us, started a whip-round. Others began muttering angrily. 'Why isn't the government helping?' said someone. 'How can they let the captain down like this?' 'Someone should call the mayor.'

It was early afternoon when the man in epaulettes and naval uniform strode into the camp. He had a long-suffering expression of one who has seen most things in the world, but is always ready to be surprised. He nodded sympathetically as Phil explained the list of mishaps that had led to the week's series of failures. The *panga* was still anchored offshore, with various mechanics hunched over its engine. 'You cannot launch a boat without proper help,' the man pronounced, finally, as if dispensing a great truth.

'What we need is a little more organisation,' agreed Phil, smiling weakly. 'We'll spend tomorrow preparing properly, and launch on Friday.'

Friday had the feel of the real thing. In reality it had to. There were only so many times we could seriously expect the people of Arica to keep turning up for botched launches before they started slow hand-clapping. The process had already taken so long that our Aymara helpers had packed up and gone back to Bolivia, and Charlie, Steiny and Ann, who must already have set some kind of record in the number of times they had delayed their flights home, had been finally forced to call it a day. The local newspaper, the *Estrella*, was beginning to show signs of severe strain in its headline department. Having begun the week, somewhat optimistically, with '*Viracocha* to sea!', it had downgraded by Tuesday to '*Viracocha* already approaching the sea!'. On Wednesday it was 'One last push!', and today it was 'Third time lucky!'. In my darker moments I imagined tomorrow's headline as 'Oh for *****'s sake!'. And perhaps a month from now, 'Arica's shame!', with a full-page picture of a rotting *Viracocha* now partially buried on this same beach, and used principally as a trysting place for amorous couples and seabirds.

Friday felt like a good day. Frogmen had appeared out of nowhere and fitted a long marker pole a short distance offshore for reasons that eluded me. We were all quietly relieved that someone else was running the show, and enjoyed simply doing what we were told – apart from Marco, who was extremely sulky when he was informed he would no longer be giving the orders. In his place came Don Prudencio Hurtado, a balloon-shaped man with motorcycle-cop sunglasses and a megaphone. He sauntered joylessly into the camp early on Friday, identified himself as the local business mogul hired to get the job done, and promptly began barking instructions. First he ordered the JCB to bulldoze a long straight strip down to the sea, then called in our suddenly attentive and energetic railway workers to lay the rails. Sand pushed from the surface of the beach was built up in protective ramparts either side of the causeway to delay the effect of waterborne sand on the rails. And a much larger tug rumbled into view and paid out a floating plastic rope. So efficient was Don Prudencio's military-style operation, that by 10.30 a.m. everything was ready, the sea was encouragingly placid, and all we had to do was await the slowly rising tide.

Little knots of Aricans were already getting quite emotional. There was an impromptu rendition of the local anthem, 'Arica, siempre Arica', with dubious tunefulness but unquestionable fervour, and we found ourselves being asked to autograph anything from driftwood to swimsuits. Roberto was doing a roaring trade in ships-in-bottles, and had painted a national flag for each of us, which he presented proudly as Miriam the Fan Club snapped her way through her twenty-fourth film. Whispering youths were clustered round the wooden tow-plates carving intense good luck messages: 'Ciao *Viracocha*, carry our dreams with you always!' or 'Phil Buck, we will always remember your brave spirit!' At 11 a.m. we were summoned up on to the deck of the *Viracocha* to say our thank yous to a crowd of 500 gathered below. Phil was the main attraction. Stephane, though, seemed to have drawn his own contingent of fans, and had just begun a suitably tear-jerking speech of thanks when several middle-aged women yelled: 'Wiggle your bum!' When he did so, cheekily, there were screams of such longing that I was fully expecting a volley of knickers to be hurled. Stephane blushed and grinned, which only made the screaming worse.

We were delivered from a wholesale riot by a barked order for everyone to take position. The tide was touching the underside of the boat, and the man with the megaphone was listening to his radio handset tensely. Greg and I stationed ourselves on the beach while the rest of the crew stood aboard the *Viracocha*. Megaphone Man raised his arm, awaited the call from the tow boat, and called for tension.

'PULL!' All at once, there was a low, whale-like moan of yearning as the undercarriage accelerated down the track, and hundreds of people roared excitedly as they pulled on the two steadying ropes. With a sudden jolt the undercarriage dropped off the end of the submerged track and for a moment the boat stuck fast there. We all watched, hearts in mouths, until a split second later, a large wave lifted the bows from the undercarriage, and the JCB accelerated forward with a final roar. The boat pitched over the wave and slid out into the bay, celebrated by applause, car horns from the road behind, and the delighted shrieks of whole battalions of helpers who were drenched by the incoming swell. I could see Stephane and Phil and the others leaping up and down on the cabin roof, waving their arms. Greg had plunged into the sea to collect the eucalyptus support logs now bobbing to the surface, helped by dozens of local men, and on the beach strangers embraced. Eli, exhausted after weeks of work, was weeping. 'It was like seeing a baby born!' Nearby, an old woman danced a strange, tottering jig, crying: '*Gracias a Dios!*'

The *Viracocha* rode the waves proudly, levelly, only a foot or so of her under the water, as the tug towed her out towards the mooring buoys. Burgos the taxi driver slapped me on the shoulder and shook my hand. 'At last,' he said. 'The adventure begins!' It was his adventure as much as mine. It was everybody's, I realised, as I looked at the celebrations around me. For all our shortcomings, we were the privileged representatives of other people's yearnings to rise above the ordinariness of life, to envisage wider horizons. I felt guilty for all my nervous fears, suddenly determined to be big enough to fill the role. It was simply that I had been here too long, on this dusty little patch of waste ground – almost long enough to lose sight of the bigger dream that had drawn me here in the first place.

That night, as we sat greasy-fingered round a campfire eating shark fillets with our Arican friends, we all knew something had changed irrevocably. With the seaward wall now missing, the camp lost any illusion of being a refuge. At its open mouth, our makeshift shower was little more than a rickety wooden frame now leaning crazily, its plastic shower curtains fluttering in wind-ravaged shreds. We sang Chilean folk songs, shared jokes and reminiscences, but none of it could ward off the sea any more, as it rushed at us, white and foaming in the moonlight. Out in the bay we could see the dark shape of the *Viracocha*, her navigation light dancing above her like a firefly as she tugged at her moorings, small and proud, impatient to be off. There was no longer anything to separate us from the wide, wild Pacific.

5

Green Luminous Froth

Picture, if you will, the image beamed back from a high-powered surveillance satellite at about 4 p.m. on Friday, 25 February 2000. Focusing on the point where the stiff edge of Chile balloons outwards into the paunch of Peru, you pick out a strange detail among the thin, chalked wakes of tiny fishing boats. 'Get me an enhanced image of that,' you bark at the imaginary surveillance geek in your technological bunker. He twitches his joystick and zooms in on two tiny interconnected specks on a slow outward trajectory, poised where whitish shallows are just beginning to cloud towards emerald. 'Strange,' frowns the geek. 'My scan's picking up a metal vessel towing some kind of . . . *vegetable matter.*'

Down in the cabin of the vegetable *Viracocha*, we were beginning to think that satellites only ever existed in the imagination. We had been trying for the best part of an hour to link up with our own supposedly space-age navigation system for a simple weather report. So far we would have been better holding a straw in the wind and guessing.

'Dammit,' said Phil, hunched over the laptop in the swaying cabin. 'This thing's a pile of junk.'

He stabbed *return* a couple more times, in the time-honoured tradition of technophobes the world over. The screen blinked and stonewalled us with the same message we had been getting all afternoon: *Log-in fail.*

'Let's try it again later,' I suggested, starting to feel a little queasy. The cabin seemed to have shrunk since we left the shelter of Arica. Every available surface, every bunk was now crammed with cartons, life jackets, camera cases, toolboxes, a bag of onions and personal duffel bags. It was like being trapped in some floating jumble sale, and I was suddenly anxious to get out on deck, watch the land recede.

Stephane, somewhere above us on the roof of the cabin, blew a flatulent, wavering blast on a little brass horn. '*Vamos a Isla de Pascua! We're going to Easter Island!*' he shouted. I stumbled out of the cabin into bright sunshine to join in the exuberance. We all felt it, after so long in preparation. The air in our lungs, the fluttering excitement in the pit of our stomachs, the reassuring solidity of the boat we had built. Even a temperamental navigation system couldn't dent the high spirits. I swung out around one of the taut, hairy mast stays and hauled myself up a rope ladder on to the cabin roof, where Stephane was lashing down a bundle of spare reeds – the *Viracocha*'s equivalent of a puncture repair kit.

The sea was sunlit and emerald green and Arica's enormous outcrop, *El Morro*, was still hazily visible about 10 miles behind us. Looking out over the bow I could see our tow boat, *Choña*, 100 metres ahead and bobbing like a bath toy in the swell. The *Viracocha*, on the other hand, seemed to absorb the waves evenly, like a sponge. The tow boat was Phil's concession to our inexperience. It would take us 100 miles offshore, far enough beyond the bulge of Peru to begin our first clumsy experiments in sailing without fear of being blown back on to the coast.

'Soon we see if our sails work, eh?' grinned Stephane, slapping me on the back. I nodded nervously, and looked down at the mizzen sail, the smaller of the two, gathered neatly along the length of its eucalyptus yard, which arced out over the water on either side of the cabin like a tightrope walker's balancing pole. We had tried hoisting the sails only once before leaving. Anchored in a light breeze, we had taken the opportunity to try them out for the TV cameras in Arica. The mainsail had fluttered and bulged magnificently and displayed its bright designs for some minutes before an embarrassed press photographer quietly pointed out to me that it was the wrong way round, perfectly rigged for sailing backwards. Unfortunately, it was a little late to try it again, and the next day my gaffe appeared on front pages across northern Chile.

In fact, there was a lot about the last two weeks I wanted to put behind me.

Naïvely, I had assumed that the physical launching of the boat would be the hardest part. But it had taken another fortnight of preparation simply to get permission to leave port, during which time the *Viracocha* had sat out on a mooring in the middle of the bay, quietly absorbing water. The first problem had been the life raft. Ever since Craig's parting words to me, I had been pestering Phil for proof of its existence, yet two days after launch, it was still proving to be more of a metaphysical idea than an actual reality. Phil kept claiming it was 'on its way', having been delayed at customs due to its classification as an explosive device. Then one day, it arrived, in a box the size of a briefcase.

'That's *it*?' I had asked, failing to hide a yelp of panic in my voice.

'It does look kind of small,' Phil had admitted, 'but it says it holds thirteen people. We're getting it authorised this afternoon.'

A few hours later, unpacked and inflated in the workshop of the naval inspector, the 'lifeboat' had been revealed to be a kind of airbed with sides a few inches high. A cheerful bright red colour, it would have made a good swimming-pool toy, and could conceivably have contained thirteen people if you packed them three deep like frozen herring. It had no sheltering roof structure at all, no chamber that could be sealed against the elements – which meant that in a storm on high seas you would probably be safer lashed to a piece of wooden wreckage. We had all walked around it, trying to make it look bigger, more substantial, until the inspector had put us out of our misery.

'I cannot authorise this,' he said. 'You must find a proper lifeboat.'

I was secretly relieved. I knew for a fact that Phil believed the lifeboat was a formality – that we would never need to use it. Now he looked incredulous. 'You don't understand,' he had protested. 'We don't have time! Every day our boat absorbs a little water, sinks a little lower!'

The inspector looked at him strangely. 'Surely all the more reason to take a proper lifeboat.'

I was getting worried about Phil. His increasingly fevered state of mind had not been helped by a fresh onslaught of criticism from Kitín Muñoz, expertly lobbed to hit the newspapers on the morning after our launch. With help from his boatbuilders, the Esteban family, the Spaniard had been busy faxing statements to the media claiming that we were concealing metal spikes in our wooden masts and rudders, and flotation tanks within the reed bundles. Not to mention the ropes: it was now claimed that 80 per cent of them were plastic.

'In Bolivia,' sneered Muñoz, 'they call her the *Plasticocha*.' The tabloids rather liked this name, and adopted it lazily alongside another favourite: *Mulacocha*, which translated roughly as Donkey-Cocha.

Had we all remembered the childhood wisdoms about sticks and stones, we would have smiled tolerantly and ignored all this. Unfortunately, it had got right up our noses. Phil, no longer able to conceal his annoyance, told reporters that Muñoz was simply lying out of jealousy after his own failure – a failure which, by the way, had nothing to do with rope-chewing molluscs. *Teredo* worms, he pointed out confidently (though as it later turned out, mistakenly) did not eat rope and reeds, only wood. Others in the camp went further, stating that Muñoz's failure was a simple result of bad construction. All of this was greedily devoured by the newspapers and splashed across the top of pages with headlines like: 'Phil Buck breaks his modesty and silence.' It brought a temporary satisfaction, like a punch swung at a bully, but we braced ourselves for the response.

It was not long in coming. Two days later a new headline appeared: 'Heyerdahl dismisses value of *Viracocha* expedition.' Phil reeled at the news, looking crushed as if some enormous Monty Python foot had descended on his head from the clouds. What could have been more devastating to him at this stage than a one-line snub coming from the childhood hero who had inspired the whole expedition in the first place? Heyerdahl's actual words were minimal and horribly familiar. Questioned during a book tour, he claimed that our use of plastic cord 'destroyed any scientific value' in our experiment. More galling still, he admitted he had got his information from his friend Kitin Muñoz.

The only solution at this stage seemed to be to make sure Heyerdahl had the facts before him. I spent that afternoon typing a group letter to the explorer, invoking high-minded principles, pertinent facts, *Boys' Own* images of pith-helmeted pioneers, respectful appraisals of Muñoz's own considerable achievements, and indeed anything else that might persuade everybody's favourite raft builder to step in and put a halt to the mud-slinging.

It was probably a futile gesture, given what Heyerdahl had already said, but at least we weren't just sitting back and taking it on the chin. Eli promised to print it out and mail it for us once she was back in Santiago.

In the meantime, ordinary Aricans went out of their way to buoy us up with a final week of truly eclectic hospitality, including a display of Cueca dancing, a presentation of individually crafted ornamental wooden sea chests by Miriam the Fan Club, and a surreal sit-down meal in the tinned fruit aisle of the local super-market. On Saturday night we were guests of honour at a 'Rock the Viracocha' beach party, sipping our beers politely as dozens of tat-tooed teenage anarchists slam-danced on the sand to the abject wailings of a punk band called Phlegm. As Arica's disaffected youth railed against the government, their mothers and other potent totalitarian icons, I found it oddly gratifying to know that we were now officially cool enough to be anti-establishment.

Unfortunately, none of this helped us much on the continuing absence of an eighth crew member. Ernesto, Jorge's mariner friend and one of our hardest workers, had been appointed in the week after the launch, only to drop out a few days later complaining of 'nervous exhaustion'. Contenders to replace him were plentiful but generally unsuitable. Meanwhile, an inevitable gravitas descended as we slowly absorbed the reality of what lay ahead. Greg went to see a priest and brought back some religious icons to hang in his bunk. Stephane purchased some shark hooks and strong fishing twine. The rest of us tried to reassure ourselves by buying life jack-ets and absurdly large hunting knives. We loaded the food, water and equipment, and – at last – a reassuringly chunky life raft, bor-rowed from a decommissioned fishing boat, with its plastic pod resprayed '*Viracocha*'. The Chilean navy, perhaps a little startled to find the trip was actually going ahead, made Phil sign a disclaimer form absolving their officials of all legal responsibility in the event of our deaths. Phil accordingly drew up his own disclaimer absolving him of legal responsibility for any of us, either. Quite where all this legal responsibility had suddenly gone, it was hard to discern. We all signed on the dotted line and tried not to think too deeply about why such get-outs might be necessary in the first place.

So it was that eight weeks into the new millennium, shortly after lunch on the afternoon of Friday, 25 February, we stepped into a launch, superstitiously touched the blood- and fish-stained dockside, and pushed off: Phil, Jorge, Marco, Erik, Greg, Stephane and I.

There was another man in the boat too, a short, stocky man equipped with a small kitbag and a wide grin. As he waved his Chilean flag at the handful of well-wishers lining the dockside, Carlos Martinez considered himself the luckiest man in Arica.

'What are you making?'

Carlos was sitting in the bow, whittling away at a stump of eucalyptus with a huge hunting knife and a look of intense concentration. He glanced up at my question.

'Hola Neeky!' he said, a broad grin spreading across his face. He had slightly Arabic features, framed by a luxuriant mop of curly, greying hair, and dominated by a prominent and sunburnt nose — a combination which had already earned him the nickname *el payaso*, the clown.

'I'm making a special tool,' he said simply. He carried on whittling at the stump until it was a pointed stake of the kind used in horror films to nail vampires. Then he smoothed its sides with a piece of sandpaper. 'Now I'll show you what it does.' He took his stake, grinned enigmatically at me, and forced its point into the centre of a tight, bulbous knot on the yard. Already shrunken solid, it had been foxing me all afternoon, but with a grunt and his new tool, Carlos loosened it in a few seconds.

'Incredible,' I said, gratefully stepping in to re-align the rope harness which would soon bear the weight of the mainsail. He looked pleased with himself.

I instinctively liked Carlos. He was as enthusiastic as he was practical, and had been one of the more industrious local helpers on the beach during our launch, though I had been too preoccupied to notice him then. Like Jorge and many of the men of Arica, he relied on seasonal work, a bit of construction, a bit of fishing, whatever he could find, and had found a temporary purpose helping the crazy gringo launch his boat. It wasn't until our final days, when the boat was afloat and most of the other locals had melted away, that Carlos began to stand out. He was in the camp almost daily, lending out his own tools, offering advice, and emitting sporadic honks of clown-like laughter. I had assumed he was a friend of one of the Chileans, but nobody seemed to know him.

In fact, even now, we still knew very little about him.

What I *did* know was that in the last week, struggling to complete the sails, I had come to rely on him. The sails had been a millstone round my neck for nearly a month, and barely a day passed when I didn't find myself envisaging their humiliating or dangerous failure. I even dreamt about them. In one particularly vivid nightmare I had been hammering my seventy-ninth grommet in a neat row across the canvas, when the sail edges rose up malevolently around me and tried to suffocate me. I had woken, sweat-drenched at 4 a.m. to find myself clawing at the inside of my own tent. The meaning of my nightmare was, as usual, disappointingly obvious: I was completely out of my depth. None of the rest of the crew seemed to realise this – they were all too relieved that someone else was doing the sails to worry about whether I really knew what I was doing. But Carlos sensed I was struggling, and had begun to offer advice: how to lash two halves of a wooden yard together; how to attach the sail to it with self-tightening knots. The more I had worked with him, the more I instinctively trusted him. So when Phil's long-promised cinematographer failed to turn up, I had begun to push hard for Carlos to take the eighth place. Phil agreed, finally, on the eve of our departure. Carlos had packed his bags that night, and kissed his wife farewell.

'Your wife must have been shocked,' I suggested now.

'No, she knew I'd been dreaming of it for weeks,' he said.

'She wasn't annoyed?'

'It was a one-off opportunity, and she knew I had to take it. She is a good woman.'

'Mine too.'

I thought of Ali. I had last spoken to her by phone two weeks ago, shortly before she was due to hike off to a remote Patagonian village with her team of young adventurers. She had sounded tired, but happy to hear from me. I missed her.

The clouds were beginning to turn peach-coloured, and Carlos was now busily arranging neatly folded tarpaulins in the V-shaped central crevice of the *totora*. I watched him as he patted them down, threw a blanket over the top to level out the surface, and unrolled his sleeping bag.

'Carlos, you know you can sleep in a bunk if you want. There are only six between eight of us, but that's because there are always two people on watch. We share them. We weren't expecting you to go without a bed.'

He shrugged. 'This is more comfortable. Jorge and I will sleep outside. Under the stars – *mas lindo*! More beautiful.' His eyes shone like a boy's.

I smiled and got up. They would both come in soon enough, once the waves had got a little larger. In the mean time, it meant each crew member would have his own berth.

In the cabin, there was a sweet smell of wine. Greg was rummaging about in his bag. 'The damn thing burst!' he said, pulling out a squashed carton of cheap white, and a bundle of wet clothes. He unearthed a bottle of red, intact this time, and looked up at me, sheepishly. 'Emergency rations — might need it later in the voyage,' he said, with a nervous chuckle.

Of the whole crew, Greg was most transparently out of his depth. Not that the rest of us had much idea what we were supposed to be doing, but at least we had learned to fake it a little. Greg was much too honest and straightforward for that. He wore a slightly lost expression. It didn't help that a Chilean documentary cameraman, Manuel Hererra, and a French agency photographer, Nicolas Le Corre, were accompanying us as far as the tow boat would take them, and were prowling about desperately trying to get footage. Whenever I saw either man shooting in my direction, I immediately adopted what I thought might seem like the actions of a well-briefed crew member — perhaps untying and retying a loose rope, or climbing purposefully up on to the cabin roof, scanning the horizon as if calculating something, writing it in a notebook, then climbing back down again. Greg didn't seem to notice the cameras at all, however, and ruined at least one of these shots by wandering up to me and asking: 'What are you doing?'

In the cabin, Marco had perfected a much more convincing impression of a navigator, standing over the map table with a pencil, ruler and sage frown, making tiny crosses on the chart.

'Where are we, Marco?' I asked.

'Exactly 18 degrees 27 minutes south by 70 degrees 19 minutes west,' he said, reading the numbers off the yellow handheld GPS.

'Oh right . . . what does that actually mean?'

'We're here,' he said, showing me a little cross on the chart, barely off the beach. 'We've come about . . . twelve miles.'

I was grudgingly impressed. Perhaps I had misjudged Marco's

competence. The trouble was, I had no way of knowing if he was getting it right or not. And more worryingly, neither did he.

Phil wasn't in any position to tell me either. He was in his bunk, asleep. In truth, he had seemed deflated ever since Heyerdahl had come out against us, and he had lately begun to exhibit one of those coughs which sounds like a frog caught in a lawnmower. This was his last chance to snatch some uninterrupted sleep before we were cast adrift and he took over. I looked at the little collection of books he had lined up along the back of the map table. There were some textbooks (*Emergency Navigation*, *The Sailmaker's Apprentice*, *The Six Volt Sailor*) and a few adventure stories (Ranulph Fiennes, *The Bounty Trilogy*), but the majority seemed to be by Heyerdahl (*Kon-Tiki*, *Aku-Aku*, *The Ra Expeditions*, *The Tigris Expedition*). Not for the first time, I felt a mixture of awe and irritation at Phil's simple faith in his own dream, and a stab of irony that Heyerdahl should choose to snub one of his most ardent admirers. It made me angry. I stepped out of the cabin.

In the kitchen I homed in on Stephane's multi-coloured jumper, the only part of him visible as he rummaged and cursed among piles of bags, boxes and pans, which swayed precariously with each pitch of the boat. '*Concha tu madre!*' he muttered, as a large bag of onions swung across and clubbed him in the kidneys.

'Need a hand?' I offered, securing a string of dried Bratwurst sausages flailing from the door frame. 'This job is impossible!' said Stephane, straightening up and clonking his head on a pan hanging from the ceiling. 'How can I organise everything when there is no room to move?'

The 'kitchen' or 'galley' was little more than the underside of the steering platform, walled with bamboo and occupying a space about the size of a small toilet. Along the starboard wall, was a long wooden box to accommodate the two-ring gas hob that would serve as our cooker. In the middle of the floor was a trap-door that had to permit clear access to the stern daggerboard, protruding through the heart of the boat and into the blue water beneath. Astern of this door, and along the port wall, was the space in which Stephane had to arrange three months' food for a crew of eight.

In his plans for feeding us, Phil had mercifully strayed a long way from the pre-Inca diet. Nobody doubted that ancient navigators could have lived on a diet of dried maize, pickled eggs, salted llama or whatever it was they ate – but why force a modern-day crew into retching mutiny by making them do the same? Instead, our cramped kitchen was a small floating supermarket outpost, impressive in its range. In addition to the basic staples and carbohydrates – rice, beans, lentils, oatmeal, pasta, potatoes, powdered milk, coffee, tea and flour – we were equipped with luxuries ranging from cappuccino coffee sachets to yoghurt-covered raisins. Just because pre-Inca civilisations hadn't got round to inventing peanut butter and Fig Newtons, ran Phil's thinking, there was no reason for us to miss out. Mindful of mariners' tales of scurvy, we also had a range of fruit and vegetables. For as long as they would keep, we planned to boost our vitamin intake with bags of apples, oranges, pineapples, pears, melons, cabbages, carrots, onions and garlic; then for the rest of the voyage we had bags of dried prunes, raspberries, blueberries, apples and oranges, all methodically dehydrated by Phil and his long-suffering mum over weeks and flown over from the US. In addition we had trail mix, a few large tins of peanuts, about 150 donated Power Bars, and an enormous sack of dehydrated soups and pasta meals given by a Chilean supermarket chain.

While dehydrated food had at first seemed an excellent space-saving idea, the initial genius of the thought was weakened by the fact that each meal would require substantial amounts of drinking water to reconstitute it. This was fine when you were climbing a mountain and could simply boil up a panful of snow or stream water. In the middle of the ocean it was somewhat more problematic. Phil refused to be daunted, and had allocated a generous ration of just over 4 litres of water each, per day, to be revised later in the voyage depending on our progress. In all, we had brought well over 2000 litres, stored in a range of plastic barrels including 12 large blue vats which were lashed carefully in place along the outside edge of the cabin and kitchen, and on the foredeck. Each was covered in dampened sacking to give a primitive form of refrigeration against the sun, which could otherwise accelerate stagnation.

Both food and water supplies had been calculated on the basis of between 75 and 100 days at sea — a rather generous allocation, until you considered the very real possibility that we would miss landfall at Easter Island altogether and be forced to sail on towards Pitcairn and Tahiti. We were therefore instructed to ration ourselves conscientiously.

Stephane had been put in charge of the food. I had assumed this was because he was French and therefore the next best thing to a Cordon Bleu chef. However, that morning we had all been a little disheartened to learn that his duties in fact only encompassed the monitoring of food supplies, and that all of us — Phil included — would be taking it in turns to cook, one whole day in every eight, followed by one whole day of washing up. Looking at Stephane stumbling around the tiny cooking area now, cursing at the various booby-traps it sprang on him, I shuddered at the prospect. Could eight men realistically be expected to produce something edible without a microwave?

Leaving our 'French chef' to cobble together the first meal, I clambered up the rope ladder to the steering platform, where Erik and Jorge were enjoying the evening sun. The steering platform was the *Viracocha*'s operations centre, raised well above the deck to enable the helmsman to see over the roof of the cabin in front, while still enabling verbal and visual contact with whoever was at the map table in the cabin. It was a stepped platform on two levels, with its lower level more easily accessible from the stern of the boat, using a wooden ladder. The person steering – in this case Erik – stood on this platform keeping an arm on the tiller and an eye on the Perspex hemisphere of the compass, which was fixed before him at waist height in a small wooden box on the platform's upper level, among a miscellany of waterproof duffel bags, kerosene cans, and life jackets. There were actually two rudders, one on either side of the platform. I wasn't entirely clear how they would work together, as neither was connected to the other. It was like having a separate steering wheel for each of a car's two front wheels. Probably for this reason, only one rudder had been lowered so far, to keep us roughly on course behind the *Choña*.

'*Mucho trabajo ese timón* – this rudder is hard work,' grunted Erik, as the tiller bumped against his ribs and the water gurgled astern. The compass was swinging 15 degrees either side of 220, which meant we were heading more or less southwest once the northerly flowing coastal current was taken into account. This would strengthen as we pushed out into it, becoming the cold, continuous Humboldt current from the Southern Ocean, the 'conveyor belt' which the *Kon-Tiki* had ridden from Peru as it curved westwards away from the continent and out across the Pacific to become the South Equatorial Current. Its lower offshoots might well have carried us on a broad arc to within range of Easter Island, had we simply drifted with it. But Phil had no intention of taking that roundabout route. Instead, we would cut across the Humboldt Current and aim directly for our goal. We were sailors, not drifters. That, at any rate, was the theory.

It was getting dark by the time Stephane dished up supper – a blend of onions, sticky rice, peanuts, carrots, sliced salami and soy sauce, which seemed to have been selected in much the same random way that many people select lottery numbers. The result was truly interesting.

'This is French food?' asked Jorge, intrigued.

'*Más o menos*,' said Stephane. 'More or less. I had to substitute a few ingredients because I haven't found the proper ones yet. You like it?'

Jorge gave a non-committal shrug. 'I suppose anything tastes better outdoors.'

Phil lit a hurricane lantern and hung it at the front of the boat. Our skipper seemed noticeably cheerier after his afternoon snooze, and took on a convincing captain-like authority as he announced the details of the watch system in front of the TV camera. 'There will be two people on watch at any one time,' he said, 'because it's statistically harder for both of you to fall asleep at the helm.' The shifts would run two hours on, six hours off, on a continuous loop throughout the day. Just in case we ran out of things to talk about, he had staggered the rota to give each of us two watchmates in our two-hour shift.

We drew lots for that first night. I landed 2 a.m. with Carlos and 3 a.m. with Stephane.

'This will be the dry run – we've just got to stay behind the tow boat,' said Phil, trying to be reassuring. 'But by tomorrow night we should be on our own.'

Stephane yowled: '*Isla de Pascua!*' and Marco grinned so broadly that his teeth seemed to shine.

'A song, *capitán?*' enquired Carlos. Jorge pulled a guitar out from under a tarpaulin and politely handed it round as if it was a peace pipe. Phil declined, but I managed to cobble together the requisite three chords for *La Bamba*, enabling us all to sing, with unwitting irony *Yo no soy marinero, soy capitán*, I'm not a sailor, I'm the captain (half right, at least). Marco accompanied the whole effort with the wailings of some kind of children's flute, until everybody begged for mercy, and we settled once more into reverie backed only by soft strummings from Jorge who, like Carlos, had made himself a bed up in the bow. Above us, the stars blazed with a clarity I had only previously seen in the desert, peppering the black velvet sky from horizon to horizon. I sat and gazed at it for what seemed like hours, the taste of hot chocolate on my lips and the night wind playing in my hair, until it was time to turn in.

We had drawn lots for our bunks, and mine was on the port side, nearest the bow on the upper level. It wasn't long before I realised why Carlos and Jorge had happily opted for the spongy hammock-shape of the bow instead. We had done such a good job with the restraining ropes designed to stop us falling out, that it was rather difficult to climb in. Once installed a few inches below the roof beams, I found the natural movement of the boat rolled me up against the ropes, and it was difficult to get any purchase on the foam mat to prevent it. Netting or hammocks might have been a better option. I lay there trying to get worked up about this, but realised after a few minutes that I was far too excited to do anything but enjoy the moment. Heavy breathing drifted from various parts of the cabin, interspersed with what sounded like the death rattle of a walrus emanating from Marco's bunk. Pulling aside the curtain by my head, I could look directly out on to the moonlit waves. I was very nearly happy.

I was sure I hadn't slept for more than a few minutes when a hand shook me awake. I extricated myself groggily from my bunk, trying to see what the time was and cursing my style decision to buy a black watch with black hands. By the time I had donned my fleece, boots, harness, life jacket and headlamp and checked the time, it was 2.05 a.m. Jorge – I assumed it was he who had woken me – was still bent over the map table writing our GPS co-ordinates into the log book, so I stepped out of the bow door and round the water vats to make my way along the side deck. The moon had disappeared behind a cloud, and my headlamp created a cone of light around which all else was deepest black. I clipped my harness on to a shroud to lean out over the starboard side. Somebody had told me, probably Craig, that an unbelievably large percentage of drowned yachtsmen pulled out of the sea were found to have their flies undone, after falling overboard while relieving themselves. I was taking no such chances.

I was, however, disconcerted to discover that I was leaving a trail of glowing water. I switched off my headlamp and the effect was positively spooky – a glowing froth of luminous green. What the hell had Stephane put in that food? A few moments later, making my way cautiously up towards the stem, I noticed that the glow was not restricted to me – the same effect was created all along the side of the boat, wherever a protruding rope or board produced turbulence, little sparks of light spun off in the splashing, like the brief burn-up of reflected stars. The effect at the back of the boat was most impressive, the gushing and gurgling around the rudder leaving an aqueous snail-trail of ghostly green light, all the more marked because of the darkness of the night.

'Beautiful, no?' said Carlos, quietly, from the steering platform above me. 'It's phosphorescence. Millions of little glowing creatures. They light up when you disturb them.'

Relieved to find I wasn't the owner of a radioactive bladder, I clambered up to join him. A light, warm breeze was blowing over the port side, and the only noise was the creaking of the cabin and the faint chuntering of an engine as *Choña*, visible only as a dirty, bouncing yellow rectangle of light, laboured onwards 100 metres ahead of us. Behind us to the northeast, a few fading points of light marked the civilisation we had left behind.

I woke hours later to the sound of shouting, and someone stomping along the starboard deck. Greg stirred in the bunk below me and pulled the door flap aside, letting daylight in. There was a lack of movement, and an odd stillness. In fact, there was no engine noise. I clambered out of my bunk.

'The tow rope just broke,' said Phil, standing up at the bow. The *Choña* was perhaps 200 metres away, turning in a wide arc. Two men were hauling the loose rope over the stern. There was no direct sunlight, and the sea was an inky shade of blue, oddly opaque, and unruffled by even a breath of wind. There was no sign of land in any direction.

'Where are we?'

'About thirty miles offshore – nowhere yet. If we were going much slower we'd be going backwards.'

There was a tension in Phil's voice, and he looked as if he had not slept well.

The *Choña* drew alongside while we reattached the towrope. She was a small fishing boat, shorter than the *Viracocha*, with a hull that must once have been red, but which was now mottled with a corrosive orange. Her tiny white cabin was striped with rust streaks too, and her crew looked sullen and tired. I waved at them, and one nodded briefly. The captain scowled across at us, weighing us up, standing in the cabin doorway with a mug in his hand. He looked bored, impatient to get back to port.

Ten miles further out, the tow rope again slackened into a lazy S on the water. 'What the hell is the problem now?' muttered Phil, looking out at the *Choña*. Nobody was visible on deck, so Jorge radioed them. 'They've got engine trouble,' he says. 'They're trying to fix it now.'

The 'engine problems' seemed to continue for much of the afternoon. As we drifted gradually sideways towards Peru, the *Choña*'s crew members would occasionally appear on deck and wave a spanner at us in a sort of helpless shrugging motion. I wondered what it was they were expecting us to do. It occurred to me, fleetingly, that Phil had paid up front for the full 100-mile tow, which meant it wouldn't exactly inconvenience the *Choña* if we decided we no longer required her services for the remaining 50 miles. But it was an unworthy thought, and I pushed it aside.

At 3 p.m. the skipper radioed to announce that, sadly, the engine trouble was too serious to continue, and they would have to radio for another boat to come and help.

Phil lost his patience. 'Marco, can you radio *Choña* back and tell the captain we're going to do some sailing trials? We can't wait all day.' After a glassy, dull morning, the clouds had dissolved and the sea's surface was now puckered and wind-rippled with a perfect southeasterly.

'Do you think we're far enough from the coast?' I said. It would only take a few false starts in the wrong direction to put us in danger. On the other hand, we had no guarantee the sails would actually work — and if they were going to fail irrevocably, we would at least be closer to rescue.

The skipper of the *Choña* seemed most understanding, and told us not to worry if we had to leave his stalled boat behind. He was sure he would manage somehow. Marco, with equally killing kindness, assured him there was no question of us abandoning an engineless boat — apart from anything else, radio communications from Arica had forbidden it. 'Just retie the rope — we'll tow you out to sea behind us if necessary.' The skipper was lost for words. I watched his puzzled crewmen walk the tow rope round to the bow of their boat.

'Positions, everyone!' shouted Phil, with a force that would have been more of a boost to confidence if I had known what my position was supposed to be. I spent several moments in the pretence of fiddling with knots on the mainsail yard as I tried in vain to visualise which way round the sail should be when it rose. After more than a month winging it as a novice sailmaker, I was about to see if I had pulled it off.

'OK people, raise the sail!' shouted Phil, who had joined Erik on the steering platform.

Carlos, Greg and Jorge all pulled robustly on the likeliest-looking rope. Greg said: 'Heave!', which sounded about right. Marco and I, down on the foredeck, stepped behind the yard and guided it upwards as it rose from the deck, catching hold of the ropes as the sails began to flap and swell in the breeze. Stephane, perched high on the mast, pulled at a restraining cord to stop the yard from being blown outwards. With grunting, heaving and cursing in three languages, all of us secured our various ropes on available poking-out bits and gazed up at the result – enormous, bulging pregnantly, and gratifyingly the right way round.

Better still, a trickling sound from the bows showed that we were beginning to move, creating little ripples like whiskers as the wind took hold of the sails. We sailed past the crew of the *Choña*, lined up blankly on deck, watched the tow rope straighten in the water, and felt a satisfying creak and jolt as we began towing her too. We repeated the whole procedure on the mizzen sail, more confident now, and sat back to admire our work: two sculpted parabolas of stretched canvas, set in parallel in a reasonable breeze. It was astonishing. We were *actually sailing!*

At the helm, Erik and Phil wrestled the tiller across until the compass showed 220 degrees, a little more southerly than our previous course, to compensate for hours of drifting. The wind increased as we experimented with different sail positions, and by suppertime there was an impressive tilt to the boat. Erik co-ordinated the fitting of four lee boards, or *guaras*, shaped from cedar wood and designed to cut the water cleanly on either side of the boat while preventing us from drifting sideways in the wind. A quick calculation over the course of a few hours revealed that we were actually travelling faster now than we had been under tow from the *Choña*, and what was more we were travelling in the right direction – a direction many of our detractors had deemed impossible for a reed boat. Marco threw his head back and laughed. 'Nothing can hold us back now!'

Except, of course, the rusting tow boat still bobbing along forlornly in our wake. As night fell we grew increasingly irritated by her, eager to cast ourselves into the great beyond. It was like going to the school disco with your little brother tagging along. Unfortunately the rescue boat showed little sign of taking her off our hands. On the VHF radio throughout the night we could hear position reports being broadcast from *Choña* to shore, *Choña* to rescue boat, shore to rescue boat, and all three to *Viracocha*, revealing that the rescue boat was having difficulty catching us. She was, in fact, closing at about one knot per hour. Phil, idling away his early morning shift, did the maths and worked out that if we maintained our present speed (about three knots) we would be towing the *Choña* for the next two days before we could finally cast her off to the rescue boat, some 200 miles offshore. Clearly this made no sense at all, so early in the morning we were summoned from our bunks to pull the sails down.

The *Judith* finally caught up with us mid-morning on Sunday, much to the relief of everyone involved. We had barely handed over our two journalists and cast off the tow line when, after an indecently small interval, there was a burst of exhaust and the *Choña's* engine miraculously healed itself. The captain revved away in a large arc around us, shrugging and pulling an oily 'Well, what do you know?' expression.

Jorge and Marco glowered darkly at this brazen maritime equivalent of a used car salesman, but we were all too energised to hold the grudge for long. Instead, we hoisted our sails again, and watched as the two dots grew smaller on the horizon, leaving us alone at last, facing the empty seas.

6

In Deep Water

'*Ballenas!*' hissed Jorge, in an excited whisper. '*Muchas ballenas!*'

It was about 5 p.m. and from my position hunched over the still non-functioning navigation system, I could see Jorge's sunlit figure framed in the end of the cabin, pointing excitedly over our port side. What was a *ballena*? A bird? A type of fish? An amusing cloud formation? I hurried outside, but could see nothing more than ocean, furrowed with dark shadows in the low sun, and endless. 'Wait,' said Jorge, his finger making little circling movements. '*Mira!*'

There was a sound like someone being sucked out of an airlock, and a sudden cloud of water vapour sparkling in the air about 100 metres away. For a moment I was stumped as to what I was seeing. Then, as the cloud disappeared, I saw the dark, humped shapes in the water below it. 'Whales!' breathed Greg, standing beside me. 'A whole family of them.' There was a second hiss of expelled air, a second glistening tree of water. I counted three or four dark bodies, each almost as large as the *Viracocha*. I hardly dared breathe, half willing them to come closer, half afraid of what might happen if they did. Greg seemed to be deep in the midst of a kind of mystical experience.

'It's like they're welcoming us,' he whispered, a look of sheer awe on his face. 'Like they're saying: *you're in our domain now!*'

It was equally possible they were still trying to work out whether to steer clear of the *Viracocha* or mate with it. Our rounded hull must have looked strangely animal from below, unlike the huge metal edges of tankers that sporadically sliced through these waters. They weighed us up for five minutes, keeping pace with the boat but keeping their distance, while we conferred excitedly. '*Orcas?*' hazarded Jorge, who claimed to have glimpsed white markings. But the fins seemed less angular than those of killer whales, and the shapes larger – possibly Bryde's, another species known in these waters. We never knew for sure – soon they dropped back, and eventually dived from sight, lost in our tiny wake. We tingled with the encounter for the rest of the evening – it seemed a hopeful omen, a peaceful transition to the deep ocean.

And it was extravagantly deep ocean, as I realised with a shudder of vertigo when I noticed a solitary number printed on the chart close to our most recent pencil cross: 7500. *Metres!* In other words, only a few bundles of reeds separated me from more than 7 *kilometres* of watery void. I traced our route back across the map like a safety rope, trying to imagine the changes in the ocean floor beneath. Our first 50 miles had been innocuous enough: slipping off the continental shelf, the sea bed sloping gently downwards to 2000 metres, the colours of a printed atlas changing from shades of cream, through pastel and then bottle green. Then the gradient had steepened for 20 miles, down to 4000 metres. But even that gave no warning of what was to come 10 miles later, when the sea bed dropped away entirely, down into the inky abyss of the Peru Trench — a tectonic chasm running parallel to the coast, caused by the slow collision of the vast plates of the Earth's crust, the puckering and downwarping of one beneath the other. Far beneath us, the world silently continued to reshape itself, swallowing a few centimetres of sea floor each year.

I climbed cautiously out on to the gunwales, hooked my arms around two mast stays, and looked down. With the sun still on the water, I guessed I was looking through perhaps 50 metres, though there was nothing to focus on, a dizzying lack of perspective. The absolute maximum penetration of light in sea water, I had read, was one kilometre. I imagined a coin dropped overboard, spinning downwards, glinting at first in the dancing sunlight, then growing steadily duller until it disappeared into the total darkness beyond, its journey barely begun. Downwards, onwards, through the thickening water, tumbling imperceptibly more slowly as the pressure increased, down past strange bug-eyed fish lit like casinos, neon oddities pulsating in the chill water, down through whole realms empty of life, kilometre after kilometre. I stood there for about 15 minutes, wondering if my coin had yet settled, finally, noiselessly in the dark silt at the bottom of the Peru Trench, home of primeval life forms, tubeworms, rat-tailed bottom-feeders. I couldn't get there, even in my mind, preferring to stay suspended above it all, as precarious and tiny as a pond skater balanced on the surface film. A haze of cloud covered the sinking sun, and I watched the water lose its shimmer, watched the darkness approaching as if from below, and felt fear settle on me like dew as the temperature dropped. I shivered and went to put on more clothes.

In the cabin, Phil was trying the Trimble navigation system again, without success. Despite adjustments to the egg-shaped antenna at the foot of the mast, the screen still kept flashing up the message: *Log-in fail.*

'I think the ancient navigators were better off without computer technology,' he sighed. 'Who needs it anyway?' He shut down the computer and closed the laptop lid. The finality of the action was disconcerting.

'*We* need it, don't we? To get the weather reports.'

'We'll think of something. Maybe we can phone the navy.'

'And the email? I've promised to send bulletins back to my newspaper.'

'Yeah, it's kind of a bummer. We need to send log entries back to Eli for the website too.' He scratched his chin absently. 'I guess we'll just have to write them up on the computer and then dictate them over the phone.'

I steadied myself against the map table, breathed slowly.

'So the satellite phone is definitely working, at least?'

'It should be. I haven't unpacked it yet. It's somewhere around . . .' He bent down to look under the bunk.

The journalistic worst-case scenarios of missing my deadlines suddenly became rather more dramatic, involving SOS messages, terrified crew members straddling widening chasms in disintegrating *totora*.

'OK,' I said, carefully. 'So we've *probably* got a satellite phone. But if all else failed, we've got VHF radio, right?'

'Well, actually the VHF only works over a hundred-mile radius,' shouted Phil casually from beneath the bunk. 'We'll be out of range of the shore by tomorrow. But yeah, we'll be able to radio a passing ship — if there's one in the area.'

The walls of the cabin seemed to close in a little as another prop of confidence was kicked away, inadvertently, by my captain. *Act rationally*, I told myself. *Think positive.* There were a few more clunks and rattles from beneath the bed before he shuffled out backwards, muttering: 'Where is that damn phone? Maybe I put it below deck. Anyway, we won't be needing it till—'

He caught my expression and stopped. A grin spread across his face.

'Hey, Nickers, you're not worried are you?' he said, with a chuckle.

'Where's the emergency positioning beacon?' I asked, stonily.

'Last time I saw it . . . in that trunk under Marco's bunk,' he said.

'Shouldn't it be somewhere we can grab it in an emergency?'

'Sure. I was getting round to that. There's a lot of stuff that needs sorting out tomorrow.'

'Well . . . what happens if a storm hits tonight?'

Phil looked puzzled. 'Does it look to you like a storm's going to hit tonight?'

'How the hell would I know? You've just informed me we don't have a bloody weather warning system!'

I yanked the plastic trunk out from under Marco's bed so hard that it hit the map table opposite. I was being insufferably grouchy, but I couldn't help it. All I knew was that my confidence seemed to be ebbing away with the daylight, and Phil wasn't exactly stemming the flow. He shrugged and wandered out of the cabin.

The emergency position-indicating radio beacon, or EPIRB, was a bright yellow, foot-long baton with a bulbous cylindrical head. Inside its head was a satellite positioning system which was activated either manually or on contact with water. The idea was that even if crew members did not manage to get to it in time to take it with them when they abandoned ship, its wall-holder would automatically release it when it became wet, and it would float to the surface and flash constantly while broadcasting to rescuers the exact position where the ship went down. Obviously, this would work better if it were not shut in a trunk, four miles below the surface. I wired the holder to the bamboo wall at the open end of the cabin.

Supper that night should have been idyllic. Erik had cooked up rice and bean stew, flavoured with onions and sliced salami, which we devoured on deck, all of us glowing orange in the last weak beams of the setting sun. Greg was still dreamily recounting the sighting of the whales, and Stephane was talking excitedly with Marco about possibilities for fishing tomorrow. I, meanwhile, was envisaging black waves smashing through the bamboo sides of the cabin, crew members scrabbling to get out of their bunks, the reed hull torn like a breakfast croissant, the masts crashing through the ceiling . . .

'*Viracocha! Viracocha!*' It was the VHF radio. I stopped chasing a bean around my plate and listened. Marco took the call, which consisted of the usual static of whistles and crackling Spanish. I understood nothing except the words 'Arica Radio' – the shore-based naval station which had now accompanied us almost to the limit of its range. Marco talked radio language for about thirty seconds, before signing off with *cambio fuera*. Over and out.

'What's the story?' asked Phil, filling a kettle from a plastic flagon, as Marco emerged.

'Just calling to check our position,' said Marco. He glanced at me purposefully. 'And they think there might be a storm coming.'

I nearly choked on a bean.

'Really?' said Phil, sounding more amused than worried. 'How about that? Specially for Nickers!'

I looked out towards the eastern horizon, and felt my stomach knotting itself. I couldn't be sure, but it seemed to me that there was a dark smudge, a stain, growing on the horizon. Clouds gathering. The wind suddenly seemed to rise, malevolently. I felt the adrenalin kick in.

Phil was fiddling with the stove. 'Tea, anyone?' he asked, cheerfully. It was a surreal moment. We had perhaps an hour to ready the boat for a hammering, and Phil was making a cup of tea. I got up, tossed my plate into the washing-up bucket in disgust, and announced that I was going to do a safety check.

I started with the safety lines running along both sides of the boat from bow to stem. Their purpose was to allow someone to clip a harness loop on at one end of the boat in bad weather and walk along its entire length while remaining attached to the boat. Unfortunately, on port side it appeared someone had commandeered this vital rope as part of an improvised duck enclosure for Pedro (Pablo had been pecking him in the other cage), which made it impossible to use a harness without getting entangled in mesh and duck-crap. It would almost be funny if it weren't so dangerous. I spent ten minutes retrieving the safety line, while Pedro pecked and quacked angrily at me from behind his netting. Avoiding the impulse to give him his first involuntary flying lesson, I scrambled up to the roof to see what might need lashing down. Almost everything. The only thing that wouldn't be washed away in the first big wave was a large bag containing our life jackets. As I stooped to put mine on over my harness, it struck me that everybody else was still in the cabin. I could hear Greg chatting about whales directly below me, and somewhere an Abba song was playing, tinny-sounding against the breeze in my ears. Did none of them have the faintest idea of what a storm might involve?

'Doesn't anybody want their life jacket?' I yelled through the roof. The conversation below stopped, and someone switched off the Abba.

'Er, no. Why?' It was Greg, sounding kindly but baffled.

'Well,' I spluttered. 'Presumably if we're about to hit a storm, you'd prefer to be wearing it, rather than be washed overboard with it still strapped to the sodding roof!'

There was a pause and a hint of whispering, in which I could imagine people exchanging glances, raising eyebrows, mouthing: *Who is this jerk?*

'Ah, no, it's OK, I'll just leave it up there, thanks,' shouted Greg, as if addressing someone senile as well as deaf. 'So I know where it is.' I could tell by his voice that he was grinning.

I was incredulous with fury. 'Anybody else?' I asked, barely controlling my voice.

A chorus of 'No!' wafted up through the roof, and presently the Abba music began again. On the steering platform to my right, Carlos waved and grinned.

I stuffed all the life jackets back into the bag, feeling clenched and murderous. What was I doing here, babysitting this bunch of amateurs? And what was our so-called captain doing to prepare his crew? The more I thought about it, the more angry I became, and the more heroic I felt – in a solitary kind of way. Eventually I decided I must act. I swung down from the roof to confront him.

'Phil, why is nobody apart from me doing anything to prepare for this storm?' I was breathing hard to keep my temper under control, and rather hot in my bulky assemblage of cagoule, harness and life jacket. Everyone was sitting on their bunks, still clad only in shorts and T-shirts, and smirking at me as one might smirk at someone's parent turning up to a teenage party.

'What storm is that, Nickers?' said Phil, with a kindly tone of concern.

'The storm! Radio Arica said there's a storm com—'

I stopped suddenly and looked at Marco. He was grinning apishly at me from his bunk, where he was lying with his hands behind his head. In my fevered brain, something clicked rustily into place. I felt my shoulders sag involuntarily.

'You *utter* bastard,' I said slowly. In the ensuing merriment of my crewmates, I resisted the impulse to club Marco to death with the positioning beacon. 'You'll have to get used to Marco's sense of humour,' said Phil, adopting an exaggerated English accent as the guffawing subsided. 'Now, old chap, why don't you come and have a cup of tea?'

The dark clouds seemed to have been wheeled offstage by the time I heaved myself up to the steering platform for my watch at I a.m. Instead, the southern skies were flecked with stars, and a full moon had turned the sea into dancing slivers of glass on black velvet. I felt too awestruck to be nervous any more, though I still took the precaution of clipping my harness to anything available, until I almost garrotted myself on the hand-rail. Carlos, I was interested to note, had rather more usefully lashed the tiller to the side of the platform with a complex series of lassoes; leaving the compass hovering more or less constantly around 220 degrees. Thus freed up, he was sitting reading a small Gideon Bible by the light of his head-torch. He shut it as I arrived on the platform.

'I didn't know you were religious,' I said, intrigued.

'I'm not,' he said quickly. 'I don't like church or anything. But this is a good book.'

'And today's reading is taken from . . . ?'

He looked at me blankly.

'Which bit were you reading?'

'*Los Salmos*. The Psalms.' He grinned nervously and reopened the Bible. 'You know this one? "If I take the wings of the morning and dwell in the uttermost parts of the sea, even there shall thy hand lead me and thy right hand shall hold me."'

'Great.'

We both lapsed into silence and stared at the stars for a few minutes, listening to the creak of rope on bamboo, and the churning of the sea around the rudder. A shiver passed from the top of my head and right down my spine.

'I'll leave the Bible here next to the compass, just in case . . .' he said, presently.

I grinned involuntarily in the darkness. Just in case of what? He made it sound like an emergency life-saving device. Once upon a time I believed it was.

'Do you believe we'll make it all the way to Easter Island, Carlos?'

'*Por supuesto!* Of course!' He tweaked one of his ropes slightly, till the compass needle nudged 220, then turned to look at me. His eyes were suddenly wide and earnest. 'I believe there is something out there looking after us, watching over us. I don't care whether you call it God, or providence, or fate. Whatever it is called, I believe it is on our side.'

'So you're not worried about what might lie ahead?'

'I didn't say that. There is nothing wrong with being afraid. Fear is what keeps us vigilant – you understand? – it is good as long as you do not let it rule you.' He gave me a knowing glance, and a chuckle, by which I understood that he too had been in on the afternoon's joke. Somehow I didn't mind with Carlos. I felt immensely comforted by his presence, by his friendly guru-like wisdom. In fact, I realised, as he ended his shift, I had found my resident Uncle Chris.

Stephane, who was supposed to replace him at 2 a.m. was less flattering.

'That stupid old arsehole!' he muttered as he climbed groggily up the ladder at 2.15, some time after Carlos had gone to wake him up. 'He shook me so hard my head hit the wall!' With his tongue hanging out, he mimed being shaken senseless in his bed.

'Are you a heavy sleeper?' I asked, diplomatically.

'No – he could have woken me gently, but instead . . .' He sat down on the port side of the platform and tried unsuccessfully to light a cigarette. '*Mierda!*' It was the first time I had seen Stephane in a bad mood. Then again, it was the first time I had seen him woken in the middle of the night.

'What the hell is this?' he said suddenly, waving Carlos' Emergency Bible. He flipped through its pages, sneering half-heartedly.

'You don't like it?' I felt suddenly protective.

'The paper's good for rolling joints,' he grunted, rustling a couple of pages together. 'Otherwise it's full of shit.'

He chuckled to himself until he realised my discomfort.

'*You* like reading it?' The cigarette end was poised in mid-air.

'Some of it. Other parts scare the pants off me — the kind of stuff that starts wars and gives people a pretext to hate each other. *Excuse me, I'm afraid God has told me to annihilate your tribe.* But I think Christ was different, a truly radical figure. He loved ordinary people, exposed hypocrites — presumably why the religious experts had him executed. I'm sure he'd disown most of what goes on in his name. That's why I still read the Bible sometimes — to try and see past the man-made rules to the more . . . I dunno . . . *visionary* bits . . .'

It was a little startling, on the first night of our unaccompanied voyage, to find ourselves pondering theology. I hadn't discussed this kind of thing with much passion for years, but here it suddenly seemed as natural as it did in those mellow, late-night head-exploding sessions in college, when you sat with friends and thrashed out the big answers, the meaning of it all. After eight weeks of often relentless minutiae — sail widths, grommet diameters, launch logistics, crew concerns — I hadn't been prepared for this spaciousness, the snail-like passing of the hours, the slow munching of miles. I tried to think what I might normally talk about on a graveyard shift, a dogwatch at the *Scotsman*, when nothing much was going on. Office gossip? A government scandal breaking on Reuters? The latest 'revolutionary' music format that will make all others obsolete? What one celebrity says about another celebrity? *Did you see that survey in the paper? Apparently, right, men are 15 per cent more likely to* . . . Almost anything, oddly enough, to avoid talking about what really mattered to me, the stuff of the heart. Here, though, it was different. There was really nothing else.

Stephane was certainly up for it that first night. He told me how he had become disenchanted with religion: a soured friendship with an embezzling priest; a period working with young adults with learning difficulties and the resulting questions about the randomness of suffering; and of course, his brazenly large appetite for the one thing which sent the Catholic Church into shuddering paroxysms of embarrassment: sex.

'Basically, I believe we are simply animals,' said Stephane, shrugging. 'We should not be ashamed of that – in many ways animals are more honest than humans, they simply follow their appetites, go after what they want. They do not pretend.'

No pretending. No masks. No bullshit. An hour later, as he grasped my fist in a complex, street-wise handshake that I predictably botched, I realised I liked Stephane for his honesty, the way he was unashamedly himself. Whether that would add up to a peaceful voyage, I was not so sure.

Sipping sugary coffee in the fresh, sparkling sunlight of the next morning, I could barely remember my fears of the previous evening. It was a different world, crackling with optimism, cushioned with warm porridge and bits of reconstituted Kiwi fruit. The sails were swollen with the playful air, and we were leaving an impressive wake behind us, suggesting our speed had rocketed almost to walking pace. Marco was howling cod-operatic Freddie Mercury songs from the steering platform, and it was a mark of the general high spirits of the crew that none of us yet felt the need to gag him.

We had come around 140 miles so far, which left about another

2360 to go, stretching ahead of us idyllically like the summer holidays of childhood. I shut my eyes and enjoyed the kiss of the sun on my lids. What were we going to do today? Or the next day? Or the one after that? Phil emerged from the cabin with squashed hair and baggy eyes to tell us. 'We've used up a bunch of power running the navigation lights,' he announced, yawning. 'So let's go for a cycle.'

It wasn't quite as strange a suggestion as it might seem. Cycling was in fact our primary means of generating electricity. A few days before departure, our electronics experts had been alarmed to discover that the two solar panels Phil had purchased for the purpose were not going to be sufficient to run even half of our growing cache of electrical appliances: VHF, navigation system, computer, satellite phone, navigation lights, video camera recharger and GPS. Phil, already weighed down with concerns over the life raft and Kitin Muñoz, had given the electricians a carte blanche and a very small cheque to assemble a pedal-powered generator. The result was an ingenious fusion of lateral thinking and bits of scrap metal.

The *Bicycocha*, as it had been christened, was essentially the skeleton of a mountain bike, welded to a metal stand by its front forks and its crankshaft, and connected to a second-hand car alternator by a rubber belt running round the bare rim of its back wheel. The alternator was linked to our double bank of car batteries with a large hose-sized cable, ensuring that while one bank was in use, the other could be charged. Not being particularly mechanically minded, I was staggered by the simple ingenuity of this design. Not only would it provide for our electricity needs, but it would also keep us fit within the confines of our small vessel.

That, at least, was the theory. The practice was not quite as simple, as I discovered when I volunteered to take an early half-hour shift in the saddle that day. The first problem was that the

Bicycocha had been installed on the roof of the cabin. This had seemed a good idea in Arica, as it kept the whole contraption clear of the work areas at deck level; but unfortunately ocean swell is amplified the higher you climb on a boat. The result was rather like trying to ride a bike while hopelessly inebriated. As the boat pitched, the bike pitched with it, and I was forced to hook my arm around a nearby mast stay to avoid being thrown sideways off the roof of the cabin.

'Come on! Get pedalling!' shouted Marco from behind me. Stephane whistled and grinned. There was a definite macho competitive thing brewing here. I began pedalling as hard as I could, while keeping one arm hooked round the stay and the other on the handlebars. It was incredibly hard work, due to the resistance of the alternator, and I was soon forced to stand up on the pedals to keep the wheel turning at all. Gradually, though, I got into a kind of Weeble-like swaying motion in keeping with the boat, and found it all oddly exhilarating. Pedalling in the direction of travel, looking down from my windswept perch high above the boundless blue, I felt suddenly inspired and heroic, like the boy in the Spielberg film *ET* who finds his bike can fly with the help of a small alien in the front basket. Of course, with the tip of the mainsail yard swinging just inches away, anyone sitting forward of my handlebars – mystic alien or not – would have found himself clubbed abruptly overboard.

The cycling continued in relay all morning, as each crew member hoisted himself into the saddle, pedalled furiously for approximately one minute, and then creaked along for the rest of his session wheezing unpleasantly. We were not the world's fittest crew, and the novelty of the exercise seemed to be wearing off, all the more so when I discovered, shortly before lunch, that four hours of cycling had increased the battery level by the merest fraction of a volt.

'That can't be right,' said Phil, when I pointed this out. 'Maybe it doesn't work unless you cycle at a certain speed?'

We yelled up to Marco to cycle faster, and watched as the digits on the voltmeter flicked briefly upwards and then actually began to decrease.

'Maybe the energy is draining back through the system,' I suggested, vaguely remembering something called reflux I'd seen in an advertisement for indigestion remedies.

Phil nodded sagely. 'Better pull the plug out before we lose any more.'

Neither of us thought to inform Marco of this decision, and there was a brief clatter and muffled curse from above as the resistance suddenly disappeared from Marco's pedals, causing him to hurl himself almost over the handlebars. I am somewhat ashamed to say this amused me.

The serious implications of our latest glitch, however, were not long in dawning. Our electricity generating system was not functioning properly for reasons that none of us were qualified to understand. We had one bank of batteries that was more or less empty, and a second that would last perhaps another couple of days. Then what? Unless we could find a reliable way of creating power, we would risk losing both our navigation equipment and our ability to communicate with the outside world.

'Am I missing something here, or are we completely shafted?' I said.

'Not completely,' said Phil. 'We've still got the solar panels, which might give us enough to maintain essential communications – GPS, satellite phone at the least. Plus we could conserve energy – only use navigation lights when there's a ship in the area, and leave the phone switched off except when we're using it.'

I didn't much like the sound of this. 'Why don't we just call the electricians on the satellite phone now and see if they can suggest anything?'

Phil looked dubious. 'Give me a while to think about it,' he said. 'I'd rather try and sort out the problem ourselves first, then maybe I'll think about calling for help. Have you checked all the battery connections?'

I made a cursory check of the batteries, moved the solar panels along the side of the boat so that they were in the full glare of the sun, and then, reassured by a slow resulting upturn in the figures on the voltmeter, went away to procrastinate over an enormous lunch of something weighty and bean-based. After lunch, perhaps fearing a resumption of the cycling regime, everyone suddenly remembered pressing responsibilities that needed seeing to. Stephane had noticed that the yards were knocking repeatedly against the mastheads so Phil asked him to install a safety rope, to prevent any sudden breakage in the yard from braining someone below. As luck would have it, this meant he would have to spend a large amount of time sitting up at the top of the mast.

Erik, meanwhile, wanted to take a proper measurement of how much the boat had sunk since her launch, and Greg was keen to join him in the water, inspecting the hull using masks and snorkels. It was a beautiful afternoon, and as I watched Greg trailing from a rope, being towed along in the boat's gentle wake, I thought how clear and empty the water seemed. Stephane, tempted beyond all power to endure, leapt screaming from the top of the mast to join him, and soon the pair were taking it in turns to leap while Phil videoed them. It seemed an unnecessarily dangerous occupation – even with the boat moving at walking pace, they had to swim quickly to its side to avoid being left behind – but I found myself yearning to join them, at least for a swim.

Then I caught sight of Jorge's face.

He was standing anxiously on the side deck, peering down at

those in the water, his forehead furrowed. He looked older than he normally did, perhaps because his jowls were grey with stubble.

'You OK, Jorge?'

He sighed and joined me sitting on the foredeck.

'*Estos niños* . . . these children are playing with death,' he said, his voice a little higher than usual. 'Don't they know there are sharks out there?'

'You think so?' I said, nervously. 'The water seems so *empty* here. I haven't even seen a fish yet.'

Jorge sighed. 'Believe me, there are sharks. We must be vigilant, only go in the water when absolutely necessary. This fooling around is madness. When sharks attack they come from below, very fast. You won't know they are coming till it is too late.'

There was something in Jorge's tone which made me suspect he was drawing on more than myths and tall stories. He was, after all, a fisherman.

'You have . . . *experience* of this?'

He paused and looked over my shoulder at the sea. 'I saw a man killed once.'

'Ah . . . I'm sorry . . . what happened?'

'I was in another boat nearby when it attacked. A diver was harvesting shellfish at 50 metres, very near shore. He had surfaced with a bagful and taken a breath of air. But at the same time the helper in his boat began cleaning and cutting fish, rinsing his bucket, while the diver was still in the water. Very bad.'

I knew the significance of this, just like anyone brought up in the era of *Jaws*. Sharks have an incredibly advanced sense of smell, able to pick up one part blood in 100 million parts water, and will home in on a victim from up to a quarter of a mile away. Washing out a bucket was like blowing a hunting horn to every shark in the vicinity.

Nobody even saw the one that got the diver.

'The man's legs were bitten off. His friends managed to drag him on board, but he bled to death before they could reach a hospital. I didn't know him well, but his brother was in my boat at the time, and worked with me many years after that. I have never been able to forget it.'

What amazed me was that Jorge was still, by profession, a diver. He took these risks regularly, presumably trying not to think of the screams as the man was dragged from the water, bleeding from stumps. 'What else can I do?' he shrugged. 'I must earn money to live. But I take care, and I only go in the water when I have to.'

I listened to the whoops and laughter of Stephane and Greg, and imagined the vibrations from their splashing rippling through the glassy water. I heard the first tentative half-tone cello notes of the *Jaws* soundtrack beginning to accelerate. I decided not to go for a dip just yet.

Bloody Steven Spielberg.

Greg looked suitably spooked too, when Jorge repeated his story, but claimed most sharks would circle before attacking, giving us plenty of time to get out of the water as long as we didn't stray far from the boat. I wasn't so sure. It made sharks sound like a pretty sporting bunch, always letting their quarry get a head start by gamely signalling their approach. Stephane, predictably, wasn't even in the same universe.

'Wow,' he said. 'Imagine seeing a shark close up!' He howled, put on his goggles, and leapt overboard again in search of the ultimate adrenalin rush – man against shark.

Jorge rolled his eyes and wandered off to talk to Phil instead.

The afternoon's swim was in fact worrying for a different reason. It confirmed that we were sinking.

While Greg and Stephane had found the hull still tight and undamaged, Erik gravely surfaced to report that the entire boat was already 5 inches lower in the water than on the day of launch. Using simple maths, it was possible to extrapolate that our deck would be swamped within two months. Two months, in a voyage that could theoretically take up to three. Erik and Phil both pointed out that all our food, water and equipment had been loaded since the first measurement, which might have caused disproportionate sinking. In reality, said Phil cheerily, we probably had plenty of time. On the other hand, I couldn't help thinking that all our hypotheses rested on the assumption that the water would penetrate the reeds at a uniform rate, rather than at an accelerating one. What if salt water acted differently to fresh water? In truth, we simply didn't know what would happen, and neither did Erik. We were part of the experiment.

I did my best to battle off such fears, but as the sun dipped lower, I noticed my anxiety was seeping back in like cold ground water. After folding away the solar panels for the night, I found that the power in the batteries had risen only slightly from a day's use. Determined not to make a gibbering fool of myself again, I nevertheless decided procrastination would get us nowhere.

'Phil,' I said, keeping my voice artificially bright and cheery. 'Here's the electrician's phone number. Now seems like a good time to call him for some advice on this power drain problem.'

'Well, OK . . . if you think it will do any good. We don't want to alarm anybody.'

The satellite phone was an interesting-looking device. Phil had eventually discovered it lodged behind a hamper of greased hens' eggs under Stephane's bunk. With its weighty black brick of a handset, and an aerial as thick as a Smartie tube, it looked like mobile phones did twenty-five years ago when such things were used only by the CIA.

Power drain or not, I wanted to see if it worked, now that we were more or less out of range of land on the VHF radio. Phil keyed in the number and held the handset to his ear.

'Ah, hello? Is that Juan? . . . This is Phil . . . Phil Buck from the *Viracocha*. Listen, we're having a few problems with the batteries and wondered if you guys . . . what? . . . No, PHIL BUCK from the VIRACOCHA . . . Yes, *really!* . . . We're calling on the satellite phone . . . so yeah, the basic problem is that the bike doesn't seem to be generating enough power to charge up the batteries . . . what? . . . Of course I'm not joking . . . why would I be joking? . . . Hello? . . . HELLO? . . . Damn it, he hung up!'

'He *hung up?*'

'I think he thought it was one of his friends pulling some stunt.'

'That's ridiculous. Didn't he recognise your voice?'

'It's different on a satellite phone. He sounded kind of weird and robotic too.'

'Well, try it again! We need to convince him!' I realised I was raising my voice again.

Phil sighed. 'Actually, you know what? I've got a better idea,' he said, putting the phone down on the map table. 'I've got to phone Eli with a progress report tomorrow anyway, why don't I get *her* to call the electricians and come back to us with suggestions?'

There was an edge of irritation in Phil's voice that told me not to push it any further.

'Uh, right. Are you sure we've got enough power for the next day or so?'

'Pretty much.'

That night, as I shuffled up to take my watch, the stars seemed even clearer and brighter than normal. It took me a moment or two to wake up sufficiently to realise why. We were sailing without navigation lights.

'Captain's orders,' explained Carlos. 'Too much wasted electricity. And anyway, you can see better without them. Lights disrupt night vision.' I went straight to the electricity panel and turned them back on again, but had to admit he had a point – it was much harder to see what was out there in the darkness when you were squinting past a red or green light. Grudgingly, I turned them off again, but still felt annoyed that Phil had taken a potentially life-threatening decision without informing everyone in the crew. How would a ship avoid us if we had no lights?

'Easy,' said Carlos. 'When we see a ship, we turn the lights on.'

'But that's assuming we see it first.'

'Of course – but that's why we are here on lookout!'

'But what if the other ship has its lights off?'

'Why would they do that?'

'Why would *we* do that?'

Carlos grinned dimly in the green glow of the compass, and shrugged.

In the end we left the lights off anyway. It made us less complacent.

The next morning, Phil phoned Eli. It was a brief, but lively conversation, and not hugely more enlightening than the previous night's exchange.

'Hi Chini, it's me . . . what? No, we're fine . . . why? . . . WHAT? . . . Chini, slow down . . . I don't understand. We phoned who? . . . WHAT? . . . No, the guy hung up – he didn't believe it was us . . . He told WHO? No way! Oh my GOD! . . . Can you call them? CALL THEM QUICKLY! Stop them!'

I had only ever heard Phil speak like this to Eli. They had a volatile but passionate relationship which seemed at odds with Phil's otherwise predominant air of measured calm. I had never seen him this agitated before. We waited earnestly to hear what catastrophe was about to befall us.

'*Goddammit!*' he shouted. '*That* is exactly why I didn't want to phone the electricians!'

I was intrigued to note that his anger seemed to be directed at me.

'You want to know what's happened?' he muttered, pacing to the cabin door and back. I nodded, carefully. 'Turns out the electrician was so freaked out by our phone call that he phoned his boss. His boss panicked and phoned the NAVY! And now – get this! – the navy is all set to come and find us! They're treating it like a kind of distress call! They've got a ship ready to set off, and a spotter plane on standby!'

'Oops,' I said, which was, in retrospect, an inappropriate response. Phil slumped down on the bunk, and ran his hands through his hair.

'Don't you understand? Eli's trying to call it all off right now, but it could be too late. They might already be on their way. And you know what that could mean? It could mean we're about to be *forcibly rescued!*'

7

The Trouble with Fish

'They have no right to rescue us without our permission!' stormed Stephane, flushing an angry red. '*Concha tu madre!* They'll have to remove me by force!'

The whole crew was in uproar. Even Jorge looked annoyed: a shark escort was apparently preferable to a naval one. Erik shook his head gravely and said nothing, thinking of all his family's work brought to shame. If we were ordered to end our expedition, there would be no second chances for the *Viracocha* — she was a one-use boat, already absorbing water fast. Either we sailed on, or we would have to start building a new boat from scratch. In our many months of dreaming about this trip, we had all imagined both the heroic climax (victorious arrival at Easter Island, garlanded by dancing girls) and the tragic climax (storm, self-sacrifice, acts of

extreme bravery). What we hadn't envisaged was the *anti*-climax —
being towed home in disgrace like errant schoolboys. It was difficult to imagine a more embarrassing end to our voyage.

Thankfully it was not to be. Within ten minutes, Eli phoned
back. She had managed to get through to the right number, report
our position, and persuade angry but relieved naval officials that
the trip was proceeding well. Neither ship nor plane had yet set off
to search for us, thanks in no small part to a fortuitous distraction
provided by one Augusto Pinochet.

By extraordinary coincidence, we later discovered, Chile's noto-
rious former dictator was being flown back to his homeland that
very day after an indignant and rather extended stay in British
custody. For the massed adoring ranks of the armed services, the
return of their revered general was evidently far too important an
event to interrupt fannying around in the Pacific looking for a
bunch of idiots adrift on a haystack.

Instead, the episode had a clarifying effect for all of us. Faced
with the prospect that we would have to go home, we realised
more keenly than ever that we were glad to be here. The only one
not smiling at the end of the phone call was Phil. Having sensa-
tionally pissed off the navy by going incommunicado for a couple
of days, he was now ordered to phone and report his position at
noon every day. It wasn't really so much to ask, but Phil looked
pained by the instruction.

'I hate making any kind of agreement like this,' he told me,
after Eli finally rang off. 'It just causes unnecessary worry.' It was
not the first time he'd almost sparked a rescue operation, it
emerged. 'I once promised to phone Eli on a sat. phone from the
top of a mountain, but a snow storm cut off our power. Poor Eli
was worried sick, and they ended up flying out a search party by
helicopter. That's why it's better not to set any expectations, just to
go it alone.' In this case, however, he had no choice.

Privately I was delighted with the new arrangement. I still couldn't quite get over the speed with which the navy seemed to have prepared itself for a rescue attempt. Never mind that we were sinking, running out of batteries, and had perilously little sailing expertise between us — at least now we knew someone was looking out for us, albeit from a distance. Wandering out on to the foredeck with a cup of tea, I felt something inside me unclench and relax for the first time in weeks.

None of this got us any further forward in solving either our power drain problem, or the non-functioning of our satellite navigation system, but in the laid-back ambience of the coming days we found that the two cock-ups seemed to cancel each other out. Now that the electricity-guzzling Trimble system was entirely non-functional, the requisite daily power requirement was less than half what it otherwise would have been, and we found that we could more or less get by on solar energy, interspersed with occasional lung-bursting bouts on the *Bicycocha* when things got desperate. We also continued to leave our navigation lights off at night, which had the not unwanted effect of making us all more vigilant for other ships — at least at first.

A general contentment reigned. For the moment at least, the boat seemed to be sailing herself, more or less straight along the pencil line drawn from Arica to Easter Island. We all began to feel a sense of pride in her. I've always found it strange that ships are automatically female, but there was no doubt about the *Viracocha*. Perhaps it was the curves of her construction or the softness of her flanks, but we began to see her affectionately as a kind of protecting mother. Every afternoon, those of us not on watch would sit in the shade of Jorge and Carlos's makeshift shelter, our bodies hinged into a shallow 'V', as we lay in the cleavage of the mother ship, comforted by the warm, musky, familiar smell of fermenting reeds.

Other smells were more recognisably male, and rather less welcome. Due to the preponderance of onions, beans and lentils in our diet, there would often be a strangled cry from inside the cabin and someone would throw himself out on to the deck making choking noises. Phil seemed most prone to this form of biological attack, and always chuckled shamelessly as the cabin emptied around him. It was one of the few ways in which he claimed any privilege as captain – the privilege to make the cabin uninhabitable for short periods of time whenever he wished. Hygiene in general was rather better than this might suggest, despite the lack of fresh water. The favoured spot for washing was balancing on the still unused port rudder at the very back of the boat, and drenching oneself in water pulled from the sea in an old paint can on a string, before soaping up with a strange ecologically friendly concoction brought along by Phil. This came in tiny plastic bottles and was supposed to be so concentrated that it would require only one or two drops per crew member. I went through my whole bottle in a fortnight, after which my hair turned stiff and bleached with salt. Our clothes, washed in sea water, felt permanently damp, however much we hung them out to dry.

We took these hardships in good spirits, however, as there always seemed to be some compensation. Our toilet system was a good example of this win some, lose some principle. There were definite shortcomings about the simple bucket on a rope. For a start it wasn't very private, being in full visibility of anyone on the steering platform, not to mention Pablo the duck, who stared psychotically from behind the string netting of his makeshift cage and looked as if he would relish a sharp stab at something that would make you very, very sorry. However, once the performance anxiety subsided and we got used to conducting conversations punctuated with occasional deep notes of nature's bluntest orchestra, even this primitive toilet system had its advantages. It was very well-ventilated, for example. And what other toilet in the world afforded such stunning views of the Pacific? The only hazard was the likelihood that in tossing the contents over the windward side, you might easily follow them, when the bucket drifted to the end of its rope and suddenly became a kind of sea anchor.

There were a few small hiccups. Some time in our second week, we realised we were all fighting over the same cutlery, seven pieces in total. It didn't take much speculation to work out where the rest of it had gone: someone had washed up the dishes in the deep bucket, and inadvertently tossed all our knives and forks overboard with the dirty water. Whether or not he noticed the brief glittering of our eating implements as they began their long tumble into Davy Jones's locker, nobody seemed inclined to own up to this misdemeanour. Not that it would have made any difference. Davy Jones clearly wasn't going to give them back. After a few days of being forced to stir our tea with enormous hunting knives, we all began carving ourselves spoons from offcuts of bamboo. We etched our names into them zealously, and it became an offence to be found using someone else's spoon. When so much is shared, such tiny boundaries become sacrosanct, as I was later to discover to my cost.

Early on we learned that the normal laws of physics could not always be relied upon at sea. Everything important had to be tied down. Casualties of this new rule were plentiful, and just occasionally rather welcome, as when Marco's seemingly endless Freddie Mercury tape fell victim to an unexpected lurch and broke free all over the cabin floor. Unfortunately the tape player too became somewhat temperamental after its tumble, like a sickly child who might at any moment vomit forth your offering in drooling loops. Eventually, the only way to be sure of hearing anything in its entirety was to cradle the player in one arm and use a finger of the other hand to press gently and continuously on the side of the cassette, as if suckling it. Inevitably, we didn't bother much.

Not that we didn't have the nurturing instinct. Perhaps it was the influence of Mother *Viracocha*, but I was rather pleasantly surprised by the 'new mannishness' that revealed itself as we drew further away from the pressures of ordinary city life. Marco, for example, became very protective towards the two ducks, and took it upon himself to feed them each day from a large sack of corn. It was he who had first noticed that Pablo had taken to pecking Pedro's feathers, and it was he who had separated them by building another enclosure on the ship's port side. Each day he would talk to them gently as he fed them, and give us a brief report of the ducks' progress. 'Pedro's feathers seem to be growing back now,' or 'Pablo seems moody today — keep your fingers away from the cage.' A psychoanalyst might have suggested that Marco was in fact using the birds as substitutes for his children whom he was missing terribly. Marco might have suggested that a psychoanalyst take a running jump.

Jorge also revealed a New Age side — I noticed he was reading *Jonathan Livingston Seagull*, or *Juan Salvador Gaviota*, as it had been tactfully renamed in Spanish, about a spiritually gifted gull who gave up squabbling over dockside fish scraps to ascend to higher planes of enlightenment.

Everybody else seemed to be hooked on Thor Heyerdahl, myself included. It was the first time I had actually got round to reading *Kon-Tiki*, and I was expecting a somewhat starchy and professional account from someone in a pith helmet. So it was a pleasant surprise to discover that the great explorer had been 'winging it' a little himself when he set out from the Peruvian port of Callao, a few hundred miles north of us, in 1947. His crew had almost missed the raft when they turned up late for the tow offshore. They too seemed to have learned as they went along, rather than knowing what they were doing to start with. Heyerdahl sounded similarly awed by his surroundings, perpetually on the verge of a religious experience.

> The whole sea was ours, and with all the gates of the horizon open real peace and freedom were wafted down from the firmament itself. It was as though the fresh salt tang in the air, all the blue purity that surrounded us, had washed and cleansed both body and soul. To us on the raft the great problems of civilised man appeared false and illusory, mere perverted products of the human mind. Only the elements mattered . . . Instead of being a fearsome enemy, flinging itself at us in foam, the elements had become a reliable friend which steadily and surely helped us onward.

It was easy enough to agree with this, sitting in the bow, looking out over the unfeasible blue, scuffed by harmless clouds. We had seen several of our own 'perverted products of the human mind' smashed or malfunctioning, and each loss became a further shedding of restricting skin. We lost track of the days, gave ourselves to this new life with something like relief.

Yet parts of Heyerdahl's account were less easy to identify with. For a start there was the small matter of fish. Heyerdahl's expedition seemed to have been blessed with fish from day one. They had scarcely waved off the tow boat before the ocean's rich and varied fauna rushed to greet them.

'There was not a day on which we had not six or seven dolphins following us in circles round and under the raft,' enthuses Heyerdahl.

> On bad days there might be only two or three, but on the other hand as many as thirty or forty might turn up the day after. As a rule it was enough to warn the cook 20 minutes

in advance if we wanted fresh fish for dinner. Then he tied
a line to a short bamboo stick and put half a flying fish on
the hook. A dolphin was there in a flash, ploughing the surface with its head as it chased the hook with two or three
more in its wake. It was a splendid fish to play, and when
freshly caught its flesh was firm and delicious to eat, like a
mixture of cod or salmon.

I was relieved to read Heyerdahl's clarification that 'dolphin'
was in fact another name for dorado, not the lovable mammal. Still,
he could have been forgiven for getting a few names mixed up
with so many creatures throwing themselves at his feet. The *Kon-
Tiki* adventurers sometimes didn't even have to put a hook in the
water. Flying fish obligingly landed onboard overnight ready for
breakfast or bait, rare species of whale shark came alongside to say
hello, huge squid rose up in the dark with luminous eyes, and one
night a 3-foot long snake fish leapt through the door of the cabin
into a crew member's sleeping bag enabling Heyerdahl to discover
its existence for the first time since prehistory. The tanned, bearded
Norwegians pulled sharks out of the water by their tail fins, ate
fish every meal and conducted research into giant octopuses for the
National Geographical Society of Washington. The most we
could muster was a request for sea-water samples for the science
class of Kennebunk Middle School, Maine.

Where were the fish when you needed them? Apart from the
distant whales, and a school of dolphins (*real* dolphins) that
sped towards us one morning only to turn round when they heard
Marco's singing, we had seen not a single sign that anything larger
than a luminous shrimp was out here with us. Marco and Stephane
had spent their first few days trailing lines in the water, but nobody
seemed to be home.

At first I blamed myself. I had offered to buy Stephane some tackle in Arica, and due to my inexperience of fishing he had found himself lumbered with twenty rubber squid lures which looked like the kind of free gift you get in particularly cheap Christmas crackers. Unfortunately they were not improved when Stephane, in a fit of boredom, started cutting off the rubber tentacles with scissors, producing a kind of punk squid.

'Perhaps the lures are not the problems,' I suggested, like I knew the first thing about fishing. 'Perhaps there are simply no fish! Have you seen a single fish yet?' Stephane shook his head and stomped away up the boat. Marco had given up long ago and was whittling a tiny wooden *Viracocha* in the bow.

One night we had a chilling clue as to what was wrong. Close to midnight, we spotted what looked like floodlights in the darkness ahead of us, and came across a factory fishing ship, its high steel walls enclosing dark secrets. We tried to make radio contact, but there was no response, only a metallic hum and a clanking sound from below the deserted decks. As we approached, the boat moved off, dragging nets behind it across our path. It seemed a ghostly, sinister omen, pared of human contact, a machine munching its way through the oceans. 'That's where all the fish have gone,' I muttered to Stephane.

The longer it went on, the more it became a kind of existential problem. My contentment shrivelled in my yearning for evidence of some other life. I went swimming on an unusually calm day, scanning the vast, empty chasm below us for some sign. Even a shark would have been better than nothing, but I found only almost-invisible jellyfish, which left streaks across my back like a penitential whipping. Jorge, enlightened and evidently at one with his psyche after reading *Juan Salvador Gaviota*, patted my shoulder gently and said, with the soothing voice of a Zen master: 'Be patient, Nick. The fish will come. Have faith. Just a little further.'

*

On our ninth day at sea, we finally got what we wanted. It was, perhaps inevitably, a shark. Marco found it almost by accident while checking his line early the following morning. We were woken by a sudden yelp and the word: '*Tiburón!*'

Wrestling our way out of our sleeping bags, we clambered to the side of the boat to see Marco's line being yanked from side to side by something just below the surface. Gripping the reed column of the ship's stern, and with Stephane holding him round the waist from behind, Marco finally managed to drag the shark twitching from the water. Thor Heyerdahl would doubtless have grabbed its tail at this point and wrestled it on-board, but we stood well back. Besides, Marco didn't really need much help, as the shark was only about a foot and a half long. 'It can still do a fair bit of damage to your finger!' Jorge reminded us, as we peered in nervous excitement at the baby Blue Shark thrashing on the floor of the boat. It sent shivers through me despite its size: the sandpaper skin, the black, staring eyes and the crescent of triangular teeth champing furiously on what looked like a yellow plastic bag. 'What's it eating?' I said, puzzled. 'A yellow plastic bag,' shrugged Marco. 'We got bored of using those squid lures and thought we'd try something else. Some sharks will eat anything.' As master fisherman, Jorge picked his moment, grabbed the shark with one hand behind the gills, and with the other sank his knife through its spinal column with a crack.

There was just enough meat for us each to enjoy a shark steak for lunch, cooked the French way with plenty of oil and seasoning. Once I'd eaten it, though, I found myself dwelling on the rather worrying implications of our first catch. Contrary to my yearnings only the day before, it was in one respect worse than catching no fish at all: if there were baby sharks in the area, there were presumably parents too. If a baby was hungry enough to try its luck with a plastic bag, what did that say about the availability of other fish? And if other fish were as scarce as it seemed, then the sharks would be hungrier, bolder . . .

Jorge ate silently, and retired to his bed shortly after lunch.

I had been nagging half-heartedly for our first man overboard drill for a couple of days. Now, with the likelihood of waters teeming with sharks, it suddenly seemed vitally important to do it that very afternoon.

'We're hundreds of miles offshore, but we've got no idea how to turn the boat round,' I argued as I brewed up some tea. 'Am I the only one who's worried about that?'

'Why do we need to turn the boat round?' said Greg, puzzled.

'Well, what happens if you trip overboard this afternoon and miss the safety line? Don't you want us to come back and get you?' I said.

Greg looked thoughtful. 'OK, I got you,' he said.

In truth, nobody really wanted to do the drill, myself included. None of us could quite believe our luck in managing to sail in the right direction for so long, and we didn't want to jinx it by sailing in the wrong one, even if it was only for a few minutes. But you only had to imagine that the man in the water was you to see the logic.

As Jorge was still feeling a little under the weather, it was decided that he should be the man overboard. Not literally, he was grateful to learn, but symbolised by our first empty water flagon. He himself would take no part in the drill, as for obvious reasons we had to be able to do it with one man missing.

Erik took the helm with Phil, and Stephane was allocated the important role of keeping his eyes fixed on the person in the water. Marco and Carlos were given the task of changing the main-sail, while Greg and I took the mizzen at the rear. Then someone kicked the flagon into the sea and Phil yelled 'Man overboard!'

For the first few seconds, it looked like it might actually work. Erik forced the tiller round, as far to port as it would go, which started the boat turning to starboard. Unlike ordinary sailing boats, which tack into the wind, lateen-rigged ones have to turn away from it. In an extraordinarily complex manoeuvre, the slanting yard has to be pivoted into a vertical position, parallel to the mast, and the sheets and sail need to be passed all the way around the front of the yard and secured on the opposite side – in other words, swung through almost 300 degrees in order to change position by 60 degrees – as the boat turns under its own momentum. This, at least, is the theory. In practice it was high farce.

Marco and Carlos seemed to manage the mainsail admirably, but Greg and I found ourselves in a kind of *It's a Knockout* contest which involved one of us scrambling up the side of the cabin, over the top and down the other side carrying three separate sheets, while the other wrestled the foot of the yard to the foot of the mast. It wasn't helped by the fact that Phil and I seemed to have very different ideas about how this could be achieved. To this day I still don't know which of us was right. 'Greg, pull towards the mast!' screamed one of us. 'Greg, drag it away and round the mast!' screamed the other. Greg, dancing a kind of involuntary foxtrot with the yard, tried to do both. Something was wrong with the steering, in that we seemed to be travelling downwind, rather than across it. Erik grunted at the tiller, and Phil yelled: 'We need to use the mizzen to bring us round! Quickly!'

Half-way down the rope ladder with three sheets between my teeth, I growled impotently. Glancing sideways, I could see an occasional speck of blue flagon between waves. Stephane climbing ever higher on the mast, said: 'We're losing Jorge.'

At that moment there was a sudden whip of sail cloth above, and the yard thudded against the mast with a sort of metallic crump.

'*Concha tu madre!*' shouted Stephane from above. 'There goes the radar reflector.'

Leaving the sheets tied loosely on port side, I scrambled up the side of the cabin again to help Greg drag the lower end of the yard back away from the mast, which see-sawed the upper end further across it. There was another gust of wind and a sharp crack from above as the radio aerial snapped and clattered down the mast, hanging by its electrical wire. Stephane had to move his fingers quickly to avoid having them crushed by the now heaving yard.

'We need to turn further!' I yelled.

'We can't,' said Phil, leaning on the tiller with Erik. 'The rudder's full across, but something's stopping us.'

'Where's the man overboard?'

Stephane looked round quickly, scanned the sea around us. His silence was all the information we needed.

'OK, abandon manoeuvre,' shouted Phil, wearily. 'Bring her back round to the same course as before!'

In ten short minutes, we had lost our man overboard, demolished a radar reflector, snapped off our radio aerial and, it turned out, splintered two of our leeboards, which hung at a strange angle in the water, shattered by the sudden resistance of turning. We had forgotten to pull them up before making the turn. Jorge seemed unamused by his symbolic death, but our anxious jokes were the only insulation against the dawning realisation that we were unable to control our own boat.

'OK, that didn't go very well, but we did learn a few things from it,' said Phil, ever the optimist, later that afternoon, when we had done our best to uncrumple the radar reflector, and Stephane had fixed the aerial back in an oddly slanted position at the mast head, using duct tape.

'We've learned that we don't have the expertise to turn the boat round, and that in all probability we won't be going back to fetch anyone. Our best hope in the event of someone going overboard would be to lower the sails as quickly as possible and then try and launch a rescue using the rubber canoe, depending on conditions.'

There was a silence, as we all paused to imagine launching a rescue in a rubber canoe in high seas.

'But look, here's the bottom line. If you fall overboard, you've got about 30 metres to grab hold of the safety rope and shout like hell. If you miss the safety line, you're probably going to die. The best idea is: Don't fall overboard.'

A few days later, Greg fell overboard.

The day had begun like any other of the preceding nine, with porridge and coffee and the feeling of being tousled gradually awake by the wind. The only difference was that we were usually driven from our beds by Marco's terrible renditions of Chilean easy-listening classics. Since the botched drill, however, our least favoured operatic singer had seemed subdued, and spent hours measuring our progress across the chart.

In fact the whole mood of the crew seemed to have quietened, focused a little on our situation. There was a realisation like never before that we were at the mercy of something larger than our own talents, or lack of them. It had different effects on different people. Stephane seemed to thrive on the renewed sense of danger, and spent quality time hanging from the yard repairing the downhaul. Jorge and Carlos muttered together like old sailors in their tent. Erik quietly repaired the broken *guaras* with reinforced planking, while I typed up a newspaper dispatch ready for dictation. I was actually feeling quite cheerful, because I was no longer 'the worried-looking one' of the boat, but a member of a unified, worried-looking crew. Greg was transparently nervous, having just lost his shoe overboard while washing.

Phil, however, had a foolproof plan to restore crew morale.

When Marco yelled excitedly, 'Six hundred miles! Quarter of the way there!' from the cabin, our captain seized upon it immediately and announced a celebration with the magic word: '*Cerveza!*' Beer! The change was almost instantaneous. Phil cracked open some emergency cans he had stashed away somewhere, while Stephane rummaged in the kitchen and pulled out some Pisco, a Chilean drink that mixed fortuitously well with powdered orange juice. Greg, meanwhile, found a canister of 98 per cent alcohol – popular with miners in Bolivia as a cunning means of passing from sobriety to unconsciousness without having to bother with the sociable bit in the middle. It had been given to us by an action-hungry Chilean TV cameraman, possibly in much the same spirit that one might helpfully offer a half-brick to an anarchist. Needless to say, our rocket fuel ended up liberally sprinkled in the evolving punch. By the middle of the afternoon, Stephane was performing pelvic thrusts on the bow deck and singing Pearl Jam songs, while everyone else sat around feeling thoroughly relaxed.

It was about 4 p.m. when Greg, coming from the kitchen with a fresh mug of punch, stepped off the side-deck, reached for a mast stay with his free hand, and missed. There was a brief 'oh!' as he stumbled forward on to the gunwale, a vista of sprawling legs, and a splash as he plunged over the side. It was both extremely shocking and extremely funny. Even as we rushed to the side to help, we couldn't hold back the sudden barks of mirth.

Luckily, falling head first into the sea seemed to sharpen Greg's reactions. Swimming quickly back to the boat, he missed the rope ladder but managed to grab the rudder, where Erik and Marco helped him out of the water. A minute later he slopped damply back to the foredeck, still holding his tin mug, which now contained only sea water.

Phil grinned. 'That was very entertaining, Dobbers,' he said.

'But maybe we should all go a little steadier on the fruit punch now, eh?'

This was as direct an order as Phil ever gave, and unfortunately Greg adhered to the letter rather than the spirit. He switched to wine instead. A couple of hours later, returning to the bow after an early watch, I found him singing 'I Believe in Angels' and hugging the mast like an old flame. An empty wine bottle rolled about the deck at his feet, and Jorge, sitting a few feet away, was looking nervous. 'Ain't thish a beautiful boat?' grinned Greg.

I picked up the wine bottle and looked questioningly at Jorge. 'The whole bottle?' Jorge nodded gravely. At that moment, Greg entered a particularly rousing part of the chorus and got up. Or at least he tried to get up.

I've often wondered why sailors traditionally feel the need to get drunk. Perhaps it's the fact that the motion of a ship feels so much like drunkenness anyway that they figure they might as well go the whole hog and enjoy the fringe benefits. But then, when an ordinary pavement feels so much like a ship when you're drunk, why make it worse and actually do it on a ship? Never having got drunk on a boat, I had wondered if the two effects cancelled each other out, and drunken sailors were left with the sensation of walking on perfectly flat ground – but this hypothesis was quickly shattered by Greg's stumbling progress towards the edge of the boat, his centre of gravity apparently getting there slightly before his legs did.

'Whoa!' he said, as I braced myself against a mast stay and nudged him back towards the middle of the boat. He looked at me in an unfocused but reproachful way for a moment, before sitting down heavily on a eucalyptus log resting across the bow. Then, in slow motion, and with a faint smile, he toppled backwards through the canvas roof of Jorge and Carlos's sleeping quarters and landed heavily with his legs still propped up in the air. He lay motionless and I thought for a moment he had knocked himself out, but presently the sound of snoring rose from among the wreckage. I breathed a sigh of relief.

'We need to look after him,' said Jorge quietly. 'Otherwise he may fall overboard again.' The sun was long gone, and the clouds on the horizon were fading into darkness. My anxiety was now rapidly becoming annoyance. What the hell was Greg thinking of? Did he expect his crewmates to babysit him all night? Perhaps he was planning on sleeping it off — but what would happen when he got up to pee in the middle of the night? Suddenly the possibility of losing Greg seemed very real. I seriously doubted his bludgeoned reflexes would save him if he were to topple overboard now. It was more than likely that we would wake up tomorrow morning to find ourselves one crew member down. And that would be that — the mayday message, the end of the expedition, the disgrace, the pointless grief. I've always had a tendency to rush imaginatively towards worst-case scenarios, but this didn't seem all that unlikely.

After a few minutes of snoring like a waste-disposal unit, Greg woke with a sort of choking noise, and looked round, dazed at the two stony faces watching him. He began, carefully, to rise to his feet, swaying with his arms out.

'How about calling it a night, Greg?' I said, trying to keep it friendly but firm. 'You've had a bit of a skinful.'

Greg looked annoyed. 'I ain't ready to go to bed yet,' he said, moving crablike into a sitting position. 'I wanna watch the stars.'

He sat down heavily on the gunwale, fell against a mast stay, steadied himself and presently began singing again. Jorge and I stood anxiously above him like security guards, unsure of what to do next. I resented feeling like an overprotective brother, but I didn't fancy jumping in after Greg. I decided to wake Phil. He emerged from the cabin sleepily.

'Phil!' shouted Greg affectionately, throwing his arms out. 'Jis look at this beautiful evening – ain't it beautiful?'

'Uh-oh,' said Phil. 'Dobbers, what's happened to you?'

Greg chuckled and got up, stumbling across to port side.

'Where are you going?' I was again standing in his way, this time blocking his route. It was beginning to feel absurd.

'What *is* this? I'm needing a piss, that's all.'

He pushed past me, tripped over a plank and only narrowly dragged himself back on to the deck, before lolloping along towards the back of the boat. I followed with Jorge in pursuit. Phil ran round the starboard side to try and intercept him.

I got to the aft deck and past the kitchen just in time to see Greg swing himself up on to the lattermost straw bundle. Beyond him was the dark water, nothing else. I felt my stomach turn with panic.

'No!' I shouted and threw my arm round his waist. This would have been less embarrassing had he not just opened his fly.

'Whoa! Mind what you're doing! *D-ay-amn!*' He slurred, half angry, half chuckling. 'What *IS* the problem here?'

Phil stepped in.

'Listen, Dobbers, it's nothing personal, we're all just a bit worried about you.' He had a kindly, unpatronising voice. 'It's hard enough moving about on this thing when you're sober.'

Greg looked sulky. Then with a sudden tipsy laugh he broke into a quick scramble up the ladder past Erik at the helm and on to the high part of the steering platform, where he lurched against the wooden handrail, breathing heavily with a victorious chuckle.

'Man, look at the moon!' he shouted. 'Ain't this all so damned beautiful? Ain't it?' We all murmured 'mmm' like a bunch of listless sheep, watching his hand on the rail anxiously from below.

'I mean, man! Have you ever wondered what we're doin' here? Like . . . just us, and this big ol' ocean, the moon and the stars . . . Don't this just make you believe in . . . something awesome . . . ?'

I'd never heard Greg so lyrical, or so drunk. It was as if the drink freed the dreamer in him, the visionary. Not to mention the complete bloody liability.

'Come on now, Dobbers,' said Phil, with exaggerated patience. 'We're worried about you. You're one of us, part of the crew. We don't want to lose you.'

'Yeah!' breathed Greg, sounding as maudlin as a floral greetings card. 'S'like this afternoon, when I fell in – I felt so . . . small. But y'all cared enough to pull me out. It's almost like we're family . . . I know if I fall in you'll rescue me!'

'Don't count on it,' I muttered.

Eventually, with much coaxing, and with a sulky look on his face, Greg lowered himself down the side of the kitchen and lumbered off to his bunk.

Phil made a pragmatic decision to let him sleep through his watch, and the next morning he woke as normal, seemingly unaware of the havoc that had followed him around the night before. I saw him speak quietly to Phil, and I waited all day for him to apologise to me, feeling the anger rise. At about teatime he ambled over to hazard a conversation.

'So, ah, were y'all worried about me last night too?'

He said it with a faintly amused air, but perhaps it was embarrassment.

'You were out of your skull, Greg, and to be honest you're lucky you're still here today.' I'd been rehearsing this lecture for the last twelve hours. 'And what really pisses me off is that you put the rest of us in danger too. It's not like on shore where it's up to you how drunk you get. When you're on a boat, everybody's behaviour affects everybody else.' He was sitting beside me on the roof, and I could only see him out of the corner of my eye, his head hanging slightly.

'It sure meant a lot to me that you all helped me when I fell in,' he said.

'Look, you screw up once, and your friends will move heaven and earth to get you out of the water,' I said. 'But if you get intentionally pissed, why should I risk my life diving in after you? Forget it.'

There was a pause, in which I became aware of my own breathing, furious and stressed, and that I seemed to have turned into some sort of temperance fascist. Greg processed the information quietly, nodding gently with a frown on his face.

'Well, I sure am sorry I gave you a scare,' he said presently. 'I didn't think I was that far gone.' He patted me gently on the shoulder and paused. Then he added, hesitantly, 'I want you to know something: I'd jump in for *you*, even if it *was* your fault. I'd jump in for any of you guys, every time.' He wandered off astern, heavy and sad.

That night, I pondered his words fretfully. It seemed ridiculous that I was now the one feeling bad, but it was true. I was the petty legalist, the Shylock, the control freak, while Greg was the openhearted man's man, generous if flawed. I was suddenly the individualist, and he the communitarian. He slept soundly and noisily in the bunk below me, while I swatted gnats of conscience and stared at the dark ceiling. How could I have said what I did? We were all, to some degree, buffoons afloat, as likely to fall overboard from inattention or clumsiness as from drinking. How could I draw up rules about life and death in such a world? I felt ashamed, and wanted to wake Greg up, tell him that of course we were in this thing together, of course I would be looking out for him. But instead I fell into an agitated asleep.

'Come quickly!' hissed Jorge, as I emerged for my watch a few hours later. 'Bring a flashlight!' He had an excited look in his eyes, and was trying not to grin. I climbed sleepily up to the platform, puzzled. 'I told you they would come!' he whispered. 'Now look!'

He pointed down into the water on our port side. At first I could see nothing but what looked like the opaque glare of car headlights against a bank of fog. It was only when I looked closer that I realised that the whiteness was moving. I let out a gasp. Swimming just below the surface of the water, were the ghostly illuminated forms of hundreds, perhaps thousands of fish. Occasionally they rippled the surface, but mostly they moved silently at the same speed as the boat, escorting us.

'You see! I told you the fish would come!' whispered Jorge, excitedly. 'Beautiful, no?'

I nodded without looking at him. The moving carpet of fish stretched beyond the limit of my torch beam on both sides of the boat. There seemed to be a couple of different species there. One, blunt-headed, swam slightly deeper, weaving inwards and outwards. The other fish were smaller, and rippled along the surface in formation. Something about them was familiar, and it was only after staring for a couple of minutes that I realised what it was.

I was looking at dozens of tiny sharks.

8

Webbed Feet and
Shark Fins

The little sharks had vanished like ghosts by the time the sun rose, but the water was alive with the iridescent blue-green of the other species. These larger, submarine-shaped fish wove from side to side, keeping pace with the boat, and occasionally more distant ones would leap, glistening from the water, arc gracefully through the air and re-enter, to a round of applause from Jorge and Carlos. Both men recognised them immediately as *palometa* and had a hunch these were the same abundant fish that Heyerdahl had described as dolphins, or dorado. Whatever they were, they drove Stephane, Marco and Greg into a frenzy of excitement. The three of them dangled hooks for fruitless hours, getting more and more frustrated as the fish cruised along sniggering at their inauthentic rubber squid lures. Stephane, reduced to a caveman-like state of inarticulate rage at the frustration of watching such large fish so close to his hook, seemed to develop a kind of tunnel vision. It was about four in the afternoon when we finally heard him snag his first quarry.

'Come on you ... yeeees ... *casi* ... no ... yesyesyesyeeeees ... YES!'

There was a sudden splashing and the sound of Stephane's bare heels stamping on the wooden side deck.

'I've got one! Quickly!'

Sure enough, a 4-foot fish was thrashing angrily in the water, jerking at the line, which Stephane held aloft using gardening gloves for protection. It was a strange-looking creature – long muscular body, beautiful armour of gleaming greeny-blue scales, yet with a grotesque, thin head on which the eyes and mouth were cluttered below a long forehead, like a large-brained scientist squashed in a vice. Its eyes now bulged with anger or fear.

'Come on you motherf—'

The fish convulsed in mid-air, knocking Stephane off-balance. Both fisherman and fish landed heavily against the duck pen, causing outraged quacking from Pedro. Recovering quickly, Stephane yanked his catch into the air again and staggering, carried it towards the foredeck. But the fish was not finished yet. At the corner of the cabin it leapt so energetically that it freed itself from the hook, landing close to the edge of the deck with a thud like a boxing glove hitting a well-toned stomach.

'Noooo!' yelled Stephane, as it juddered sideways towards the gunwales in a style reminiscent of bad breakdancing. He leapt furiously on top of it and hugged it tightly to stop it convulsing, until the two of them finally lay still in a pile of old netting, breathing heavily like warring but exhausted lovers. Much cheering and air-punching ensued, and I picked up the video camera to record the moment. Which was when Marco, standing nearest the edge of the boat, suddenly stiffened and pointed.

'PEDRO!'

In the chaos of landing the fish, nobody had noticed that one end of the duck pen had been torn open. Nobody, that is, apart from Pedro himself, who was now waddling in a dignified manner along the gunwale towards the back of the boat, looking interestedly over the side at the water below.

'OK, no sudden movements,' whispered Marco. 'Somebody creep through the cabin and try and coax him back in this direction.'

We closed in like pantomime villains in slow motion, until we were within a few feet of Pedro. At that moment, the duck looked up, and I knew we were rumbled. With a disdainful shake of his tail feathers, Pedro plopped off the gunwale into the sea, and paddled off quickly towards the sun. I did the only thing I could think of in the circumstances: I videoed him.

Marco was frantic. 'Quick, let's launch the canoe! We can still save him!' What Pedro had not perhaps appreciated was that he was now 700 miles from the nearest landmass. He was a domesticated freshwater duck and as far as we knew he couldn't fly. Could he drink salt water? It didn't look good.

Phil shook his head sadly. 'I won't allow a rescue attempt,' he said. 'If we launch the canoe and paddle back after him, we may lose two crew members too.' We were travelling at a good speed, and in the opposite direction to the one Pedro had decided to follow. Instead, we all stood, twitching and speechless, and watched his profile grow smaller against the glittering reflection of the sun, until he was the merest dot in our wake, impossible to distinguish from the shadows of wavelets.

I thought for a moment that Marco was going to burst out crying. He shook his head, and sat down heavily on the gunwale. We all felt his grief. Over the past two weeks we had grown fond of Pedro's bad-tempered quacking, his vibrantly coloured excretions underfoot, his simple presence by our side as we ate porridge

The *totora* hull takes shape by Lake Titicaca.

The *Viracocha* hits the road to Arica.

After copious shoving, the long-awaited launch . . .

Hmm, which way round does this go?

'Where the hell are we?' Jorge, Phil and Stephane, puzzled.

Erik sympathises with a
crash-landed flying fish.

Carlos, foghorn in
hand,
enjoys a spin on
the *Bicycocha.*

Phil can't quite
believe the sails
are working . . .

Greg and Jorge,
noble ocean
gladiators,
parade van-
quished foe.

NICOLAS LE CORRE/GAMMA

In memoriam: Pedro takes a morning stroll.

If in doubt, kick it: Marco leans on a leeboard.

Easter Island navigation: 'Aim between the two rocks . . .'

Phil and Carlos helming it: 'Okay, maybe not *that* close . . .'

A *moai* statue presents its mysterious backside to the arriving *Viracocha*.

Our motley crew cunningly disguised as a row of stone *moai*: (left to right) the author, Carlos, Erik, Marco, Phil, Jorge, Greg, Stephane, the real *moai*.

looking out over the sea. Now, it was as though we had sacrificed our web-footed crew member for the passing thrill of our first big fish.

For a moment, sitting with our shared sense of shock – Stephane still lying with his fish, the rest of us in a ragged semi-circle around him – it was as if our sadness seeped under our emotional defences, transcended the simple clichés of manhood. Could it be that we rose, in that instant, from the hunched status of hunter-gatherers and stood straight-backed, somehow refined as noble human beings, united in our sense of loss? Had we discovered gentler emotions than the mere lust for blood?

Stephane got up, and dragged his fish, still twitching, to the centre of the foredeck. 'Now you die, amigo,' he said, and beat its brains out.

Supper that night had a subdued mood. Even the huge helpings of succulent white flesh could not compensate for the loss of our feathered crewmate. I decided to cheer myself up by requesting a satellite phone call to Ali.

Anyone who has ever tried phoning a loved one long-distance on a dodgy line in a public booth will know a little of the frustration I experienced in the ensuing eight minutes. Yes, there was the simple inadequacy of words to express the yearning of such a long separation; yes, there was the two-second delay which posted awkward pauses on to each heartfelt utterance, causing each of us to believe the other was for some reason reticent about replying. But thanks to satellite technology, there was also a periodic fading of the signal, and an odd metallic tinge in each of our voices that lent us the resonance of amorous androids. In the ensuing miscommunication, Ali mistook the news of Pedro's sad demise for the punchline of an extremely funny joke and giggled happily until she noticed I wasn't joining in. The realisation that I was serious –

and that eight grown men were indeed in mourning for a duck —
only seemed to make things worse, and I lost her for what seemed
like a whole minute in helpless hoots of android laughter. This
proved too infectious to resist, and soon I too was laughing. We
spent a few more minutes cooing metallically at each other's competing tales of hardship (Ali won, having endured three weeks of
unrelenting lavatory humour in the Patagonian wilderness with a
group of gap-year school-leavers) and relishing that delicious ache
of mutual yearning which is the payoff of separation. Then I
rang off, feeling much better.

Marco, still deeply upset, looked at me suspiciously. 'Whatever
you do, break the news gently for the sake of my mother,' he said,
in a gloomy, Eeyore-like voice, as I carried the phone back into the
cabin. He knew I was due to write up a log for the expedition website, which must inevitably include the Duck Drama.

'I'll do my best,' I said, sitting down at the computer. An hour or
so later I had produced, I felt, a minor masterpiece. I did not shy
away from hinting at Pedro's probable fate — effectively flightless,
unable to drink salt water, and therefore eventually destined to die
of dehydration if a shark didn't take him first from below — but I
made sure I infused the whole thing with a certain nobility. I felt
certain Gloria would find it a sensitive and compassionate tribute
to a remarkable duck.

Unfortunately, I reckoned without the system of technological
Chinese whispers that was necessary to transmit the report back
home. In the absence of email, Phil had arranged with Eli that he
would dictate the entire log directly into her answer machine, so
that she could subsequently transcribe it on to the webpage at her
leisure. This would have worked fine were it not for the facts that:
a) the satellite phone was unclear at the best of times, forcing Eli
to guess at large sections of unintelligible text; b) English was
Eli's second language; c) the Chilean press corps seemed to be

using our website not so much as a factual record, but as a source of inspiration for creative writing.

Perhaps I should have foreseen, then, that Gloria would find out about Pedro the deceased duck a few days later when she picked up her morning tabloid to read the following concise front-page report:

FIRST *VIRACOCHA* CREW MEMBER DEAD!
Sharks Ate Reed Boat Pet!
Pedro the duck has been devoured by sharks after plunging into the ocean. The savage attack on the mascot of the reed boat *Viracocha* occurred 800 miles from Arica, and was radioed to the Navy by the English reporter Nick Thorpe.

Stephane pursued fish obsessively for the next few days, sitting poised for hours on the side of the boat, watching his prey inscrutably from behind his oversized *Terminator*-style sunglasses. Increasingly, he found the rubber squid lures redundant, due to the seeming eagerness of real squid to throw themselves on board during the night. The best place to find them each morning was on the waveguard at the front of the boat, which seemed to catch their jellied forms as they squirted themselves out of the slanting sides of waves like gymnastic snot. The first person along the side decks each morning could also expect to pick up at least one flying fish, its long aerodynamic fins dried out like paper fans. By disguising a hook inside either one of these unfortunates, and jerking it along in the water so that the creature appeared to swim, it was usually possible to attract something big enough to feed the whole crew for the day.

Marco, Stephane and Greg were the keenest fishermen, pulling in dorado and tuna with the wide-eyed delight of city boys let loose in the wild. I preferred to spectate, fascinated but still repulsed by the proximity and messiness of death: the casually wielded club, the final convulsions of packed muscle, the gradual clouding of those large eyes, little scales lying like broken finger-nails on the deck. Jorge observed all this with the bored half-interest of a professional, but obliged us by gutting and fil-leting with spellbinding speed. A nonchalant expression hung on his grizzled chin as he slit behind the gills, cracked through the spine, tossed the fish head over his shoulder, gripped both sides of the severed cross-section and pulled the greyish tube of skin back as if peeling off a woman's stocking.

Fresh tuna bears no resemblance whatsoever to the greyish meat scraped from supermarket tins. It is crimson like raw beef, can be sliced off the bone like a prime steak, and tastes rather like tender pork. For the first few days at least, before 'tuna surprise' began to accumulate irony, we ate it joyously for every meal: mar-inated in lemon juice and eaten cold with spices and raw onion like sushi, pan-fried with onions and garlic and (tinned) cream; or simply picked from the pan in succulent chunks as we passed the galley.

Mealtimes still took some getting used to. Having grown up in a London suburb dining on processed fish fingers or the occasional cling-wrapped supermarket fillet, I found it disconcerting to glance up from a fresh-caught tuna steak and meet the unblinking gaze of one of its live relatives flashing along the clear glass barrel of a rearing wave. There were always dozens at our side, often at eye level as we skidded down into watery canyons. Never had the food chain seemed so intimate.

For Greg, it apparently still wasn't intimate enough. One after-noon he pioneered an eccentric form of underwater fishing, which involved harnessing himself to the redundant port-side rudder in a snorkel and mask and brandishing his fishing line like some aquatic cowboy with a lasso. Needless to say he only ever caught one fish this way – the presence of a large human in full view on one end of a line somewhat denting the authenticity of the bait at the other end – but Greg claimed it put him on a level footing with the fish, and enabled him to take part in breathtaking gladiatorial close encounters. I was intrigued – particularly when he roped me into constructing a 6-foot snorkel out of some unused plastic hose.

'Now you can stay under for ages without swallowing water,' he grinned, surfacing with eyes like saucers. 'You wanna try it?' If he harboured any grudge after my overreaction to his drunkenness, he showed no sign of it now, and I secretly envied his boylike delight in the sea. I climbed into the harness, declined the fishing line, and clambered cautiously down to the end of the rudder, clipping on to the safety line as I went. Then I jumped in.

There's something about the disorienting first seconds below the surface of any ocean that bypasses ordinary emotion and takes you straight into A-grade terror. Having spent weeks training myself to trust the supportive qualities of this undulating sheet of mirrored sky, I now stepped through it as though it were a cloud, and found myself dangling as if from the undercarriage of an air-craft. When the airbubbles cleared, the vertigo kicked in.

Fathoms below me, like an accompanying air squadron viewed from a high-altitude jet, a huge school of tuna kept pace, tiny-looking as minnows in the bluish haze. Lifting my head slightly, I almost coughed out my 'snorkel' to see others just within reach of my arm, weaving towards me and away, unblinking. They were all around us. Where were we all going, in this unbidden forma-tion? What was in it for the fish? I felt a shiver of wonder and unease. One dorado, wounded by Stephane's hook, had followed us for hundreds of miles. I could see it now, a few feet away, the pink rag of torn flesh eaten away by its fellows, the raw wound still visible. Its eye stared, giving nothing away.

I lay there swinging slowly on the harness, listening to the peaceful rumble of water over my ears, watching the big fish making minute fin adjustments in the muted sunlight. Then I swung myself to the other side of the rudder, under the boat, feeling my way beneath the tight packed reeds and ribs of rope, all of it now covered in a thin slime of plant growth. In the cleavage where the rear centreboard cut through the water, I noticed four or five small black-and-white striped fish, not more than 6 inches long. There was something uneasily familiar about them.

Most were staying well out of reach of the tuna and dorado, but I noticed one swimming out in the sunlight, jerkily as if injured. I watched the inevitable happen, the almost effortless quiver with which a dorado accelerated and swallowed the tiny fish whole. The law of the ocean, I thought, as I swam outwards again.

But now something was wrong with the dorado. Very wrong. I clung close to the rudder as it swam frantically back and forwards. There was a faraway shout from above, and I realised with a start that it was hooked. The small fish was bait! The dorado thrashed at the surface for a moment, then disappeared upwards through the shimmering curtain of light, as if ascending to fish heaven. Only a fine mist of air bubbles marked its passing on.

The remaining fish carried on swimming, carried on staring, their emotionless eyes neither fearful nor reproachful. They seemed not to have noticed the sudden, violent passing of one of their number, though in ten minutes or so they would probably get to feed briefly on its discarded, severed head. Was that the only reason they were following us? A mutually beneficial arrangement?

Suddenly I remembered where I had seen the striped fish before. A wildlife documentary. They were pilot fish – so named because they generally swam a few inches in front of a shark, riding the bow-wave caused by its snout, appearing to be guiding it, piloting it. The two species nearly always travelled together, the little fish attracting medium-sized fish for the sharks, while the shark acted as a kind of bodyguard for the pilots.

Which prompted the sudden question: why were there pilot fish under our boat? I took a nervous look behind me and climbed out of the water.

'Ain't it awesome down there?' grinned Greg, who had been sitting keeping watch. 'I could do it all day.'

'Beautiful,' I breathed, pulling off the mask, snorkel and harness and handing them back to him. 'But sort of unnerving too. I've got a feeling there are sharks out there, quite close by, and I want to stay at the top of the food chain. Take care, eh?'

Greg grinned and prepared his hook. 'I'll be ready.'

In fact, that night's emergency came from another direction entirely. We staggered out into the darkness at 2.15 a.m. to find the sails blown on to the wrong side of the mast, the yards bowed and quivering. Marco was lying on his back atop the steering platform using his feet to try and force the tiller back round, but we were being blown helplessly sideways to the north. The water resistance had again cracked the *guaras*, only recently repaired after the fiasco of the man overboard drill.

'What happened?' asked Erik, sharply.

Phil looked sheepish. 'We took our eyes off the compass for too long and veered too far south,' he said. 'The wind just caught the backs of the sails, and now we can't pull her back round.'

We spent more than half an hour straining at ropes, tiller and *guaras* before the sail edges flapped, caught the wind and finally bellied forth, back into the right position. Yet the tiller remained unresponsive, and when Greg tried pulling up the forward centreboard he found half of it missing. For a moment, peering in the torchlight, I imagined I saw teethmarks in the jagged mess of wood that presented itself, but on closer inspection it had splintered away, probably wrenched off by the sheer sideways force of the water. Another casualty of our inexperience.

Erik improvised a couple of pine planks to act as emergency centreboard for the rest of the night, but he was clearly unhappy. Next day he worked more or less in silence at repairing the fractured *guaras* once more. They were supposed to serve two functions: firstly to prevent sideways drift, but also a more ancient function as an aid to steering. By raising and lowering them in certain combinations, Heyerdahl and others had found they could supersede the rudder.

'But if we keep breaking them at this rate, we won't have any left to experiment with,' muttered Erik. 'More care is needed.'

Yet the sails seemed to slam across with alarming regularity, almost always due to inattention on the part of a sleepy helmsman in the early morning watch or during a lazy afternoon shift. Once even Erik himself lost control. We were, in conventional yachting terms, doing uncontrolled gybes before the wind, but with no easy way of restoring our course. It was the most hated emergency, requiring seemingly fruitless straining at ropes for ten minutes at a time until someone managed to flap the sail outward enough to catch the wind from the right direction again. One afternoon, as we struggled with the same problem in a brief flurry of rain, Greg forgot to let go of the corner of the sail when the wind filled it, and was lifted off the deck and into the air by the ballooning canvas. It flung him back and forth above our heads like a rag in the teeth of a Rottweiler, before he finally dropped into the sea in the dramatic fashion that had by now become his trademark. But even this was not as embarrassing as being the helmsman who caused the gybe in the first place, feeling the groaning disapproval of the rest of the crew like a goalkeeper who fumbled the easy save.

It was an obvious flashpoint for any incipient crew frustration, and one afternoon it was Marco who bore the brunt. He had been distracted by the sight of a large marlin on the starboard side, and in the process of shouting and pointing had lost control of the helm. Half an hour later, dragging yet another fractured *guara* inboard for repairs, Erik couldn't contain his anger.

'That dickhead,' he muttered to me. 'Does he think this is just a game? Doesn't he know this is serious?'

Phil looked up from tying off a rope, and frowned. 'Whoa, wait a minute. Marco made a mistake, but we've all been there, right? Including you, I think. Let's not let our frustration get out of hand, OK?'

If Erik had been meaning to test allegiances, he had his answer. He said nothing, and walked away to retrieve the second *guara*, shaking his head. From then on, his mood seemed only to darken.

A few days later, I was out in the canoe with Erik and Phil on a more or less windless afternoon. We were taking photos of the boat. Erik cleared his throat, nervously.

'Phil,' he said. 'I would like permission to remove the Chilean flags for the next photo.'

Marco had dressed the boat in Chilean flags for our departure from Arica, and they had remained in position ever since: two small ones flying from the tip of the bow and stern, and an enormous bed-sheet sized one that kept getting tangled in the mizzen stays. It dwarfed the single Bolivian one below it.

'Why do you need to take them down? You've got the Bolivian one up,' said Phil, uneasily.

Erik's voice grew stiff with suppressed anger. 'Because it is not a Chilean boat — it is a Bolivian boat.'

Phil chuckled briefly. 'Well if we're going to be technical about it, the hull's Bolivian and the cabin and rigging are all Chilean. Personally, I'd rather stick with an international boat.'

'But this is very important for the dignity of my country,' said Erik, barely keeping his temper.

'Well, if you have to – but it sounds a bit racist to me,' said Phil.

'It is not racist!' stormed Erik. His raised voice caused a head to turn on the *Viracocha*, and he coughed nervously.

He was silent and did not bring up the subject again. But a few days later he quietly and temporarily removed the flags and took his photo.

Once you began looking for the faultlines it was not hard to see where problems might arise in our international crew. Erik's antipathy towards Marco was as much political as personal: to Bolivians, Chile was a greedy oppressor that had taken away their country's only corridor to the sea. It made sense that Marco, being the middle-class managerial Chilean, was automatically more suspect to Erik than either Carlos or Jorge, who were both working-class. Yet Carlos and Jorge seemed to disagree on who their political enemies were, as I discovered eavesdropping on their conversation one afternoon.

'The trouble with our country,' Jorge was saying, 'is that all the money is being siphoned off by foreigners and rich Chileans who don't want to share with the rest of us.'

Carlos blew a raspberry. 'Rubbish!' he said, wagging his finger back at Jorge. 'The problem with most Chileans is that they are stupid – they are poor because they don't use what is given to them.'

Carlos's argument seemed a peculiarly self-defeating one, and it only made me more determined to prove that we could all forget our differences and work together. I was forgetting, however, that I too – along with Phil and Greg and Stephane – was not only a person, but a symbol of a system, of a certain kind of privilege. Before long I found myself exposed on the web of interpersonal politics in a way I had not expected.

It was getting dark, I had just finished listening to the BBC

World Service news, sitting on the starboard side deck, and I was beginning to feel peckish. Peering into the kitchen I was concerned to find it empty: nobody seemed to be making supper yet. Thinking back to our lunch of rice and beans, I recalled that Carlos was on cooking duty today, and went down to the foredeck to enquire when he was thinking of serving up supper.

Carlos raised his eyebrows and turned to Jorge. 'Are *you* hungry?'

'Not really,' shrugged Jorge. 'A cup of tea and some crackers would do me.'

'You see?' said Carlos. 'One big meal a day should be enough, I think.'

I experienced the usual light-headed flutter of panic I get from hearing that I might not get to stuff my face as soon as I thought, combined with a wave of righteous anger. What kind of team spirit was this?

'I'm glad you're feeling fine, Carlos, but in case you hadn't noticed, you're part of a crew. Today is your day for cooking, and personally I'm extremely hungry, so I'd appreciate—'

'Hungry?' said Carlos, cackling unpleasantly. 'You people don't know the meaning of the word. How can you be hungry after the amount you ate this lunchtime? Don't you know that most people in the world feel lucky to have one meal a day?'

You people. So that was it. I suddenly felt cornered and uncomfortable, cast as the greedy middle-class westerner to his hard-working mariner.

It was not the first time someone had pointed out my abnormally large appetite. I've always eaten staggering amounts of food while retaining a disappointingly rake-like profile, a phenomenon which is attributable either to my torpedo-speed metabolism or an undiscovered army of tape worms. Since sailing from Arica it had if anything got worse, perhaps through the amount of nervous energy I was burning up worrying about imminent death. On a few occasions, I had looked up momentarily from shovelling down my second full plate of 'tuna surprise' to find my crewmates staring at me with appalled fascination.

'That's incredible,' Jorge would whisper, as if watching an anaconda swallowing a whole warthog.

'Must be the sea air,' I would stutter, guiltily.

And now my sins were being named in public. Yet it seemed a cheap political shot, especially when only that morning I'd seen Carlos worriedly poking at his own beergut and resolving to diet. I was pretty sure it was middle-aged spread, not global justice, which lay behind his sudden campaign for frugality.

But I couldn't bring myself to carry on arguing, so instead I stalked off angrily to cook up some western individualist boil-in-the-bag pasta. Luckily, before I even got to the kitchen, I was rescued in time-honoured western tradition, by a friend in a high place.

'Hey Carlos, I'm getting kind of hungry,' yelled Phil innocently from the steering platform. 'How about cooking up some of that great pasta?'

'Ah, OK *capitán!*' said Carlos, scrambling to his feet.

Food has always been a central theme of long sea voyages. Partly because it is by necessity a limited commodity, and partly because mealtimes form comforting and solid fixtures in an ocean of fluid time, it assumes an exaggerated significance, far greater than its sustaining power. In many ways it becomes a kind of currency – the only currency worth fighting over when you're a thousand miles from anywhere. Reading *Mutiny on the Bounty*, I was intrigued to discover that the entire tragic rebellion had been triggered by Captain Bligh's histrionic reaction to the alleged depletion of his coconut ration:

'Now, Mr Christian, I wish to know the exact number of coconuts you purchased for your own use.'

'I really don't know, sir,' Christian replied, 'but I hope you don't think me so mean as to be guilty of stealing yours?'

'Yes, you bloody hound! I do think so! You must have stolen some of mine or you would be able to give a better account of your own. You're damned rascals and thieves, the lot of you!'

Thankfully, our own captain was as far from the tyrannical Bligh as it was possible to get without recourse to Prozac, running not so much a 'tight ship' as a sort of floating focus group. He had a fundamental trust that we would work things out between us in an adult way — an optimistic view of human nature which showed its deficiencies most keenly when it came to sharing out the contents of the Goody Bag.

The Goody Bag, our equivalent of the *Bounty's* pile of coconuts, was a large zip-up holdall which sat on the roof. When spirits seemed to be flagging, Phil, Guardian of the Goody Bag, would extract a ten-pack of, say, Fig Newtons, and toss them like Scooby Snacks to whoever happened to be in the area. Unfortunately, Phil could never be bothered to do the necessary maths for an equal share-out, which lent the whole exercise a frustrating randomness. On the day the Fig Newtons made their appearance, for example, I was busy doing something worthwhile in the bow and didn't notice what was happening until I saw Jorge walk past screwing up his wrapper. I rushed immediately to the kitchen and poked my head up to the steering platform:

NICK: (Trying to sound casual) Er, did someone mention Fig Newtons?

PHIL: You didn't get one? Huh. You *should* have got one.

NICK: (trying to hide irritation) Well, maybe someone's saved me one?

PHIL: (Pause) Marco, you see what happened to the rest of those Fig Newtons?

MARCO: (Hamster-cheeked, shrugging guiltily) Mmmmff.

Marco had, like me, grown up in a large family and was therefore instinctively attuned to the survival-of-the-fittest psychology of mealtimes. I mourned the lack of anyone willing to be the adjudicator, the fair-minded mother dingo to ensure all the pups were present before dragging the succulent animal carcass into their slavering midst; perhaps even putting a little aside in case anyone misses out.

In some ways, I reflected moodily one unlucky day, Phil's laissez-faire distribution system was a microcosm of the capitalist system, reliant on the 'trickle down' which never happened. Carlos had his own way of subverting it, by accepting all offers of chocolate and promptly storing each one in a plastic bag 'to take home for my daughter'. This was greeted with a kind of mute outrage by the rest of us, for whom delayed gratification — particularly the delayed gratification of someone who wasn't even on the boat — seemed an alien concept.

But he was wise to take his chocolate when it was offered, as was demonstrated by the Power Bar scandal — a chilling indictment of human behaviour in an unregulated economy of confectionary snacks. Power Bars were the one form of rationed sweet that would not fit in the Goody Bag, as there were 150 of them (exactly 18.75 bars each, I worked out feverishly when I first clapped eyes on them) donated by one of Phil's long-term adventure sponsors. Instead, they were placed in a sack in the kitchen, with only the most half-hearted guidance from Phil ('Make sure you all share them out fairly'; 'Once they're gone, they're gone').

They were, of course, gone by the end of the second week. In the solemn post-mortem that followed, a crestfallen Greg declared he had only eaten two because he thought they were for special occasions only, and the majority of us claimed we had each eaten fourteen (at the rate of one per night watch), which meant that Marco and Stephane who admitted they 'hadn't really been keeping count' had somehow consumed eighty between them.

It was a dark day for idealists, though not, in the end, for human nature. Greg, after all, did not shout: You're damned rascals and thieves the lot of you! Instead he looked perplexed and said: 'Oh. OK.' And Marco, stricken with conscience, came to me some time later bearing a crumpled and forgotten Power Bar.

'I found this in the pocket of my cagoule,' he said. 'Can you give it to Greg?'

I am lying on the side deck, eyes closed, faintly conscious of uneven, sun-warped planks in the small of my back.

The boat rises and falls gently, like a warm chest. I can smell salt on the light wind, and fermented reeds, and the sharp tang of something cooking.

Time has almost stopped. I lie back in it gratefully as in a slowly cooling bath, seeing only the blurred pink glow on the inside of my eyelids.

I open them to the play of sun on water.

Around me, herds of clouds graze slowly across the endless prairies of the ocean, and a solitary column of rain smears the distance. Here is unfenced existence, the mind shorn of landmarks. The horizon never gets any closer.

I am almost free of me.

'There's something following us!' yelled Phil. It was Thursday afternoon. I peered out from behind *The Bounty Trilogy* as others padded past to the back of the boat, following the line of his finger. At first I could see only the lazy upwelling of the seas, foam-flecked parallel ridges running back towards the horizon.

It was only when I climbed to the fourth rung of the aft mast for a higher perspective that I saw what Phil was pointing at. It was much closer than I had been looking, swimming a few metres behind our trailing safety line, a dark but familiar shape with a sharp dorsal fin occasionally breaking the surface.

'A shark!' yelled Stephane, rushing to fetch his fishing line.

'It's gotta be nearly five metres long!' said Phil, peering backwards from the tiller.

The shark had a blunt nose and long pectoral fins, and was cruising lazily in our wake, barely needing to move its tail to keep pace. It seemed very interested in our safety buoy. Presently, it closed in with a firm thrust of its tail, and bit experimentally on it. The safety line, tied high on the stern of the boat, whipped momentarily above the surface in a sparkle of scattered drops of water, then slackened again as the shark let go, unimpressed with the texture of plastic.

Stephane and Marco were preparing a line, impaling raw cubes of tuna over the hook.

'You're not seriously going to try and haul that thing in, are you?'

Stephane ignored me, his face taut with excitement. He swung the hook backwards and forwards, then tossed it into the water, paying it out towards his quarry. The bait floated slowly closer to the shark, which twitched sideways slightly to investigate. It made an experimental approach, seeming to sniff the meat. Marco clamped a precautionary hand on the back of Stephane's belt. This was one occasion when nobody wanted to find himself in the water. The shark gave a last sniff, a quick flick of its tail, and took the bait. Stephane yelped, yanked on the line.

'Pull!' yelled Marco.

Stephane tensed and fell suddenly backwards, picking himself up to find only a severed fishing line in his hand. The shark didn't seem to have noticed the hook it had swallowed.

'*Concha tu madre!* He cut through it!' he muttered.

'Let me try,' said Marco, ready with his own reinforced nylon line on the starboard side of the stern. This time he tried to lure the shark alongside the safety rope, closer to the boat to make it easier to reel in. Jorge, I noticed, was wide-eyed and nervous. Perhaps he was wondering, like me, what we were going to do with the shark if we actually hooked it.

Again the shark seemed to scent the meat, and accelerated towards us.

'Go on . . .' whispered Marco, tightening the line in one hand, and bracing himself against the back of the boat. A closer look, then a lunge for the meat. This time the hook stuck. There was a sudden thrashing as the shark realised the trick, and Marco pulled back on the tautened rope. A roar of excitement went up round the boat. Even Jorge grinned nervously.

'Help me pull it in!' yelled Marco. Stephane locked his arms round his waist.

For a moment, the shark allowed itself to be led by the nose. But then in one contemptuous motion, it writhed back on to its side, and the line went slack.

'What happened?' yelled Stephane, red-faced with frustration. 'Did it cut the line?'

Marco reeled in and whistled, holding up the end of his line. The hook was still there, but its ½-centimetre diameter shaft was now stretched out, effortlessly, in a useless straightened spike.

'Man, imagine the power of that thing!' said Phil, laughing, as the shark retreated, chastened, and was lost from view.

'You see?' Jorge was saying to Greg. 'This is why it is dangerous to go swimming!'

Greg looked thoughtful. 'Huh,' he said.

Pablo, watching all the action from his cage at the stern, made satisfying stabs at whichever ankles were in range.

Stephane, meanwhile, was reeling his line silently on to a hunk of wood. His cheeks were flushed red, and when he stood up he did not look at anyone.

'This equipment is shit,' he said sullenly, walking away along the side deck.

Stephane still seemed agitated that evening, when I joined him on watch. '*Hola hermano*,' he muttered, his cigarette tip glowing at the helm. He didn't say much else for some time, looking out over the sea, tapping his foot absently, ensconced in his woolly hat. The tiller was lashed on a 240-degree course, and the sails were quiet and bulging. Finally, he spoke.

'*Hermano*, can you do me a favour? Keep watch while I go up the mast?'

'No problem. Something need fixing up there?'

He paused. 'You could say that.'

I watched him climb, determinedly. I thought perhaps he had spotted a loose rope, but when he reached the top he wrapped an arm round the yard, and just stood there looking out over the moonless seascape, his black silhouette blotting out the stars as the ship swayed back and forth. Five minutes passed, then ten, and he made no movement. Finally, after what must have been fifteen minutes, he descended quietly.

'Better?' I asked.

He grinned bashfully and nodded.

I thought I knew how he was feeling. There was something about hanging high above the sea which sharpened the senses, gave a different perspective on life. I often went up there myself to think, or to escape, though usually during the day. The only difference was that I needed to clip a harness on to something if the exhilaration was not to be overwhelmed by the fear of falling.

I told Stephane this and he shook his head.

'Nah. Better to rely on your own strength. Anyway, I like the danger. It makes me feel more . . . I don't know . . . alive. Like that shark today! I felt no fear! But it was frustrating . . .'

He looked as if he was about to say something else, but instead sat back and sighed.

'Is this trip turning out like you hoped it would?' I said.

'*Mas o menos,* more or less. Sometimes I get a little bit . . . what's the English for *nervioso?*'

'Nervous?' I suggested.

'No, no, not nervous.' He sounded embarrassed. 'More like angry, agitated. It comes and goes.'

I stayed silent, waiting for him to give birth to whatever it was. The only noise was the flapping of the sail edge, the creaking of bamboo, and the chuckling of water over the rudder. Then the tick and brief flare of Stephane's cigarette lighter.

'I began to travel because I wanted to get away from a bad situation at home . . . a woman I loved too much. I went crazy for those months in Arica, partied a lot, trying to forget about her. That wasn't so good either. But I thought it would all change out here: the sea, the natural world, the simple life. A chance to escape from complicated problems, but . . .' He made a vague hand gesture, and the cigarette end turned small circles.

'There's a lot of time to think out here, eh?' I ventured.

'*Exacto!* Too much time — I keep turning it all over, there's no escape. Everybody thinks of me as laid back, because I hide it well. But sometimes I feel like I will burst with it. *Kaboom!*' He chuckled nervously at his approximation of an exploding head. 'You know what I'm talking about?'

I nodded enthusiastically, trying to think of some way to reciprocate.

'I get worked up about different things,' I offered. 'I like a little bit of danger, but I think a lot about all the things that might go wrong. I waste time imagining terrible disasters that might happen to us, and trying to prevent them. I suppose I'm just a control freak trying to break the habit. I hate the idea that I might be limiting my experience of life through being afraid. That's why I came on this trip – to put myself in a situation where I had to trust someone other than myself. Other people. A higher power.'

I couldn't see Stephane's reaction in the darkness. He tossed his cigarette butt overboard.

'One day,' he said suddenly, 'I will get married. Maybe I will find a country woman on my travels, someone *tranquilo*, who won't want other men, who will help me live a more peaceful life. I don't want any more *locas*, any more crazy lovers.'

I gave his shoulder an affectionate pat.

'Well, good luck *hermano!*'

It was the afternoon of Friday, 17 March, exactly three weeks after leaving Arica, when Marco burst excitedly from the cabin shouting '*Mil millas!* One thousand miles!' He began drumming on one of the water vats, setting up a rhythm. 'Come on! We need a rock band to celebrate!'

Erik looked up from his notebook and grinned sardonically at me. His dark antagonism towards Marco had lifted remarkably that morning after Marco had helped him to pull in his first fish of the voyage. It had turned out to be as long as Erik was tall, the largest tuna any of us had ever seen. Erik was still grinning with pride an hour later.

'Come on,' I said now. 'Grab your flute.' Carlos was already on his feet, and began fiddling with the remains of Greg's 2-metre snorkel, blowing through one end and swinging the other to make a curious oscillating farty noise. I picked up the canoe pump and pumped it under my arm as an improvised squeeze-box, Jorge strummed random chords on his guitar, Erik played his recorder, while Stephane and Greg attempted a pseudo-native American war cry.

The result was surely the most appalling cacophony ever to issue from the lips of men. But there was a strange beauty to it too, a surreal harmony after the frictions and the conflicts. Never mind that we were perhaps the oddest bunch of misfits ever to set foot on the high seas. For that moment, even without Pedro at our side, we were family.

9

The Perils of Steel
and Dreams

'I'm piss bored,' announced Stephane, throwing himself down on the foredeck, where I was being beaten at chess by Erik for the second time that morning. 'We need some action.'

Jorge, who was whittling himself a new spoon from a piece of bamboo, looked up and eyed Stephane sceptically.

'I never thought I'd say it, but I agree,' I admitted, as Erik took my queen. 'Almost seems too easy if we get to Easter Island without even needing to change tack.'

Stephane grinned slyly. 'What we need, *hermanos*, is a storm! Then we'd really see what this beautiful boat can do! Yes?'

I grinned at him. 'Maybe just a little one . . .'

I stopped to find Erik's hand clamped on my arm. He was

staring at us with an expression of dark anger. Jorge too had stopped whittling, and was shaking his head.

'What you are saying is very bad, very foolish!' said Erik, urgently. 'Never speak like this!'

'Why not?' said Stephane, puzzled.

'You put us all in danger with this reckless talk — don't you realise it is bad luck?'

'What, just *talking* about a storm?' I said, incredulously. Erik wagged both hands at me, made shushing noises, looked around nervously.

'There are forces at work that you don't understand,' he said sternly. 'Do not bring bad luck upon us all through your ignorance.'

I was speechless, unsure whether to smirk or frown. Eventually, edging forward through the verbal minefield, I hazarded a clarification. 'So Erik, can you explain what it is about . . . what I said . . . that might . . .' I tried again. 'Which forces are we talking about?'

So Erik explained, keeping his voice low.

According to Andean traditions followed by his people, there were spirits all around us, many of them malevolent and demanding, to be appeased. Most dangerous in our current situation, however, was Supaya, the God of Evil, who apparently scanned the airwaves of our words and thoughts like some kind of Nazi radio operator, waiting for things he could trip us up on. '*Cuidado!* Be careful what you say,' warned Erik, gravely. 'Because Supaya may just take you at your word, and give you what you so flippantly request. He is most attentive on Tuesdays and Fridays.'

It was a Wednesday, I noted.

'I'm sorry if I offended you,' I said, 'I've never heard about these superstitions befo—'

'Not superstitions, *beliefs*,' hissed Erik impatiently. 'You westerners think you know everything, but you seem to know little of the spiritual realm. Listen my friend, the gods are on our side so far – do not turn them against us.'

I'd never seen Erik so worked up about anything before, except perhaps the Chilean flag. Stephane looked flabbergasted. Jorge nodded slowly.

'You believe this too?' I said to him.

'More or less – men of the sea are the same across the world. Everybody knows it is bad luck to mention bad things.'

Carlos was equally convinced, as Phil had discovered only the previous afternoon when he leaned over the side to play with a large green turtle swimming just off our bow.

'Don't touch it *capitán!*' Carlos had shouted, panic in his voice. Phil drew his hand back as if burned. 'It's very bad luck to meddle with a turtle – better to let it go on its way.'

The turtle continued snapping lopsidedly at small fish, and turned over to reveal it had only three fins. '*There!* It's an *injured* turtle too – *very* bad luck, you see?' confirmed Carlos, nodding sagely as if vindicated. Phil rolled his eyes and watched frustrated, as the creature dived below us and disappeared.

Sailors, I discovered, were up there with your average cult-member when it came to drawing up rules. *The Ocean Almanac*, an invaluable tome subtitled *Being a Copious Compendium on Sea Creatures, Nautical Lore & Legend, Master Mariners, Naval Disasters, and Myriad Mysteries of the Deep*, contained a section that read like Deuteronomy for seamen. Running my finger down the list of lucky and unlucky omens, I found nothing that bode particularly well for the *Viracocha*:

'Black travelling bags bring seamen bad luck.' That condemned most of our crew at a stroke.

'Avoid people with red hair.' This left Greg, whose hair was a distinctly reddish shade, with an unfortunate conundrum – how to avoid *himself*. It would also have faced the rest of us with the diffi-cult decision as to whether to pitch our resident Jonah overboard, had he not already beaten us to it.

There were a few straws of hope: 'It is good luck to pour wine on the deck.' Greg had certainly done that, albeit inadvertently. Perhaps it cancelled out the red hair. But then again, he had also burst a carton of wine *in his black travelling bag*.

The more I read, the more obscure and desperate the traditions seemed. It was bad luck to spot a curlew; lose a mop overboard; drop a stone into the sea; cut your nails or hair at sea; hand a flag to a sailor between the rungs of a ladder; or see a dog near fishing tackle. From the rationalist viewpoint, it was easy to see how such traditions had arisen. 'Women aboard a ship make the sea angry' evidently sided with the hen-pecked old soaks wanting some peace. But rather conveniently, 'A *naked* woman aboard a ship calms the sea.' You could see the thinking behind that one too.

Some traditions seemed to operate with a kind of reverse logic. It was almost certain death to utter the word 'drown' – presumably because of Supaya the eavesdropping literalist or his cultural equiv-alent – and yet it was considered pointless to learn to swim, due to the belief that if you did fall overboard, all resistance to the sea was futile.

I tried to imagine the dark crucible of pain in which these blunt rules were forged, as survivors scrabbled to give some reason for random acts of nature. A cabin boy swept overboard in a storm. Was it easier to believe that the ocean is an unpredictable, awesome force with no regard for those on its surface, that we could all die at any time for no reason? Or that the cabin boy brought it on himself by passing the flag between the rungs of the ladder? Clearly, it had to be *somebody's fault*. Anything was better than random, pointless suffering, there had to be a reason for it, some force, however arbitrary or cruel, at work behind the universe. I

could understand the thinking, but I preferred to believe in someone more benevolent and creative than Supaya — generally
hands-off, but sometimes known to tip the chaos towards a surprising good.

'It is unlucky to start a cruise on a Friday.'

It gave me a perverse satisfaction to recall that the *Viracocha* herself had been both launched and towed to sea on a Friday — we
would be the proof that this was nothing more than the pathetic
scrabbling of tiny fears. Then I read the next sentence: 'In the nineteenth century the British navy tried to dispel this superstition.
The keel of a new ship was laid on a Friday, she was named HMS
Friday, launched on a Friday, and finally went to sea on a Friday.

'Neither the ship nor her crew were ever heard of again.'

A few days later something happened which made me wonder if
the superstitious sailors weren't on to something after all. I was sitting on the sack of duck feed, listening to the BBC World Service
in what had become a reassuring ritual. Whatever else was happening across the globe — wars, famines, elections — and however
far we were from land, BBC announcers would always sound
like elocution tutors to Her Majesty the Queen. Yet tonight, at
9.30 p.m., all was not right with the world. As the last light bled
from the horizon, and a chipper-sounding reporter skipped
through the business round-up, one item in particular caught my
attention: 'The bankrupt US phone company Iridium is to send
66 satellites worth $6 billion out of orbit to burn up in the Earth's
atmosphere, after failing to find a rescuer for its ailing business. A
bankruptcy judge has given the firm permission to cut off service
to its 55,000 customers, and 'de-orbiting' of the satellite network
may begin in the next two weeks over the Pacific Ocean . . .'

I got up and wandered a few steps along the side deck to where
Phil was up on the cabin roof.

'Phil, what's the name of our satellite phone company again?'

'Iridium, why?'

Phil was first disbelieving, then outraged, as I relayed the information.

'They can't switch off the whole system just because they happen to have gone bankrupt!' he protested. 'I spent 3200 dollars on that piece of crap! What are we supposed to do now?'

It was such incredibly bad timing, you could almost believe there was something more than random chance involved. (Supaya, gleefully: 'You called it a piece of crap! I heard you! Well now it really is!') We were, at that moment, almost exactly at our half-way point, more than 1000 miles from land in any direction. Not only were we to lose our last remaining mode of long-distance communication, but we ran an admittedly outside risk of being bombarded by the smoking remains of its space-age hardware as it dropped into the ocean around us. It had a certain symmetry to it, anyway.

There had been no information in the broadcast about exactly when we could expect the service itself to end – for all we knew it could be a matter of hours. But the next morning it was still working, so both Phil and I took the opportunity to make contingency plans. Phil phoned Eli and told her to explain to the navy that we were likely to go out of contact imminently, and therefore not to panic if they didn't hear from us for a while. He seemed rather less concerned about this than I was. Then I phoned a colleague, Dave, on the news desk at the *Scotsman*. He picked up the phone with the harried voice of one whose day has already been surreally bad, but who fully expects it to get worse.

'Oh hello. Still bumming around South America?'

'Sort of. I'm on a boat made of reeds in the middle of the Pacific.'

A strangled laugh. 'Oh. Of course. And what can I do for you, apart from have you certified?'

'I've got a story you might be interested in — "Daring Adventurers Left in Lurch by Heartless Satellite Phone Giant" — that type of thing . . '

Surely even a bankrupt company could find a way to delay switching off their satellites (or whatever you do to a satellite) until we'd stopped using them? I gave Dave all the details and rang off so that he could get on with harassing the liquidators in the most emotive terms possible.

As it turned out, we weren't the only ones relying heavily on Iridium at that point. Norwegian adventurers Rune Gjeldnes and Torry Larsen were attempting a 2100-kilometre journey, the first unaided trek across the entire Polar Ocean; French yachtsman Philippe Monet was making a bid for the westabout round-the-world solo record; and Frenchman Jo Le Guen was in the Southern Ocean, attempting to row across it solo. All faced the same possibility that their only means of outside communication would disappear at any moment.

In the mean time, we got used to the idea of a little more involuntary downshifting. We'd already had to come to terms with a non-functioning navigation system, a dodgy bike generator and the removal of our means of playing Freddie Mercury tapes — what was a little more technology wrested from our grasp? In the end, wasn't it all just one expensive lucky charm, waved at a complex universe to convince ourselves we were in control? The inventors of Iridium, I later discovered, seemed to have swallowed their own hype. 'If you believe in God, Iridium is God manifesting himself through us,' boasted Ray Leopold, one of the three Motorola engineers, in a statement that would later acquire unexpected ironies. His colleague Ken Petersen, had similarly inflated views of his own importance: 'After millennia of people looking up at the same night sky, we're the first to put up a new constellation since God.'

I decided to start relying on the old constellations instead. They seemed rather less likely to fall out of the sky. Astronomy had never been a particular gift of mine, a fact which had emerged in one celebrated incident earlier in the voyage when I roused Marco from his bed one night to make emergency radio contact with a mysterious ship showing a bright red light. It was only when the 'ship' was levitating noticeably above the horizon that Carlos had informed us dryly that we were in fact radioing Antares, a rising red star 170 light years away.

Since then, Carlos had taken any available opportunity to show me round the southern sky. Antares, I had learned, was part of the Scorpius constellation, which skulked above the eastern horizon just as Orion the hunter fell away in the west soon after midnight. On earlier watches you could supposedly see not only Orion, but his two dogs, a dead hare and the seven sisters of the Pleiades taking refuge from his oversexed advances. Presumably this was what Greeks and Romans did for entertainment in the days before soap operas.

Personally I found the characters elusive and unconvincing, like bad dot-to-dot puzzles.

'I can see his armpit, but where are his arms and legs?'

'Neeky, you need to use your imagination!'

But one constellation even I could distinguish at a glance was the Southern Cross. None of its bits were missing, and it was more or less what it said it was – a slightly crooked cross, like an X on the otherwise incomprehensible map of the night sky. I used to watch it turn slowly along our port side each night until it stood upright, pointing the way south, according to *Emergency Navigation*, a book with a red cover I had found on Phil's bookshelf. The skies above us, I was beginning to understand, were as reliable as the waters below were fickle. All I had to do was learn to read them.

Growing up in a London suburb, I'd never really bothered much

with stars, scuffed faint as they were against the sickly orange of
sodium street lights, somehow less interesting than the brief, violent slashes of fireworks. Out here, they were so bright they burned
themselves on to your mind. As the moon waned the Milky Way
flicked its white paint ever more brilliantly across the sky, and I
learned I was looking at our 'home' galaxy side-on: 100 billion
stars among which earth hung as tiny as a grain of pollen. I felt
none of the cosmic loneliness I expected. In an odd way, the slow
scrolling of the same stars above us brought our only recognisable
signposts, a sense of place. We were in our own neighbourhood,
even if the neighbourhood was 100,000 light years wide.

The pre-dawn watch always brought the biggest high, a sense
that we were barely clinging to the surface of the planet as it spun
us round towards the sun again. I would watch slack-jawed as the
black horizon smudged grey, then coral pink. Wisps of cloud
turned silver, then warm gold, and suddenly that first gobbet of
molten lava would spill over the horizon, burning its glittering trail
across the sea towards us, distorting vision, warming my cheeks. In
those moments, cradling a warm mug of coffee, listening to the
flapping of the stern flag and the gentle creak of rope and
bamboo, it seemed that I was standing in front of an empty stage
before the first grand entrance, the orchestra poised under the
raised baton of the conductor. It was the creation of the world, and
we were the first men alive, floating on uncreated wastes of water,
awaiting our calling.

'*Marco!?*'

Carlos quavered as he scrambled out of his shelter, his sleepy
eyes suddenly round and white with fear. The rest of us, seated
around the bow in the warm glow of the lantern, stopped our quiet
evening banter, nonplussed. Marco was on the steering platform.
Carlos scurried to the edge of the deck, shielded his eyes against

the warm glow of the lantern, and peered urgently along the horizon. Almost immediately he stiffened.

'BARCO! BARCO!' he bellowed frantically, and ran off down the side deck towards the steering platform. *A ship.* We all strained our eyes in the darkness and finally saw what Marco, at the helm, had missed. A green light, only a short distance behind us on our port side, was getting steadily larger. There was no mistaking it now. A ship was bearing down on us, on a converging course.

There was a sudden bustle of movement as we realised our predicament. Apart from the lantern, which would be hidden behind the cabin end, we were invisible. Phil dashed into the cabin and switched the navigation lights on, while Marco, relieved at the helm by Carlos, picked up the radio.

'*Atención! Atención! Todos barcos!*' he began tensely.

Nothing but radio static. Had we tested the radio since we knocked the aerial off? I couldn't remember. I felt the adrenalin wash through me and scrambled outside. More lights had become visible. Judging by their wide spacing, it was a big freighter, perhaps even a tanker. It was too dark to make out its form yet, but we could already hear its metallic whine, getting louder, getting closer.

'Damn thing's probably on autopilot,' muttered Phil in the cabin. 'Nobody's listening in.' A new fear gnawed. What would happen if our dented radar reflectors failed to trip the ship's auto-alarm? A large ship could cut us in two without even noticing. Marco's voice was rising inside the cabin.

'*Atención todos barcos! Aquí esta la* Viracocha! *Cambio!*'

There was a silence, then a crackle of another voice, unintelligible. It said something like: '*Osi yoyo aki scuh stuzz.*'

'What the hell was that?' I heard Phil say. 'Let me try it in English. *Viracocha* here. We are a sailing boat made of reeds. You are on collision course with us. We cannot manoeuvre. Please alter your course.'

Again, a burst of static, then more unintelligible words, oriental-sounding. Probably a huge factory fishing boat, the lights now swelling, brightening, as they came closer.

'Do you speak English? French? Spanish?' asked Marco in Spanish, more urgent now.

'No comprendie,' crackled a voice. There seemed to be some conversation at the other end.

'THIS IS AN EMERGENCY,' said Marco. 'WE ARE A BOAT WITH SAILS. NO MOTOR. NO MOTOR!'

'Ahhhh! No motor!' came a new voice, in an oriental accent. 'We make quickly now.'

We rushed out on deck again in time to see the vast silhouette loom out of the darkness, slicing across our path. The night air was suddenly laden with the oily roar of her engines. We stood and stared as a wall of black steel towered, less than 100 metres from our bow – a soiled, dark product of an industrial revolution we had almost forgotten aboard our vessel of spongy reeds and uncomplicated dreams. The two ages coexisted uneasily for those strange moments, anachronistic icons against the neutral, ageless backdrop of the oceans. We squinted into the grainy darkness, trying to find something human out there to at least wave at, but there was only the line of eerie green lights, the jagged silhouette, and then, abruptly, a deafening blast of a klaxon. The lights slid steadily to our starboard side and began to shrink into the night.

Somebody began to laugh, crazy, high-pitched – some kind of delayed stress reaction as the relief flooded over us. Stephane did an impersonation of Carlos's frantic warnings, making rushed waddling movements to hoots of mirth. Phil videoed a few of us making flippant, laddish comments, while Marco went back to the radio, swapped pleasantries in broken Spanish and found out that the freighter was Korean and en route from Valparaiso, Chile, to

Osaka, Japan. Even Jorge, normally wise and measured in his comments, seemed unable to think coherently. 'How beautiful!' he said, inexplicably. 'I've never seen a boat pass so close before!' Erik allowed himself a chuckle.

Only Carlos, impassive at the tiller, kept his silence. Nobody thanked him for his intervention, and in the endless post-mortem that followed the near-miss, Jorge actually criticised him for causing panic among his crewmates by overreacting. Marco, obviously piqued by his failure to spot the ship, assured us that he would certainly have done so within seconds had Carlos not got there first. Later, the story morphed further, and he and others claimed they had already seen the ship before Carlos began to shout.

It was only during a shared watch, three days later, that I coaxed Carlos – who had been angry and withdrawn since the incident – into giving me his side of the story. What I heard made me shiver.

'Something very strange happened that night,' he told me, quietly. 'Even now I can't talk about it without emotion. The thing is, I didn't see that ship – I *felt* it.' He swallowed, looked into my eyes to see my reaction. I nodded slowly for him to continue, not quite understanding.

'I was lying inside the tent – how could I have seen it? In fact it was – what is the word? – it was a sort of *premonition*. I was just settling down for the night when my chest went very tight, as if something gripped my heart. I knew suddenly, without any doubt, that we were in terrible danger.' He pummelled his chest softly with a clenched fist, looking for words.

'You mean a kind of supernatural . . . prompting?' I whispered. I could feel myself breaking out in goose pimples.

'Exactly. I started shouting *before* I left the shelter, before I even knew what the danger was. I only saw the ship as I rushed towards the stern. Nobody else had seen her, coming from behind us – Marco was not paying attention.'

My mind was reeling with the implications of what he was saying. Carlos looked at me with a sad half-smile. 'Now you think I'm crazy too?'

He saw my awed expression and continued.

'The thing is – who knows what could have happened? You think Marco would have seen the ship in time to switch on the lights, let it know we were out here?' He shrugged. 'That premonition was for a reason . . . it's happened once or twice before in my life. It's like someone out there was looking after us. But all those idiots could do was laugh at me.'

He almost hissed the last phrase, and I was grateful that he hadn't included me in it – though I wasn't entirely sure I deserved the favour. I thought of us all, prattling like children at the bow that night, and his silence.

'They were laughing at their own deaths.'

He stopped and we both stood silently, listening to the ripple of the water and the muffled sounds of guffaws and chat from the front of the boat. The night air seemed suddenly charged with wild, benevolent magic. I breathed it in, grateful and awed.

'Carlos,' I said, finally. 'I'm extremely glad you're here.'

He chuckled quietly for the first time in days, and patted my arm.

'But I shouldn't be here at all,' he said, pointing to his wristwatch. 'I should be in bed.'

The story never did convince anyone else.

I mentioned it to several other crew members in an effort to rehabilitate Carlos in their affections, but was greeted generally with embarrassed frowns. Even those who believed in the supernatural powers of inanimate objects and the unquestionable rules of good and bad luck couldn't bring themselves to believe that any supernatural power would be short-sighted enough to choose Carlos as its conduit.

'It's all in his imagination,' said Jorge. 'He gets these funny ideas sometimes.'

Carlos, I was now realising, was something of an acquired taste. Qualities in him that I found delightfully eccentric at worst, my crewmates were beginning to find irritating. Even Jorge, with whom he had struck up a natural friendship, seemed occasionally to put up with him much as one might put up with a particularly cantankerous old husband, uttering a long-suffering, 'Whatever you say, dear.'

Phil, always diplomatic, acknowledged that 'something weird happened' on the night of the freighter incident, and left it at that.

Meanwhile, I began to see ships everywhere.

One night, in the early hours of the morning, I woke groggily to find myself gazing at the looming side of an ocean liner, its stacked ranks of portholes lit up merrily, mirrored in a shiftless sea, somewhere off our bow. I could hear the sound of shouts, the tinkle of music somewhere. My immediate thought was that Phil must have made contact, perhaps arranged to buy fresh vegetables, but I was confused to see that everyone seemed to be asleep.

'I assume we're aware of the big ship?' I said, to nobody in particular.

'What?' said Phil's voice, suddenly alert.

'Astern. Massive liner — I can nearly see into the ballroom.'

There was sudden movement from all bunks simultaneously, as my crewmates threw off blankets, scrambled out through both doors. I was finding it hard to feel alarmed. It all looked rather beautiful. There were seven deck levels, and people in dinner jackets walking along them. None of them seemed to be looking in our direction.

'Where, Nickers?' yelled Phil, now outside.

'Right there! Straight ahead . . .' Oddly, the lights seemed to be fading. 'I just thought you might be interested . . .' Phil came back through the door, slowly, and stood in front of me. I became aware that I was sitting up on the edge of my bunk.

'Point to it,' he said, with sudden fatigue.

I tried to point out the liner, but found myself pointing at the wall. I blinked, tried to think.

'Um, it was just there . . .'

I looked round the cabin at haggard faces, all staring at me, wild-eyed. Marco dashed into the cabin from the stern, panic etched on his creased face. 'Where is the ship? I can't see it!'

'It's OK, Marco. There was no ship, right, Nickers? You dreamt it.'

I blinked again.

'Shit! I'm sorry . . . I . . . it was *there!*'

'OK,' said Phil flatly, turning away. 'Panic over everyone, back to bed.'

Erik shook his head darkly, muttering something. Marco just looked uncomprehendingly at me.

In the morning, I tried rationally explaining myself to my crewmates. Ali often amused herself chatting to me during particularly surreal dreams, I said. She loved recounting how during a Turkish holiday she had woken to find me sitting upright but fast asleep at the end of the bed, operating an invisible tiller, convinced I was at the helm of a sailing dinghy. Then there was the time I woke in a stuffy boarding house in Jamaica, to find myself standing in the middle of the bedroom wielding a bottle of deodorant as if it were a powerful flashlight. When I tried to go back to bed, I discovered the duvet was missing. After an exhaustive search, I found it rolled up on top of the wardrobe.

'I've still got no idea how it got there. Weird, eh?'

'Wait a second,' said Phil, slowly. 'Are you telling us you can walk around while you're still asleep?'

'Occasionally,' I admitted. 'It only tends to happen when I'm disorientated or stressed, in an unusual place.'

'Like, for example, on a reed boat in the middle of the Pacific?'

I took his point, and decided to change the subject.

I only realised quite how much this rattled my crewmates a few days later, when I got up for a pee in the early hours of the morning. On my way back along the side of the cabin, I noticed one of the rope ends dangling untidily, and as I was tying it off, I heard Greg cough nervously behind me.

'Howzit goin' buddy?' he said, gently, easing his way along the side deck towards me.

His voice had the calm of a trained negotiator trying to persuade a suicidal man from jumping off a window ledge. His hands were open and ready at his side, in a kind of no-sudden-moves posture.

'Oh, it's OK, I'm just fixing this rope . . . it was a bit untidy . . .'

It occurred to me this wasn't the most rational priority at 3 a.m.

'U-huh, that's just fine. Nick, buddy, can you tell me where you are right now?' He spoke even slower than usual, as if to a child or a foreign tourist. He probably thought I was about to walk casually overboard. I thought of the role reversal since Greg's drunken evening, and had to chuckle. Now it was his turn to babysit.

'Yeah, Greg, it's OK mate, I'm on the *Viracocha*, heading back to bed. I'm not sleepwalking.'

Greg didn't look totally convinced. Could a sleepwalker be aware of the concept of sleepwalking while actually sleepwalking? I could tell he wasn't sure, but his arms relaxed slightly, and he patted me on the shoulder.

'OK buddy – just wouldn't want to lose you.'

Erik was the most intrigued by my sleeping habits.

'Pay close attention to what you dream,' he told me, as we sat dangling our feet over the side one day. 'Often you will find a message or a warning from another realm.' He had his own example of this, it emerged, which had disturbed him greatly during our land-based building phase. 'One night I dreamt that the *Viracocha* was on fire,' he said, 'and however hard we tried we couldn't put it out. I kept throwing buckets of water on to the flames, but they just got higher, more intense. I knew it was some kind of warning, but I didn't know exactly what it meant. Then the very next day, Kitin Muñoz began his campaign against us, the controversy engulfed us like flames. And still we haven't managed to put them out. You see?' He raised his eyebrows sagely.

I was semi-convinced. 'Why did you assume the fire was a metaphor, and not a real fire? Surely that was just as likely, on a reed bo—'

Erik shushed me, waved his hands. Supaya listening. Oops.

'These things are usually symbols,' he assured me quickly.

I hoped so. The next night I dreamt that I was trapped under bars that held me down as the ship sank. I woke sweating to find my hands scrabbling at the restraining ropes. I was aching all over. Perhaps the dream was just a metaphor for my sinking chess scores, I thought, trying to put the best face on it. I was losing so badly that my crewmates were beginning to invent excuses not to play with me, sudden jobs that needed doing. Stephane as usual, gave it to me straight: 'You're crap, *hermano*.'

It was nearly 9 p.m., watch time, and I was exhausted. I had spent all day wrestling with the tiller, writing up diary entries, typing up a log – anything to keep my mind off a growing tension inside. My confidence in our abilities had haemorrhaged since the freighter incident – a trend not helped that afternoon by the nerve-shredding howls of Stephane and Greg leaping recklessly from the mast – and there were times when only manic DIY seemed to stave off panic.

Now, having missed my much-needed afternoon siesta, I was sitting at the map table trying to make a compass light out of a 12V bulb, a salad-dressing container and (of course) duct tape.

'Why are you doing that?' said Marco, who often seemed puzzled by my relentless succession of activities. He had nicknamed me Torito, Little Bull, meaning 'one who rushes about doing things.'

'The built-in light on the compass went out last night,' I said, noticing a new humourlessness in my voice. 'If we can't see the compass, how will we steer?' I felt sure that what I was doing was utterly vital to the survival of the expedition. But why had nobody offered to help?

'Can I do anything to help?' said Marco, peering over my shoulder.

'Nope. I've nearly finished,' I said irritably, taping a wire to the bulb and watching it flare into life.

I stopped in the kitchen to make a hot chocolate on my way up top, and the exhaustion rolled in like a white mist. The boat was unusually unstable, and I cursed as I fumbled for a cup, failed to find a lid and slopped Milo powder on the floor of the kitchen, which had taken on the texture of coarse sandpaper. There was no cutlery as usual, and someone had taken my wooden spoon. I stirred the cocoa with the tin-opener, muttering blackly, reached up to put my cup on the platform, then climbed up the rope ladder after it.

'OK?' said Stephane, missing my usual grin.

'More or less,' I grunted. 'We've got to fix this light before it gets dark.'

It was already dark. Stephane held the torch as I muttered my way through taping the new light to the side of the compass box. Finally I put the battery in its protective plastic bag and connected the wires. The bulb flickered briefly and went out.

At that moment the boat gave a particularly violent lurch and my brimming cup of cocoa slid gracefully across the Nepali matting, hit a rope and emptied itself across the platform, and my trousers.

Something in my head short-circuited.

I picked up the cup with its clinging lumps of cocoa and hurled it with all my might towards the sea.

'*This sodding boat!*' I was surprised by the screech of my own voice, the tightness of my jaw, the recklessness of my gesture. It was a good cup, after all, and we only had five left.

As it happened, my aim was not very good. The cup struck the bamboo railing with an empty 'pock' sound and ricocheted, spinning back over our heads, spraying us with chocolate drips, to clatter to the floor somewhere in the kitchen. I swore again, more half-heartedly, my spectacles flecked with brown. A head bobbed up quizzically at the other end of the cabin, then disappeared again. There was a conspicuous absence of sound from Stephane, apart from a strangled nasal squeak. Out of the corner of my eye, I realised he was rocking with suppressed laughter.

I sagged.

I am a joke to my crewmates, a neurotic fool. My anger is too ridiculous to take seriously.

Slowly, I descended the ladder to fetch some toilet paper. By the time I reascended, Stephane was peering closely at the compass, trying to ignore a large clot of cocoa on its spherical summit as he used Scotch tape to adjust the position of the bulb.

'Sorry,' I mumbled. 'Bad day.'

Stephane grinned and looked up at me with a faintly victorious glint in his eye, a mixture of intrigue and enlightenment.

'So!' he said. 'I am not the only one who is *nervioso*, who hides his anger inside!'

We checked the wiring together, Stephane chuckling, me muttering, until eventually we coaxed the light to work. It burned brightly for about ten minutes, faded to the colour of urine, and went out. I gave up.

The next morning I woke up determined to reinvent myself. Today was the day, and there was really only one solution. I stripped resolutely to my swimming trunks, climbed trembling to the highest rung of the mast, and threw myself screaming from the top.

Even the scream did not seem to be my own, oddly reminiscent of the operatic death-yodel of the hapless extra who always gets mauled by a lion in Tarzan films. I found myself shaking in every limb in my body as I fell, feeling my lungs emptying as the water sped upwards to smack my backside. There was a split-second silence as my shout petered out, then the explosive hiss of entry almost immediately muffled in booming submarine bass. I hung for a moment in chilled blue limbo, the soles of my feet tingling from the impact, and trillions of air bubbles rushing over my body, then kicked back towards the light. When I surfaced, close to the rudder, I was grinning.

'Are you OK, *hermano*?' said Stephane, offering me his hand as I scrambled up the rudder shaft.

'Never felt better – want to join me?'

As I slopped along the side deck punching the air, the gaping expressions of my crewmates brought to mind the audience at a community concert I'd once attended, where the vicar had turned up in drag to perform 'The Dance of the Sugarplum Fairy'.

'Well, Nickers!' said Phil, chuckling. 'Here's a side of you we don't often see!'

That only made me more determined. Still panting, I climbed the mast and leapt again. And again.

And again.

In truth, there was a dangerous magic in that day that loosened something in us all. On the other side of the boat, Erik and

Stephane and Greg were clowning about in the canoe, which was being dragged alongside the boat by its painter. I joined them, and when Erik belly-flopped a dive, we all laughed so hard that we tipped ourselves overboard and had to swim to catch the rudder as it came past. Leaving the canoe trailing upside down, we found a new game. One of us would leap on to the platform of its upturned base, and challenge the others to unseat him in a wrestling match. There was much chest-beating, roaring, laughter and splashing, but more importantly some long-held grudges dissipated harmlessly, for the moment at least.

You could still see something hard in Erik's eyes as he grappled with Marco, their wet bodies glistening as the rubber squeaked comically beneath their braced legs, but the relief of actual combat seemed to wring the anger out of him. After more than a month pacing, yawning and occasionally snarling like caged zoo animals, we were finally getting the chance to cuff each other overboard. I found I loved the moment of adrenalin as the water dragged you away, knowing there was a chance you wouldn't make the rudder in time, always catching it as you went past. I thought fleetingly of the shark that had followed us, but it only sharpened the tang of the moment. I was beginning to enjoy this risk business.

So much so that I barely noticed when the wind picked up that afternoon. Marco, Stephane and Jorge had gone paddling in the canoe, and it was Phil who noticed first that they had fallen behind.

'Are those guys keeping up?' he wondered, watching all three of them paddling fast astern, well out of shouting distance. I looked up, heard the distant guffaw of Stephane's laughter.

'Sounds like they're still having fun,' I said, going back to my novel. Someone else could worry for a change. Phil said nothing, and watched them for the next fifteen minutes as they paddled a zigzag course, a few hundred metres behind us, scarcely keeping pace. But still Stephane's laughter reassured us.

It was only when they finally drew level with the emergency buoy half an hour later, and Marco lunged for it, dragging the boat alongside with it, that we realised how close we had come to losing them.

'Didn't you hear us shouting?' said Marco, almost sobbing with fatigue as he staggered on board.

'No, just Stephane nearly wetting himself laughing.'

Stephane lay panting on the side deck. 'It's not real laughter, it's a nervous reaction,' he explained, his eyes shut. 'I laugh like that when I'm afraid.'

None of this seemed to have any lasting effect on the adventuresome spirit of the crew, however. We were approximately 500 miles from Easter Island, but less than 300 miles from another isolated crumb of land which could be seen on the map, a little to the south of our projected course: Sala y Gómez Island.

'Anybody fancy trying to land there? Just a brief stop?' asked Phil that night. He handed round the pilot's guide:

'Scarcely more than a heap of stones, less than 0.5 miles long NW–SE and about 0.3 miles wide. During a gale it would be hardly distinguished amidst the spray . . . A submerged rock lies about 183m SW of the S point of the island. Anchorage can be taken about 0.3 miles off the N side of the island . . .'

'It's not exactly a holiday resort, is it?' I said.

'No – I guess we'd just be having a look, anchoring well away from the rocks and taking a couple of us ashore in the canoe,' said Phil.

'Excuse me, *capitán*, but it seems a little dangerous to me,' said Carlos hesitantly. 'The rocks will be sharp. Are we sure we can control the boat well enough to land there? Supposing we are driven on to it – it could tear us apart.'

'Yes, what are we going to get out of this visit?' asked Jorge.

'Well, it's got an interesting part in Heyerdahl's theories. I'd like to tell him we stopped there.'

In his voluminous research, Heyerdahl had dug up testimony from a wizened 115-year-old Peruvian Indian named Chepo, who had given remarkably precise information about an island uncannily like Sala y Gómez. Interviewed in Peru in the late nineteenth century by a Spanish captain, the elderly native said that after sailing two months by raft from Arica or Ilo, his people had reached an uninhabited desert island 'in which there are three high mountains and many birds'. From a distance, Heyerdahl pointed out, Sala y Gómez did indeed look like three large rocks rising out of the ocean, and was covered in seabirds. But more tantalising still was the elderly Peruvian's volunteered testimony that one week's journey further on lay a thickly populated island known by his people as Qüen, whose chief was Qüentique. The timing was about right, and Qüentique sounded remarkably like Kon-Tiki. Was Qüen in fact Easter Island? Chepo's testimony seemed to suggest that his Peruvian forebears had not only travelled there across these waters but also returned to Peru at least once to pass on their knowledge.

'So anyway, don't you think it might be interesting to take a closer look at this bird island?' concluded Phil.

'*Vamos a* Sala y Gómez!' grinned Stephane, excitedly. He seemed already to have forgotten his afternoon ordeal in the rubber canoe. 'Let's claim the island for the *Viracocha*! Maybe we can leave a flag?'

In the end, Phil took a vote. It would mean a slight change of course to ensure we passed near enough to visit the island, and he didn't want to force anyone into it. The vote system was based on Heyerdahl's own form of leadership, which required a unanimous vote by private ballot for any potentially life-threatening decision.

In our case, however, the ballot was not private. It was a show of hands. Seven of us, including a nervous-looking Jorge, voted to take a look at the island, while Carlos abstained from voting at all.

'Sala y Gómez it is then,' grinned Phil, to whoops from Stephane. 'Set a course for two hundred and thirty degrees.'

Newly energised from our day in the surf, we felt brave and invincible, able to take on whatever the ocean dealt us. I slept a deep, dreamless sleep, for that one night untroubled by fear, feeling lucky.

Had I known what lay in wait for us in the days ahead as we steered straight for the rocky bird kingdom, I wouldn't have slept at all.

10

A Proper Storm

'Where'd all the fish go?' asked Greg, spitting out his snorkel with a frown.

We were standing dripping on the aft deck, after a dive beneath the boat with the underwater video camera. We had been hoping for some good marine footage of our accompanying tuna squadrons, but found instead a vast loneliness of water, utterly empty of life. Looking around us now, the waves were clearly bereft of their usual friendly flashes of darting silver, but nobody had noticed them go. It was 2 p.m. on an autumnal April Fools' Day.

'Kinda spooky ain't it?' continued Greg, demasking pensively. 'Even the little stripey ones are gone. *Absolutamente nada*. Do they know something we don't?'

'Maybe we've just reached the edge of their territory,' I flannelled.

'Pity. Looks like we'll have to eat those tinned sardines after all.'

The sun had dimmed behind a chilly haze, more like mist than cloud. The sea was dark and uninviting, and neither of us felt like doing the dive again. The boat was barely moving in the light breeze. Somewhere a sail edge flapped listlessly. I found myself shivering, and went to put on some more clothes.

In the cabin, Marco and Stephane had commandeered the map table as a bakery and covered it in flattened pats of white dough. Marco was putting the finishing touches to his prototype oven, improvised from an old skimmed-milk tin and some wire, while Stephane was amusing himself sculpting a large dough phallus. The two of them looked thoroughly contented. Soon they were busy at the stove and outside we began to get homely wafts of baking bread in the wind. I remembered something I had to do.

Installing myself at the front of the boat, I dialled a familiar number on the satellite phone, hoping it would still work.

'He-hello?' said a voice, endearingly vague and instantly recognisable, even through the android filter of the satellite phone.

'Happy Birthday from the South Pacific, Dad.'

'Good gracious me!'

My dad was the only person on the planet who still used that phrase (barring seventies sitcom actors) and it made me instantly homesick. Doubtless he had also, only moments before, made two strong cups of tea using his precise count of twenty dunks of the teabag (each), and taken one through to mum, who was probably doing the ironing in front of a mind-expanding TV quiz show in the other room, having just beaten somebody half her age at the local tennis club. I could see Dad now, in his favourite rattan lounge chair, cooing enthusiastically as I gave him carefully selected highlights from our five weeks afloat. I had inherited my love of the ocean from him, just as I had inherited my wavering confidence. I knew he would quietly read between the lines for what I wasn't telling him.

'Listen, Dad, we're not far from Easter Island now – maybe four hundred miles – but we may lose contact for the last part of the journey if this phone goes down. So tell Mum not to worry if you don't get any news for a bit, OK?'

'Everything's all right then, is it?' I could hear an edge of concern creeping in to his voice. A gust blew over the bow and flapped at the shelter.

'Yeah, Dad, no problems at all.'

I ended the call and sat looking over my shoulder in the direction of the gust. A bank of impressively sculpted cloud was building ahead of us, low on the horizon, solid-looking like a motorway crash barrier. To our right, it was buckled and torn as if in a collision, and a vision of apocalyptic red was showing through the gash.

'What the heck does that mean?' I asked Phil, who had emerged with his camera. 'Red sky at night, shepherd's . . . delight? That's good isn't it? Or do shepherds like rain for some reason?'

'Beats me,' said Phil, whose weather forecasting ability was about as sophisticated as mine. 'But it sure is beautiful.'

We sat looking at it for a few minutes longer, while the last dying rays of sun clawed through the hole, set fire to a small patch of sea, and then retreated. I noticed Phil was munching something. He noticed that I had noticed.

'Haven't you tried Marco's bread yet? Better get through there before it's all used up.'

The bread was, indeed, perfect. In the cramped confines of the kitchen we ate our scorched offerings in strict rotation as Marco pronged them from the two tiny ovens, and put in new dough balls. We gathered in the warm glow of the lantern and pored over the charts together, poking fun at each other, keeping the night at bay by turning our backs on it. Like hunters round a campfire in the forest, we tried not to think about our surroundings, oblivious to what was rumbling towards us through the darkness.

As most of us slept, the wind began to play games. Phil and Erik, on watch towards midnight, found themselves with the impossible task of anticipating its next move. It would blow briefly from an unexpected direction just long enough to persuade them to reset the sails, then die altogether. Gradually, what little prevailing wind there was seemed to be shifting northwards across the stern. Phil noticed the air growing damper, the temperature dropping. The gusts began to strengthen in a petulant, unpredictable way, whipping across their faces without warning. And around midnight the first needles of rain arrived, growing steadily more heavy, hissing on the bamboo roof of the cabin, whispering insidious things in our dreams. Then around 1 a.m. the wind seemed to die for a moment, steal around the boat and kick in half-heartedly from the south, throwing both yards against the masts with a heavy flop of wet canvas. As if waiting for the cue, the rain became torrential. Phil decided it was time to rouse his crew. So it was that in the early hours of 2 April 2000, I awoke to the roar of rain and the glare of Phil's hurricane lamp, and found myself facing what I had most wanted and most feared: a proper storm.

What was immediately apparent, as we stumbled out of the cabin, was that we were no longer in control of our boat. Forces much larger than us had taken over, and our task now was to survive what they threw at us. The drenched sails, blown against the mast, were pushing us sideways, our *guaras* were hanging uselessly in the water, and the seas around us were confused, ominously dark, gathering their strength for something. We were within 20 miles of a treacherous, rocky and deserted island. The water poured into our faces and down our necks as we stood on the foredeck looking uselessly up at the twisted sail cloth quivering above us. Phil, evidently exhausted after four hours of trying to second-guess the wind, seemed at a loss. 'Looks like you got the storm you asked for, Nickers,' he said.

But it wasn't the storm I had asked for. The storm I had wanted was one in which we fought heroically against the sea, bonded by adversity and friendship. Whereas I am ashamed to say that what most characterises my memories of the early part of that night – more than I could admit in the opening account of this book – is my own barely repressed anger. It began, as most anger does, with fear. Standing waiting for my orders, still only recently awake, I found my mind rushing to all kinds of lurid worst-case scenarios – shipwreck, shark attack, drowning, or perhaps a foolish crack on the head from a yard end. Cut to the tearstained, uncomprehending faces of Ali and my family at my funeral. 'Hare-brained raft trip ends in disaster.'

Before me, Stephane was whooping with joy, beating out a drum rhythm on the water vats with Marco, Jorge and Greg, all of them laughing, shouting in the rain, defying it ignorantly. 'Laughing at their own deaths' as Carlos had put it. A ship of fools.

I noticed that Greg was still wearing the headlamp that I had lent him earlier that evening. Suddenly this seemed outrageous, symptomatic of the human condition, a cardinal sin. I needed my headlamp! Where was his own headlamp? He'd used up the batteries! In fact, nobody seemed to be wearing a headlamp – they'd all run out of batteries long ago. Which begged the question: *why weren't there any more spare batteries?* I strode up to Phil, who was still contemplating the sails.

'Phil, if you're ever thinking of doing this again, try bringing a few more batteries,' I muttered angrily. 'It helps if the crew can see where they're going.'

Phil looked tired. Water dribbled from his beard. 'Thanks for the helpful advice, Nickers. Just what I'm needing right now.'

I retreated in search of Erik. Together, we dragged the stern *guara* out of the water, Erik with a rope tied round his waist. Erik told me the boat would probably sink faster because of the downpour. I fled back to the stern, where Phil had made a decision.

'We'll change the sails at first light,' he pronounced. 'As long as the wind doesn't get any stronger, we can afford to drift for a while. I've got to get some sleep. Keep an eye on the GPS and wake me if there are problems.'

'You're going to bed?' I asked, incredulous.

Phil sighed and looked at me. 'I'm right here if you need me,' he said. 'There's nothing we can do till morning.'

'Fine,' I muttered darkly.

Couldn't someone at least *pretend* to be in control of the situation? Here we were, drifting twenty miles from a jagged reef in the middle of a torrential thunderstorm, and everybody was going to bed! Where was Uncle Chris when you needed him? Carlos, wailing for help at the stern, suddenly seemed a pathetic parody of himself. 'I can't get us on course, Neeky!' he said, relinquishing the tiller as soon as I joined him for his early watch. Not that it really made much difference which way we were pointing – the wind was pushing us wherever it wanted in any case – but we strove to keep *Viracocha* headed on 240 degrees for the sake of form. We stood there, wordlessly, watching the lightning flicker in the low cloud all around us, for once having nothing to say to each other. As the rain eased and the sails began to hang more limply, I felt my anger and fear subside into disappointment with myself and with my crewmates. Not one of us was a hero. We were all just people you might meet at a bus stop – in one case, *had* met at a bus stop – an ordinary rabble, with ordinary flaws.

At 6 a.m. relieved by Marco, I crawled miserably into a damp sleeping bag and tried to sleep. Perhaps, I thought joylessly, we would make it after all.

Then again, perhaps not. The violence with which the boat was pitching when I awoke an hour and a half later, suggested that our night-time drenching had been merely the taster. Now the drumming on the roof sounded like an approaching buffalo herd, and outside the wind was moaning in the rigging. As we scrambled back into sodden raingear, and frantically tried to stuff our clothes into refuse sacks, water poured through the ceiling, spattering us from a dozen different leaks. Outside, dawn had never struggled beyond a faint grey glow through sheets of rain. The sea was foam-streaked now, the tips of enormous waves dissolving into spray as they heaved towards us, shouldering us up and over their peaks. Down in their troughs, they seemed ready to engulf us, bearing down in walls the colour of concrete before we rose up and crested them at the last moment. Visibility extended just beyond the second wave at any given time, all else cut off by cloud so dense and wet that it seemed simply a continuation of the sea spray.

'Quickly, let's get the sails down!' yelled Phil. The wind was gusting strong enough to blow me off balance already, and the sails were hugging the masts so tightly that their shapes were perfectly shown in the wet canvas. The yards were bent like longbows, quivering under the pressure. Which was presumably one of the factors in Stephane's unprecedented decision to wear a harness – my harness.

'I'm going up the mast,' he said sheepishly, back in the cabin. 'Phil says I will need it.'

I shook my head and said: 'Fair enough.' How could I refuse? I didn't much fancy going up there myself. Phil, stuffing his computer into a rubber 'dry bag', seemed not to have heard.

Reluctantly, but with more resignation than anger, I took off the harness and made do instead with a spare webbing strap and karabiner clipped to my trouser belt. Stephane put on my harness, barely hiding his distaste.

Pulling up our hoods, the three of us squelched out into the driving rain to be greeted by a curious phenomenon. Framed neatly against the mountainous seas was Greg, standing stark naked on the wave breaker happily scrubbing himself with soap.

'Greg, would it be impertinent to ask what the hell you're doing?'

He looked up, swayed slightly and grinned though the rain. 'Takin' a freshwater shower!' he said. 'It's fantastic! Y'all should try it! Scrub all this darn salt off my body . . .'

Behind him, a large wave loomed and dropped away, grey and foam-streaked. We all stared blankly, trying to process the information before us from deep inside our rain jackets.

'You didn't happen to notice that we're in the middle of an emergency here?'

Greg picked up a towel to cover himself.

'Right now? Oh, OK . . .'

Phil shook his head incredulously, and laughed in an odd, unhinged kind of way. 'Dobbers,' he muttered, before clambering off aft in search of rope to lash down the foremast foot, which was lifting 6 inches from its portside housing with each pitch of the boat. Unless we got the sails down soon, there was a real danger that the mast would topple, ripping off the cabin roof as it went. We made our tottering way down the windward side of the boat, passing ourselves between fixtures, watching the water droplets firing off horizontally as we grabbed each sodden shroud for support. The wind shrieked in our ears, and at our feet the water boiled and slapped the spongy flanks of reed. Clambering up on to the cabin roof, we found the rainwater pooling into reservoirs caused by sagging in the canvas and bamboo sandwich that formed our only covering. We were discovering our main design flaw.

'We need to try and get a tarp over the whole roof before we put the sails down on it,' Phil yelled at me through the rain. 'See if you can find the big blue one – it's up front somewhere.'

I made my way painstakingly back to the deck, and pulled the tarp in question out from under the shelter in the bow, where Carlos had been using it to bulk up his bedding. I realised with a sudden slap of revelation, that I was now really rather enjoying myself. It was all about having something to do and doing it. No time for neurotic daydreaming – just action. I turned to find myself staring into the outraged eyes of Carlos. He looked accusingly at the tarpaulin in my hand.

'Oh – sorry Carlos, Phil needs this to protect the roof of the cabin,' I said, hurrying past. '*Una emergencia.*'

Erik and Greg followed me up on to the roof again, each of us keeping his centre of gravity low as the boat pitched and tossed. The wind was now so strong that it blew the rain horizontally through the small tubular openings of our hoods and directly into our faces. The water was lukewarm.

We dragged the tarpaulin over the roof, cut slits for the cabin stays and secured it using twine half-way down the outside of each wall. Inside, the water was pooled on the map table and on each plank of the floor, giving a strange reflection of grey-lit door frame, as if our entire cabin was under water. This was not completely out of the question, it seemed. The waves were beginning to slobber around the gunwales on occasion, and the whole boat seemed lower in the water. Underfoot, the *totora* was spongy and wet in a way we had not seen before.

'Quick – we need some help with the sails!' yelled Phil from above. I looked up to see Stephane crouched high on the mizzen yard, his form swinging crazily above us with the nonchalance of one of those fairground attendants who jumps on and off fast-moving rides while collecting money. I was only mildly surprised to notice that although he was wearing the harness, he still hadn't bothered clipping it to anything.

'Stephane is going to try and help free the sail as we lower it,' shouted Phil. 'Otherwise it won't come off the mast.'

He was right. The soaking canvas was plastered across the jagged protuberances of the mast, and the yard was still juddering with the force of the wind. Without some kind of downward pull it would simply stay there, however much we slackened the ropes. So, with the mast swinging like a metronome, Stephane began to jump up and down on the yard as Jorge and Greg loosened damp knots. Erik and I pulled at the bottom corners of the sail, trying vainly to drag the canvas. The sail began to wrinkle and flap harder at the top, but at the foot there was no budging it. The ends of the yard started to quiver and Stephane had to do some nimble aerial foot-work as the heavy wooden centre bumped and scuffed heavily on the mast.

'Try dragging the sail corner this way,' I shouted at Erik. The two of us pulled horizontally until the wind began to tip the sail around the mast. Stephane jumped some more, monkeylike aloft, and the yard slipped another foot or two. I realised now why he hadn't clipped his harness on. As he came down with the yard, the harness would have left him hanging. Inch by agonising inch we pulled and furled the wet canvas until at last it was gathered and tied, and the yard was balanced across the tarpaulined roof of the cabin. The larger mainsail ought to have proved much harder to manage, due to the excess weight of water, but the bow of the boat seemed to turn downwind a little, which made it easier to free. I climbed the mast, positioned myself a little below Stephane with my legs locked round the spars, and pulled the wet canvas down-wards as it crumpled. The yard jerked on down past me, followed by Stephane still standing on it, and I found myself alone above the chaos, clinging to the mast.

All around me, for a hundred metres before the rain cut off vision, I saw the fury of the ocean, the telltale gashes of white foam that signified a gale force wind. I pulled my hood off, clung to the mast, my cheek pressed to the wet polished eucalyptus, feeling the jolts and pitchings through my skull. Below me on the foredeck, Jorge and Greg were tying the sail and yard down, and Marco was out at the end of a long eucalyptus spar over the water, trying to tie the sail up sufficiently to stop it trailing — a task made considerably more difficult as every third wave would dunk both him and the sail. The rain stung my face like flung gravel, and I closed my eyes against it.

I was not wearing a harness, but my arms encircled solid wood. It felt like a victory of sorts.

Climbing carefully down to deck level, I found my fingers had turned greyish-white, prunelike, seemingly no longer my own. I tried drying them on a tea towel in the kitchen. They stayed wet. I was shivering. It was nearly noon, and I was extremely hungry (which was not particularly unusual), but before we ate there was an urgent need to tighten up all our supporting ropes — the ones that held the mast and cabin rigid. The rain was easing slightly, but the waves prowled round us like jostling bullies, looking for a fight, and the wind kept up its battering. Jorge and Erik and I moved round the boat for the next hour, taking it in turns to crank up the tautness in our guy ropes. I also took the opportunity to tighten the trapeze of halyards that held each yard aloft. It was impossible to do this under sail. Then, finally, we reconvened in the kitchen, where Marco was baking some of yesterday's unused dough in the frying pan, handing it out spread with *manjar* — a sweet, sticky, goo guaranteed to give a sugar high in seconds — and cups of tea. He had found the only dry place on the boat, and was wearing rather

unorthodox storm gear. While most of us peered out of voluminous sou'westers, he had changed into shiny black shoes with silver
buckles, burgundy jeans, and a skin-tight 'Prince' T-shirt.

'Going out to the disco later?' asked Phil dryly.

Marco grinned. 'They're my last set of dry clothes.'

Stephane found this highly amusing until it was pointed out that
his own minimalist approach to stormwear – bare torso with shiny
yellow waterproof dungarees hooked over his shoulders – gave
him an uncanny resemblance to a member of the *Village People*. He
frowned darkly at the suggestion.

'Shhh – listen!' said Phil, suddenly. We all listened, straining to
hear anything more than the patter of rain on the tarpaulin and the
slop of waves.

'I can't hear anything,' said Marco.

'Exactly!' said Phil. 'Where's the creaking?'

He was right. The sound that had become the constant accom-
paniment to our travels was for the first time completely absent.
The sudden dousing had caused all the ropes to swell, tightening
the knots and clamping the normally loosely connected cabin
framework rigidly in place. It occurred to me with vague misgiv-
ings that untying and tightening the mast and cabin stays and yard
harness *while wet* had not been such a good idea. What would
happen when they dried out?

Jorge stuck his head round the corner of the kitchen cabin
looking pained.

'Who has upset Carlos? He's in one of his moods again – says
someone stole his bed.'

I glanced at Phil. 'He's talking about me,' I said. 'But I only took
the tarpaulin because it was an emergency . . .'

'You didn't ask him first?' asked Jorge, pleadingly.

'Well . . . not exactly. It was an emergency.'

Jorge rolled his eyes.

'Tell him you were following captain's orders, Nickers,' said Phil. 'See if that helps.'

It didn't. Carlos was sitting pouting at the back of the boat in what was evidently one of the most satisfying sulks he had enjoyed since the Korean freighter incident. I sat down heavily next to him on the squashy gunwale.

'I hear you're annoyed with me,' I said, feeling not particularly sympathetic.

Carlos waved me away, haughtily. 'Too late now – you have to think more about these things before you do them. Think of others before—'

'Carlos, we're in the middle of some very bad weather, I was carrying out Phil's orders, using Phil's tarpaulin, and the alternative was that all the communications equipment was ruined – no radio, no computer, no rescue . . .'

Carlos made a kind of grunt which indicated he had nothing further to say.

I got up, and wandered back towards the kitchen. There was nothing to do but drift until the storm blew itself out and it was safe to raise the sails again. I trudged into the cabin, mopped water off my bunk, and tied myself in.

When I awoke, later that afternoon, it was to the returned creakings of the bamboo cabin, and a warm breeze blowing through the curtain by my head. Looking out, I could see a shadow flapping hazily on the deck. My whole body ached deliciously. I swung myself down on to the still-damp floor and put on a pair of sandals. Outside, breathing in the dry, salty air and feeling my eyes open properly, I saw not only that both sails were back up, but also what looked like the entire wardrobe of the crew. The *Viracocha* had become a giant clotheshorse. A damp jumper had thrown its arms like a drunk around the shoulders of the mast; discoloured socks hung by their toes from every available bamboo crevice; a mal-odorous green sleeping bag swung from the mast stay like some recently vacated alien cocoon. Stephane's poncho seemed to be breakdancing on the roof, with a long line of Marco's shirts threaded on to a length of climbing rope. Stereo snoring wafted softly from within Carlos's and Jorge's sleeping chamber, which had been expanded with the help of grain sacks and bits of plastic attached with string, and now resembled a homeless encampment.

The seas were still exuberantly steep, perhaps even steeper than at the height of the rain, but I noticed with delight that our accompanying squadrons of tuna and dorado were back, now almost looking down on us from above, as they darted to the peaks of their glassy wave chambers. Visibility had cleared on our port side, opening up vistas of slate-grey cratered seas as far as the eye could see, while to starboard the visibility was cut off after a mile or two by a smudged grey wall fissured by silent bolts of lightning.

The storm, retreating. It seemed that Erik's god of evil had lost this round: *Viracocha* I, Supaya 0. I breathed a sigh of thanks, added my own clothes to the flapping display of dirty laundry, and wandered aft along the port-side deck, watching the wide-eyed fish. They would tell us if the storm was going to return.

Phil was on his knees in the kitchen, sweeping up with a dust-pan and brush.

'You've been busy,' I said, filling the kettle. The place looked somehow roomier, simpler, tidier than it had before.

'We've lost a bunch of food,' he said. 'The flour's gone lumpy – don't know if it's usable – plus the sack of pasta's looking pretty ugly. And I've just noticed we're running low on milk powder and hot chocolate. I can't believe we got through it so quickly.'

'What's the damage in the cabin?' I asked. 'Communications stuff still all right?'

'The laptop's ruined. I put it in a dry bag early on, but it turns out the dry bag had an inch of water in the bottom.'

'Ah. Good job we weren't using it to navigate.'

'Right.'

I poured a couple of mugs of tea, handed one to Phil and sat down on the step from the cabin. Reaching down I levered the lid off a large tin of powdered milk, and dumped a heaped tablespoonful in my tea.

'That,' said Phil, staring at my mug, 'is why we're running out of milk.'

'Right. Sorry. Won't do it again.' This anxiousness was unchar-acteristic of Phil. I, on the other hand, felt buoyant and confident for once. The fish had come back, and we were on the home stretch. I was in too good a mood to worry about powdered milk.

Cradling my tea, I stepped up carefully into the cabin, where Marco, still in his preposterous dancing shoes, was updating the chart with our recent progress. This appeared to consist of a scrawly loop-the-loop, indicating that we had drifted northwards, backwards, and were now steering southeast in an attempt to regain our position before the storm. If his sketchings were correct, we would now pass a few miles to the north of Sala y Gómez.

'We're not going to land on Sala y Gómez?' asked Marco.

Phil looked over our shoulders. 'It'll mean a detour now, which seems a waste of time.'

This was good news. Having spent much of the last twenty-four hours worrying about hitting the rocky island, suddenly nobody seemed to have much objection to missing it altogether. More concerning was the possibility that we would miss our main desti-nation too.

'We're about two hundred and fifty miles away from Easter Island,' said Phil, leaning on the map table. 'If nothing goes wrong, we could be there the day after tomorrow. But that's a pretty big "if". The seas round here are the hardest part of the voyage – that storm could just be a taster. The wind could come from pretty much any direction, or we could lose it altogether. With the weird currents too, there's a good chance we'll have to sail right past.'

I'd never really accepted that this was a serious possibility until now. During long afternoons on the foredeck shelter, we had all pored over books, immersing ourselves in the mystery of the island, until it had become more than real, a mythic archetype, a rugged kind of paradise. Now that we were so close, the yearning grew almost tangible in the close quarters of our pilgrim boat.

The name Easter Island didn't really do justice to a place that had no contact with Christianity until 1722. That was the year the Dutch navigator Jacob Roggeveen arrived on Easter Sunday, imposing the title colonial-style to carve out his place in history as the first European to record a landing there. The island had been born in prehistoric times, progeny of three volcanic eruptions which belched up through the sea floor, leaving a triangle of three intersecting larva hills. Roggeveen had arrived to find it mysteriously peopled by a mixture of fair- and dark-skinned people, who lit fires and prostrated themselves before enormous stone statues each morning as the sun rose. They had their own name for the island: *Te-Pito-o-te-Henua* or the Navel of the World. This too seemed a strange name for one of the most isolated landmasses on the planet. More recently in the late nineteenth century, Tahitian sailors had referred to it as Rapa Nui, meaning Great Rapa, as distinct from Rapa Iti or Little Rapa, an island in French Polynesia. But whether its original umbilical link was with the west or the east, the island's mysterious statues and the shadowy origins of its people had aroused fascination from around the world. It seemed to offer the key to one of anthropology's enduring puzzles – the peopling of Polynesia.

We had all now read *Aku-Aku: the Secret of Easter Island*, Heyerdahl's

account of his 1955 archaeological expedition. In a year on the
island he had unearthed what he claimed was substantial evidence
of a possible link with South America – though he had sailed there
in a 150-foot-long Greenland trawler, and had never himself
attempted the reconstructed journey we were making. Heyerdahl
found an island recently converted to Christianity, but still heavily
imbued with its more ancient folkloric traditions. The *aku-aku* of
his book title were spirit-gods that could inhabit both places and
people, sometimes acting benevolently as a kind of conscience,
other times wreaking havoc. According to Heyerdahl's own
account, it was the islanders' awed belief that he himself was a
spirit-god that enabled him to carry off a large selection of their
ancestral statuary to the Kon-Tiki museum in Norway, where it
remains. I wasn't entirely convinced that modern archaeologists
would approve of his methods. On the *Viracocha*, however, he
remained a hero. Whatever anyone thought of the finer details of
his theories, I could not help but admire his spirit of adventure. He
had brought the island alive for me on the page, and very soon we
would see the myth solidify into land on our horizon. But first we
had to sail some of the most unpredictable waters in the Pacific.

More immediate, however, was the delicate matter of navigating
around Carlos' bruised ego. Climbing up on to the steering platform for my watch at 10 p.m. on that first night after the storm, I
found him still nursing a huff that was now fourteen hours old. At
first I thought he was joking, but there was something about his
averted eyes, the way he held his head up and crossed his arms,
which persuaded me otherwise.

'Look, Carlos,' I said. 'I'm really sorry about your tarpaulin. I'll
see if I can get you another one as soon as everything's dried out.
But for the mean time you can swap beds with me if you want.'

'It's not the same,' said Carlos, staring ahead of him.

I was stumped. This was the same man who, days earlier, I had revered as some kind of mystic, my mentor. Now he was five years old. In the requisitioning of something he had counted as his own, I had evidently activated some deep emotional tripwire. The tarpaulin was his Linus blanket, and I had taken it off him without asking.

I thought momentarily about taking a rational approach; appealing to him to think less in terms of who owned what on board the ship, and more in terms of what worked best for everybody's good. But then I remembered I was hoarding my own private stock of AA batteries while the rest of the crew wandered round without flashlights. I could rationalise it — I needed them for my minidisk recorder, without which I could not record the radio documentary I was making — but I wasn't thinking about everybody's good any more than Carlos was. We all had to balance our own private needs with our responsibilities to the rest of the crew. In 16 feet of deck space, some things mattered more than others.

Early in the trip I had noticed that whenever a tool was missing, it was always worth asking Carlos. He would invariably rummage about inside his shelter, perhaps shake a shoe, and the pliers would fall out. 'I'm looking after them,' he would explain, unapologetically. 'To stop people losing them.' Life, I gathered, had not been effortless and privileged for Carlos — he had had to work hard, scheme, perhaps hoard a little, to stave off hunger. He had learned that people would take things away from you if they could — and that you should guard all you had tenaciously.

So I took a pragmatic approach. I grovelled extravagantly and at length. I agreed how devastating it must have been for him to have lost his prized tarpaulin in the height of the storm, how thoughtless of me it had been not to ask him first, what an inspiration he had been to me on the trip. None of it was untrue — just one-sided. I elicited my first chuckle at exactly 10.27 p.m.

Unfortunately, the negotiations were so intense that both of us rather neglected our watch duties. For an hour or so the wind had been unsettled, sometimes blowing almost astern, other times seeming to come from further south. In retrospect, we should have paid more heed to the ominous buckling of the back edge, or leech, of the mainsail, which any sailor recognises as a warning that the wind is about to blow the sail across in a dangerous and uncontrolled 'gybe'. We could have called for adjustments, perhaps for a sail change to the other side of the boat. I had also noticed that, as feared, my earlier tightening of the three-strand harness that supported the yard had loosened as the rope dried, leaving the eucalyptus poles sagging precariously. Ideally, we should have taken the sail down and re-tightened. Instead, we winged it – tweaking the rudder slightly to push away from the threatening wind when it looked as if we might gybe. It was 10.30 p.m. half-way through our watch, when the inevitable happened. There was a sudden splintering crack from somewhere up ahead, a lurch of the boat, and we looked down to see that we had again veered away from the compass tracking. 'What was that?' yelled Marco from the bow. Both sails were flapping against the mast. We heaved the tiller round until they filled again, but there was obviously something wrong.

'That didn't sound good,' I muttered, straining my eyes. The mainsail seemed an odd shape, saggy and unfamiliar. It took me a moment to see why. The entire upper half of the yard had broken off, and was flopping against the sail, taking off at least a third of the sail area at a stroke. Crew members, only recently retired to bed, were now shuffling back out on to deck. Phil looked terrible, scrutinising the mast head with half-closed eyes from below the fleece hat that hadn't left his head for hours.

'Just when I was almost asleep . . . now what's happened?'

'Someone wasn't paying attention,' reported Marco officiously. 'So the sail blew across hard and broke in two. I was sitting right underneath.'

The thin-lipped silence of the other crew members confirmed that the blame had indeed already been placed for this misdemeanour. None of them would make eye-contact with me, and Carlos was still back at the helm.

'I, ah . . . the wind's been pretty unpredictable for a while,' I blustered. 'I guess we should have let the sails out a bit . . .'

'Stephane, can you go up and see what the damage is?' said Phil, pointedly ignoring my prompt for reassurance. 'If there's anything jagged up there, cut it off so it doesn't rip the sail.'

Stephane monkeyed gamely upwards with a handsaw wobbling between his teeth, and a torch in his back pocket. Marco and Erik positioned themselves to pass duct tape and other useful extras aloft. We heard sawing sounds from above, interspersed with cursing, and presently two splintered ends were passed down the chain. There were a few low whistles, a couple of tuts.

'Dammit,' said Phil quietly. 'Just when we were starting to make headway again.' He looked upwards at the sail, filling and flapping uncertainly like a collapsed lung. 'We'll leave it as it is overnight, at least use what sail area is left, then pull it down for repairs first thing tomorrow.'

I slunk back to the helm in disgrace, to find Carlos was looking at his wristwatch. If he felt any sense of shared responsibility for the cock-up, he wasn't showing it. 'I should have been in bed half an hour ago,' he said curtly, and left the tiller before I'd even reached the top of the ladder. I muttered 'sorry' and immediately had to spring forward to prevent it swinging round and putting us in danger of another gybe.

The storm, still visible on the northern horizon, flashed silent white forks. I felt as if it was hanging uniquely over my head.

Carlos was his normal chirpy self the next morning, and worked on the repairs together with Jorge and even Stephane for much of the day, lashing a new section of eucalyptus into place on the broken yard, and retying the whole sail. Phil looked impatiently at the chart, and paced about frustratedly. 'Shit, we're wasting all this good wind with only the mizzen to catch it,' he muttered, to nobody in particular, as Jorge strained at a final lashing. I still felt like I was wearing a dunce cap.

Thankfully, at exactly 6 p.m. Marco shifted the attention away from me with an exciting new development up in the rigging.

'*Tierra!* Land!' he yelled, clinging to the masthead and with a pair of binoculars clamped to his eyes.

There was a sudden stampede to the front of the boat, as almost the entire crew clambered up the A-frame mast and hung there, swaying, in the shape of a motorcycle display team. Everyone strained in the direction of Marco's frenzied pointing. I'm still not convinced there was anything visible to the naked eye, but when the binoculars finally made it down to my corner of the wobbling human pyramid, I imagined that I glimpsed the saw-toothed profile of Sala y Gómez, quivering on high magnification. In terms of an adventure destination it had about as much appeal as a nuclear test atoll, and I was relieved we hadn't bothered landing there. It was, however, something of a kick to realise that after more than 2000 miles, and 5 weeks, we had glimpsed our first piece of solid ground.

The significance to Phil turned out to be much greater. All through the voyage we had been relying on satellites and failing gadgets to tell us our position. Now, for the first time, we had concrete proof that we were where we thought we were. The ensuing celebrations coincided nicely with the completion of the repairs to the yard, and by 7 p.m. we finally had the mainsail aloft again.

And that, unfortunately, was when the wind died altogether.

11

Still Ocean

All that night, the sails barely stirred. There was nothing to do on watch except trace the reflected stars in the dark mirror of the surface. It was as if we were hanging in space.

'Looking forward to seeing your wife again?' said Carlos, breaking a long silence.

I grinned. 'What do you think? It's been nearly three months. She should be on Easter Island by now, with Eli, chartering a boat. The two of them are coming out with Nicolas the photographer to join us for our last day or so – whenever that might be.'

Carlos stared at me. 'They are coming to live on the boat with us?'

'Just for the last fifty-mile stretch.' I chuckled nervously. 'Why, is it a problem?'

'Nobody told me about this.'

'I guess Phil hasn't got round to announcing it yet. It's no big deal, is it?'

'No offence to your wife, Neeky, but boats are not a place for women. It's bad for *solidaridad*.'

We woke next morning to an indifferent sea and an incipient male mutiny. Early on, sitting on the side deck with a bowl of porridge, watching the last tiny hair-like eddies in the water, I could hear whispered mutterings in the kitchen. By 10 a.m. the boat had come to a complete stop, leaving a glass window on the depths. The tuna and dorado hung around in small gangs for a while, their bodies morphing strangely beneath the lens of the surface. Then they discreetly disappeared, as if sensing a different kind of storm brewing.

'So, I hear Ali and Eli are coming on board to join us,' said Greg, amicably, when he caught me on my own in the kitchen.

I looked at him. 'That's the plan. Is that OK with you?'

'Fine with me — but there's a lot of murmuring goin' on among the other guys.' His voice was lowered, friendly but serious. 'You and Phil might wanna deal with it before it gets outa hand.'

I had a quiet word with Phil, who was loudly outraged.

'What kind of a problem?' he said, incredulous, in a voice that was meant to be heard throughout the boat.

He immediately called a crew meeting on the bow and stood waiting with an aggrieved expression, arms folded.

'I'm hearing rumours that some of you are unhappy that Eli and Ali are coming on board for our last fifty miles,' he said, when everyone was assembled. 'I ought to have announced this earlier, but I didn't think it would be any big deal. But apparently it is. So I'd like to know what the problem is.'

Everyone seemed suddenly fascinated by the texture of the deck. Somebody coughed.

'It's not a personal objection to the women,' ventured Erik, after a long silence. 'It's just that we have sailed together as a team for forty days . . . we feel we would like to finish as a team. It's a question of solidarity.'

Phil nodded, thoughtfully. 'But you don't mind Nicolas the photographer coming on board? You didn't find Manuel the TV cameraman a problem for our first two days at sea?'

'No problem at all,' said Marco, generously, to the agreement of the others. They had fallen straight into the trap.

'Huh. That's strange, because neither of them are part of the team either. But for some reason they don't affect this 'solidarity'. Why is that, do you think?' Phil was just managing to control his voice. 'Could it be because this is an entirely sexist argument?'

More intense study of the floorboards. *Women aboard a ship make the sea angry.* Nobody dared say it.

Jorge piped up. 'The problem is that the Chilean media is very *machista.* When we arrive there will be lots of cameras and reporters. If we have women on board, the expedition will seem less . . . serious.' He shrugged. 'I don't agree with the media, but what can you do?'

Carlos nodded. 'And — excuse my bluntness — where will they go to the toilet? The ladies will not want to use the bucket in front of us all.'

'I'll rig up a curtain,' I said quickly.

Phil held up his hand to speak, his eyes narrowed as if in pain. 'I want you to know that I'm deeply disappointed in your reaction. I can't imagine how hurt Eli and Ali would feel if they could hear you. Eli in particular is already part of the crew. She has already done more than all of you put together to make this expedition work. You've no idea how many months — years! — of work she's put in. Right now she and Ali are working their butts off on Easter Island to smooth the way for us — and this is their reward?

I said I would take a vote on important life or death issues, but this isn't one of those. She has more right to be on this boat than any one of you. And that's final.'

There was a stunned, respectful silence. The captain had spoken. Democracy had been overruled. Jorge and Carlos looked grudgingly impressed. But what of Ali? I felt her place on board was less than assured. I decided to resort to more underhand tactics.

'I'm sure Ali wouldn't want to muscle in on our dream-team if she's not wanted,' I said, with studied casualness. 'But you might want to bear in mind that if it's just the original eight of us on board, there will only ever be a maximum of seven of us in the expedition video. One of us will have to be shooting the film . . .' I watched this sink in. 'Ali's a good photographer, and I'm sure she'd be happy to video us all together for our victorious arrival . . .'

Stephane nodded thoughtfully, followed by the others. 'He's got a point,' said someone.

At that moment, the tense calm was broken by the electronic trill of the satellite phone. Phil picked it up, shot a significant glance round the circle. 'Hi Chini, we were just saying how much we're looking forward to seeing you two.' He wandered off up the sidedeck. When he came back, five minutes later, it was with an ironic look in his eye.

'Well, you guys got what you wanted,' he said, sighing. 'They've just been told the charter boat has fallen through, so they're not coming after all. They'll meet us just off the coast of the island instead.'

The release of tension was as visible as if someone had pulled the plug out of an airbed. Everyone shrugged, grinned and slunk back to the shelter of the cabin. I too found myself strangely relieved. Two more days without Ali were a small price to pay for what the episode had revealed, in its skewed, prejudiced way: that for all our mutual annoyances, our cultural clashes and sporadic huffs, we actually rather liked the life we had carved out for ourselves.

I had never really done teams well before. The very word summoned up terrifying memories of school rugby, of people bellowing at me across sodden pitches to do things that were entirely against instinct, such as throw myself at the fast-moving ankles of large men in studded boots. Why would I do that? I much preferred solo sports where one was only responsible for oneself, or team sports where the only responsibility you had was to perform relatively simple actions – pull on a rowing blade, or on a halyard – under orders from someone else. Any more complex form of physical collaboration had always seemed far too messy and dangerous. When men alone were involved, there didn't even seem to be any emotional payoff.

Here, however, things were different. On the *Viracocha* I had both found a different kind of team, and begun to adopt the slower, more fragile pace of male friendship. Looking round affectionately at my crewmates – Carlos with his Linus blanket, Stephane seeking his thrills – I felt I was at last beginning to understand their emotional landscapes, just as they knew mine. The only person who still remained something of an enigma was Phil.

By lunchtime there was not even the slightest breath of wind. Climbing the mast and standing on the limp yard, I looked in vain for our accompanying schools of fish, seeing only cobalt sky and tufts of cirrus reflected in the sea. Occasionally you could hear them – a noise like a round of applause as a patch of ocean the size of a tennis court erupted in a thrashing maelstrom of fish. They leapt frantically out of the water, then plunged back in to veer away in a flash of silver.

'What are they doing?' I asked Jorge, who was watching with me.

'Trying to escape from something that is hunting them,' he replied. 'Something big.'

Swimming gingerly at the side of the ship a little later, I discovered what that something was. Straining through the mask, I had caught a glimpse of huge shoals moving quickly many fathoms below, like streetlife viewed from the top of a skyscraper. Then, from nowhere I saw another shoal closer to the surface, flashing as they turned towards me in unison. I watched them pass a few metres below me at speed, then change direction again. Then I saw their pursuer — a long, sleek monster of a fish with a metre-long spike aimed straight for the heart of the shoal, seemingly biding its time, keeping up with lazy sweeps of its tail. It was perhaps five times as long as most of the tuna, which meant it was a good four metres. I have never left the water so quickly.

'Bloody hell! Did you see the size of that?' I panted, scrambling up the side of the boat.

Greg, it turned out, came close to being run through by the thing. He was, at that moment, 10 metres beneath us with a lungful of air and the waterproof video camera. Erik, who had lowered him there on a sort of weighted trapeze made out of a large metal bar and a long length of climbing rope, peered anxiously over the side. 'Strong lungs, no?' he murmured. We watched the mob of tuna sweep round and engulf him. The swordfish stopped abruptly a few feet from Greg. We held our breath as it eyed him, uncertainly. Then it turned tail and swam away. Greg resurfaced gasping, moments later, with the distant gaze of one who had either misjudged his oxygen levels or had some kind of out-of-body experience.

'Aw ma-yan! That was INCREDIBLE! Wait till you see this footage! I was THIS close!' He put the palm of his hand a few inches in front of his mask. In fact the film seemed to indicate he was even closer than that, due to the fact that he had accidentally pressed 'zoom', resulting in a dizzying wall of flashing silver bodies, and wide eyes — fish so densely packed on the tiny video screen that for a few seconds there was no hint of blue. The swordfish occupied a brief corner.

The day passed in a leisurely blur of marine colours and stinging

eyes, as we swam, leapt from the mast, and paddled the canoe in
pursuit of elusive shoals. Erik inspected the waterline for the first
time after the storm's dousing and reported with some concern that
we had sunk almost a foot since the last measurement, and 16
inches since launch. Clearly we wouldn't be afloat indefinitely. Yet
Phil's mind seemed occupied elsewhere, and towards the end of the
afternoon I noticed he had retreated indoors. I found him ferreting
under the deck, looking for something. He pulled out a rucksack,
and from its side pocket extracted a clay pot, brightly coloured and
about the size of his palm, its lid secured with sticky tape.

'Don't tell me — your secret stash of powdered milk?'

'Actually no,' said Phil, looking up with a faint smile. 'This is my
friend Mark Fogarty — what's left of him.'

A shiver of realisation passed down my spine.

'Some of his ashes. Ann gave them to me to scatter out here. I
thought today might be a good day.'

'I'm sorry.'

'Don't be.'

He put the pot on the map table, fished a sachet of Kool Aid
from the kitchen, tore it open, tipped the contents in a plastic jug.
The silence thickened.

'So . . . what happened, if you don't mind me asking? With
Mark, I mean.'

Phil looked up, surprised.

'You mean how he died? You don't know?'

'Not exactly.'

He filled the jug with water, stirred its surface fruitlessly with
one of our remaining teaspoons.

'You got a spare hour?' he said, pouring us each a glass.

Mark Fogarty was Phil's oldest and best friend. They had met in
fourth grade, and grown closer through high school. Mark was the

kind of friend who was always getting into scrapes, and Phil needed little encouragement to join in. At university the two of them shared a love of baseball and the great outdoors, and sparked a local emergency after their canoes were swept over a waterfall in a remote and flooded creek.

'We were always egging each other on, going a little bit further. I'm sure my parents wanted to disapprove of him, but they couldn't help liking him. Nobody could. There was this incredible energy about him.'

He took a gulp of his drink, sat down on the edge of the cabin.

'Anyway, we'd been wanting to do Mount Rainier in winter for a while. It's the highest mountain in Washington State – 14,000 feet, with the largest winter snowfalls recorded anywhere in the world. Easy enough in summer – we'd done it dozens of times, people get to base camp in tennis shoes – but in winter it's a different beast altogether. Not many people make it to the top.

'So we planned the trip for Christmas 1990. There were three of us: Me, Mark, and Mark's girlfriend Binget. The two of them had just gotten engaged, so I felt like a bit of a third wheel. We made it to 8000 feet when the weather turned real ugly and trapped us in our tent with a blizzard. We ended up sitting on our asses for four days waiting for it to pass: catching up on each others' lives, feedin' our faces with all the food we'd brought, and taking it in turns to shovel snow off the tent roof every few hours to stop ourselves getting buried. Binget told me later the two of them would have headed back home at the first break in the weather if I hadn't been so determined to finish the climb.'

On New Year's Day, their luck seemed to change. The storm passed, and they were able to move up to high camp at 10,000 feet, ready to attempt the summit. 'It was one of those scenes you remember for the rest of your life. The valleys were still clouded, but there were volcanoes poking through, and the sun was setting.

We knew we were on a roll and we wanted to finish the job, so we put on head lamps and started the final ascent at 1 a.m. It was a textbook climb, good conditions, and we reached the summit in seven hours. It felt like the mountain had finally allowed us to do the winter climb, and we got back to the camp feeling great. We all assumed that the hard bit was over.'

The trio rose late on the morning of 3 January 1991, emerging from their tent into brilliant, almost springlike sunshine and perfect visibility, ready to begin the long descent back to the car. Below them stretched a wind-blasted apron of ice, 600 metres of it on a shallow gradient. They had crossed it on the way up, Mark managing fine in crampons while Binget and Phil used skis with 'skins' – synthetic strips designed to prevent backward slippage – and found the surface more slippery than they had expected. For the downward segment, both opted for crampons while Mark announced he was going to ski down.

'I told him there was no way he'd stay upright, and as usual he took it as a personal challenge. I just laughed and let him go. He was the best skier I knew, and it wasn't a particularly dangerous slope, just potentially painful. I was secretly hoping he'd fall on his ass and prove me right. I guess we all thought the real danger was behind us.

'He said: "See you in a minute," and we watched him traverse the slope, and disappear over a small ridge. We assumed that he was trying to skirt the worst of the ice. We strapped on our crampons and backpacks and made a pretty safe descent directly downhill. Twenty minutes later, crossing the final patch of ice, we still hadn't seen him.

'We stopped and waited, and tried yelling for him. There wasn't even a breath of wind, yet we heard no reply. It seemed kinda odd, so we left our packs and went across the hill and over the small ridge until we found his tracks. We followed the tracks down for a hundred metres, but then we spotted a skier thousands of feet below, and assumed he'd gone down ahead of us. It was a relief, because the terrain looked pretty rough – just as icy as the higher section, but steeper, dropping away at an ever increasing angle to the edge of a 200-metre cliff, and the Nisqually glacier below.'

The pair trudged back to their packs, strapped on their skis and attempted to catch up with their miscreant companion. But as they descended, they became more puzzled. Each time they thought they saw him ahead, it turned out to be a rock or tree jutting out of the snow. Surely he would have waited? When they reached the car park, and found the car untouched, buried under several feet of snow, their fears grew into panic.

'I was desperately hoping it was just some kind of equipment failure, but both of us had a bad feeling by then. It was already late in the afternoon, so I skied back up as fast as I could to try and find his tracks again. I kept hoping to see him dragging himself down the mountain somewhere but there was no movement. I yelled for ages, near the glacier, but only heard my own echo. When it started getting dark, I realised I needed to go and get more help.'

Several hours later, following the ski-tracks with two members of the search and rescue team, Phil found signs of a slip and a sharp turn down the slope. A story began to emerge, etched graphically in the snow. Seven metres further down, a single ski pole, then tracks again as he tried to regain control; then scuffs from another tumble, and streaks of blood as he tried to brake using an elbow or knee; 150 metres lower, an ice-hammer embedded in snow, ripped from his pack at speed, followed by a long, straight trail leading to the edge of the cliff.

'That's when I knew it was over. The moon was up and we could see a few scattered objects, two hundred metres below, that were probably Mark. We called down and there was no response, no movement. The two rangers just said they were sorry, and that was it. We couldn't get down there, so we called in a helicopter. That was the last I saw of him — this frozen body dangling below a chopper. Not a great way to say goodbye.'

His neutral tone faltered suddenly, and he stopped talking, turned away from me, gazed out to sea.

'I'm sorry,' I said again. I had almost forgotten where we were. Somewhere outside I could hear the laughter of Jorge and Stephane. I poured some more Kool Aid.

Phil stood up abruptly, turned round to face me. His face was strong and composed again, though his eyes seemed sad. He picked up the clay pot, cupped it in his palm, weighing it absently.

'So anyway,' he said, at last. 'I was thinking today would be a good day to dump some of Mark's ashes in the sea. Maybe have a bit of a ceremony. Open some wine. What do you say?'

Half an hour later, for the second time that day the entire crew gathered in an awkward semicircle on the bow deck. The amber glow of the sinking sun bathed everything in a kind of warm benevolence, and the sea lapped tamely as a cat.

'OK everybody,' said Phil, standing on the wave breaker with the coloured pot in his hand. 'Most of you will know that about ten years ago I lost my best friend in a climbing accident. If he was alive today, there's no doubt at all that he'd be with us here. In fact, he kind of *is* here with us.' He took the lid off the pot. I saw Erik crane his neck to see inside.

'Today seemed a good day to remember Mark, because today is opening day of baseball for the Boston Red Sox, and Mark and I were pretty much religious about the Red Sox. Mark always said if he ever missed a whole season without attending a game, it'd be really bad luck. Which is weird, because he actually missed his first full season right before he died . . .'

He coughed suddenly.

'Anyway, ah . . . here goes.'

He took a pinch of ash from the pot and sprinkled it like fairy dust on the pooled ocean. It spread out like an expanding galaxy, and seemed to disappear. He sprinkled some more, and put the lid back on. Somebody started clapping, uncertainly, and then stopped. There was a lot of sage nodding, and thinking. What did one do on such occasions? I did what western society now does at any kind of ritual: I videoed it.

'I'll save the rest of it for Easter Island,' said Phil, vaulting back over the wave guard, still clasping the pot. 'Now, where's that bottle of wine?'

The molten sun gradually extinguished itself in the ocean, leaving a sky of dusky blues and pinks littered with tiny flecks of cloud. We sat and watched it happen, awed and quietened, with the sweet lubricant of wine. There was no sound save our own hushed voices, the occasional splash of leaping fish, and the clicking of a fishing reel as Stephane and Greg tried, entirely fruitlessly, to catch them. It seemed the perfect evening for a little philosophising.

'I had a hunch you weren't quite the pure rationalist you made out,' I said, sitting down next to Phil. 'Now you've *proved* you're not.'

He looked perplexed. 'Does anybody else know what Nickers is talking about?'

'I mean that Red Sox superstition – bad luck if you miss the game. That's not so different from Carlos's turtle, or Erik's Supaya is it? Are you saying Mark died as a result of a kind of a jinx? Bad luck?'

Phil pondered for a moment. 'No, I guess he died of bad judgement. Everybody who knew him knew he'd make a bad call one day. For a while he was absolutely set on paragliding off the Angel Falls in a canoe. It was like he lacked the fear gene. The ironic thing was that he died making a pretty routine descent.' He took a swig of wine.

'I guess it took a while before you went climbing again after that,' I ventured.

'Actually no. If anything I went more often. I was back on Mount Sajama in Bolivia within a month and a half – it was an expedition I'd already planned before Mark died. A pretty rough one as it turned out – I ended up stranded above a crevasse in a storm, thinking, What the hell am I doing here again?'

'And what the hell *were* you doing up there again?'

Phil squinted up at me, sensing a critical edge to my question. 'You think I'm irresponsible?'

'I just can't relate to it – I mean, I spend half my time on this boat worrying about dying. Aren't you ever *afraid*?'

Phil put his cup of wine down suddenly on the deck and turned to face me. His expression was shadowed with anger. 'Of *course* I get afraid! Not a day goes by when I don't think about what happened to Mark.' He was breathing hard. 'If you have no fear, there's something wrong with you, you shouldn't even be out here.'

He looked at me, weighing me up, and his anger seemed to subside.

'The thing is, Nickers, you need to *use* that fear to stay alive. But you've also got to be able to *control* it.'

I nodded, flushing. He knew me pretty well – perhaps better than I knew myself. He had been observing me during all my panicking, watching my fear control me, looking for the right moment to tell me. He was a good man. A good captain, even.

Above us, Stephane whooped and punched the air, swinging round the masthead, star of his own private circus performance. Phil glanced up, and rolled his eyes.

'Actually, Stephane is a lot like Mark was,' he sighed. 'He has a lot of energy to burn, he hasn't yet grasped the fear. Sometimes I watch Stephane standing up there, doing the things he needs for that adrenalin rush, and I think: "If you do that enough times, you're going to die." You've got to mature enough to get past that constant need for a fix.'

'Is that why you stopped climbing mountains?'

Phil looked surprised. 'I haven't stopped climbing mountains, I just happen to be doing reed boats at the moment. I guess I need some kind of adventure to feel alive. I can't imagine doing anything else. But you won't see me leaping about up there on the mast. I learned what Mark never lived long enough to learn: *use the fear.*

'Actually, what's sad about it is that Mark had really matured a lot in the months before his death. He was just coming to the point where he knew fear. He'd had this weird experience on Anconcagua in Argentina, said he met God on the mountain – a kind of vision of Jesus – and it had changed his life. He couldn't say much about it. I guess it was kind of personal, but we all certainly saw the effects of it. He'd got engaged, finally gone back to finish his degree, changed himself to the point where he was probably the happiest I'd ever known him. Then he slipped and died.'

The pink skies had faded, and the first stars had pricked their way through the dark dome of the heavens. I sat back in silence, pondering, as Phil drained his wine cup. Stephane was still hanging on the yard, Jorge was strumming a love song, Greg was lying on his back looking up at the galaxies.

He met God on the mountain.

Wasn't that why anybody wandered into the wilderness, or on to the sea?

Wasn't that why we were all here?

The next day was my thirtieth birthday. There were worse places to be, I reflected, as I padded out into the sunshine for a bowl of morning soup. I was now officially of the age when I should find something sensible to do with my life: try a bit of social climbing; hold more dinner parties; get a pension. So it gave me intense satisfaction to find myself adrift on a sodden bundle of reeds with a gang of oddballs.

It was a somewhat subdued celebration. There had, apparently, been an attempt to bake some secret chocolate cake in the tin-can oven the previous night, but it had been such a runaway success that Stephane and Marco had been forced to eat it on the spot. The last wine and beer reserves had also disappeared the previous evening, so my birthday was marked only by an off-key rendition of 'Feliz Cumpleaños a Ti' and Stephane's bashful presentation of a new wooden spoon on which he had carved 'Nick'. I found this simple gesture inordinately moving, and spent several minutes wandering grinning round the kitchen showing it to each embarrassed crew member individually.

Then we all went back to what we had been doing before, which wasn't a great deal. Greg kept dropping himself over the side on his trapeze in search of a better angle on a swordfish, but soon gave up when it transpired that even the fish had got bored and swum off somewhere else. Carlos, Stephane and Jorge paddled off in the canoe in pursuit of a line of intriguing white blobs on the horizon, all but one of which flew away at their approach. They did, however, bring back a diamond-shaped polystyrene fishing buoy covered in small shellfish. Greg had previously found a few of these attached to our bow, causing us to wonder fleetingly if we were finally under attack from the rope-eating molluscs. But the creatures, which Jorge called *picorojo*, showed no sign of burrowing. Erik was now convinced they would make good eating, even though each one was about the size of a thumbnail. He spent the rest of the morning scooping little crumbs of flesh out into a plastic bag, where they stayed, reeking progressively, for the rest of the voyage.

At around lunchtime I phoned Ali on Easter Island for a birthday chat. She was, in fact, my birthday present – my parents had paid for her flight out to meet me. Unfortunately, I was unable to tell her when I might be joining her.

'We're totally dependent on the wind,' I said. 'Maybe it'll come back tomorrow.'

Or maybe not. In truth it could be days, even weeks before the wind returned. A flat calm has always been the psychological scourge of sailors, perhaps never more so than in an overstimulated technological age when everything else is so instantly available. In theory, I felt, there should always be something to do in life, even if it is only to think of loved ones, turn over the great questions a few more times. But in practice, out there on the millpond of the Pacific, silence and heat and endless hours of waiting became oppressive, began to blot out even thought, like pressure building in an oven. I listened to Greg and Phil's conversation slowing down as if coated in quick-drying cement.

PHIL: Ever wondered how a swordfish gets a fish off its . . . beak?

GREG: (pause) Uh-uh.

PHIL: I mean, it spears a fish, but *then* what?

GREG: Hmmm?

PHIL: (pause) How do you eat a big ol' tuna when it's stuck on your nose?

GREG: (pause, with effort) It's not like they have little hands or nuthin'.

PHIL: Right. Maybe they swim backwards, real fast.

GREG: (looks puzzled) They can do that?

PHIL: Good question.

GREG: (nodding slowly) Huh.

(pause of approx. 40 seconds)

PHIL: Interesting.

Carlos, ever resourceful, kept himself busy by digging out a small tin of blue paint from beneath the cabin, cutting out some stencils from a cardboard box, and setting up a *Viracocha* T-shirt printing workshop beneath his awning. He also repaired a broken sandal for me with some noxious-smelling glue – a quiet act of friendship which left me free to edit hours of minidisk recording or read a book. Marco kept climbing the mast with a pair of binoculars and scanning the blank horizon for something, anything, which might provide some distraction. Phil finally pulled out his long-neglected Kennebunk Middle School water temperature experiment and discovered that water temperature was 25 degrees celsius – two degrees warmer than it had been two weeks ago. 'Fascinating,' I heard him mutter irritably. In the evening we tried playing basketball on the foredeck using a pair of my rolled-up socks and a plastic hoop. This lasted approximately three minutes before Phil lobbed the socks neatly overboard in an ill-advised long shot.

On the third windless day, things began to get a little desperate. Marco emerged from the cabin, took one look at the glassy sea and turned distinctly peculiar. He roared till he was red, he stamped up and down, he bunched his fists above his head in the way that Bluto does when Popeye has got the better of him. We were all nervously amused by it, but relieved when after a few seconds of cartoon tantrum, he resumed his serious expression and went back into the cabin. He was busy most of the morning counting off each fraction of a mile using the GPS, and emerged later to announce we had travelled 10 miles in the last 24 hours, thanks entirely to local currents.

Stephane was not quite himself either. Later that morning I found him grimacing into a shaving mirror, trying to pluck stray whiskers with a pair of rusty pliers. I kept an eye on him. I had read of at least one other raft expedition on which a crew member had to be restrained after trying to saw through the raft in order to make his own escape pod. Stephane, I felt, was the most likely to resort to frenzied sawing if his mind was not sufficiently occupied. I agreed immediately when he suggested taking the rubber canoe out for a photography session with him later that afternoon.

We were perhaps 200 metres behind the boat, snapping away as the low sun cast an orange light on its still listless sails. A breath of wind was at last beginning to stir the waters, creating shadowy ripples, and I was experiencing the mixture of awe and nerves that I always did when away from the boat.

I had just changed a film spool when I heard Jorge's warning. We were too far away to hear what he was shouting, but he seemed to be pointing beyond us. I looked round but saw only shadows, the reflection of clouds. Marco was also shouting from half-way up the mast, and Greg too, both increasingly urgent. And now I could hear the single word they were all shouting: '*Tiburón!!* Shark!!'

Picking up my paddle, I realised I was already trembling. 'Stephane, let's get out of here. There's a shark out here with us somewhere.' Stephane was looking around us in quick urgent movements. When he looked in my direction he had a familiar manic gleam in his eye.

'I know there is, *hermano*, and I want to see it!' He was laughing with excitement. Then he picked up his paddle, and began hitting the rubber side of the canoe with it, making a slap that would reverberate through the water. 'Come on Mr Tiburón – come and find us!' he shouted.

For a moment I could only gape at him, then came a fury. I gripped his paddle in my free hand and wrenched it away from the side. 'STOP THAT, YOU IDIOT!!' He stopped, taken aback but still grinning. 'That's the stupidest thing you've *ever* done!' I hissed. 'Now paddle hard!'

Stephane sniggered, then shrugged, then began paddling. It was the longest 400 metres of my life. Every shadow in the darkening depths was a shark about to rip the flimsy rubber from under us, every small ripple or splash the sound of a dorsal fin breaking the surface. Our crewmates were no longer pointing but scanning the sea around us, searching for signs of the familiar shape they had seen. Had it dived in order to make its attack from below? I prayed that most sophisticated of prayers as we covered the last 100 metres to the boat: 'Pleasepleasepleasepleaseplease . . .'

By the time we scrambled out of the canoe and up on to the safety of the *Viracocha*, I was just about hyperventilating. 'Listen, Stephane,' I said, presently. '*If you do that enough times you're going to die.*'

Well, someone needed to tell him.

Stephane laughed, still not getting it. Jorge shook his head at us, pityingly, and said nothing.

'It looked like a big one!' said Marco. The shark, however, had sunk from sight.

'Y'all know what?' said Greg, sensing the tension and smiling sympathetically. 'I think we've been sittin' on this ocean too darn long for our own good!'

It was the simple truth. The wind, almost as if it had heard him, picked up through the evening, turning the little ripples into wavelets, and the wavelets into jostling troughs and peaks. By nightfall we were moving forward again, the sails swollen. Our final approach was beginning.

12

Last Tango
Before Landfall

Overnight, our terrain changed, from endless glassy plains to mountainous waves rolling at us from behind, pitching us up and jolting us sideways, leaving us skidding to the foot of huge craters, the wave tips climbing towards the level of our mast head. Even in the midst of the storm we had not seen such seas, such shredding wind. This time the wind blew almost directly from astern, piling up enormous rollers that moved in on us relentlessly, causing the rudder to lurch violently as they hit it. We doubled the daytime watch, and lowered the second rudder to give extra leverage against seas that threatened all the time to drag our stern round. Our ribs grew bruised and sore from the constant clubbing of the tiller.

Sitting in the bow, we began to notice still more worrying effects as the waves for the first time began to flex the boat along its length, like the back of some giant hairy caterpillar, writhing forwards. With the muscular motion came a whisper of reeds pulling against each other, stretching, separating. 'I don't like the look of that,' murmured Phil, as four of us watched the gunwales bloat and contract. Until now the waves had hit us either at a 45-degree angle, or side-on, causing little or no flexing. Now the following seas came from directly astern. Kitin Muñoz's boat, at twice this length, had been torn apart by the effect of similar motion. Would our smaller craft withstand the waves where his failed? We had just over 200 miles in which to find out.

By the following morning the wind had shifted a little, adding a violent sideways pitch to the longitudinal flexing, and I was woken by the yank of my own body against my bunk's restraining rope. The other two top-bunk dwellers had already evacuated: Phil had taken his bedroll out on to the foredeck (where, somewhat unluckily, he had been hit in the small of the back by a flying fish), while Erik had wedged himself among the spare reeds on the roof. I wondered if Erik had deliberately chosen the higher ground; every once in a while the waves now slavering around our stern were hitting the uppermost flanks of totora, splashing flecks of sea spray on to the kitchen floor.

Marco, up on the steering platform, was grunting beneath his woolly hat as he tried to restrain the right-hand rudder, which was scooping great slabs of water to one side, creating swirling, sucking eddies on the other. At the second rudder was Carlos, who had devised a labour-saving rope sling to do his restraining for him. Each time the boat pitched sideways, the entire roof of the cabin shifted across with a crackling noise oddly reminiscent of someone delving into a bag of Scrabble tiles. It was the sound of the cut bamboo ends splintering. Erik, still asleep on this

shifting carpet of logs, didn't seem to notice. I half-filled the
kettle, which didn't prevent it slopping water all over the stove,
then got to work trying to wedge and lash the bamboo roofing
with wood offcuts and oddments of rope. Jorge was already busy
tightening the mast stays. He looked haggard and unshaven, but
smiled weakly at me.

Wedging myself into position by the map table, I studied the
long wavering line of pencil, now only 2 inches from the triangular blob marked Isla de Pascua. We were aiming for the
north-eastern coast of the island, a sandy bay known as
Anakena, where it was believed the ancient king Hotu Matua – and
perhaps *Viracocha* himself – first landed after his long journey.

The waves continued to intimidate us all day, still reassuringly
full of tuna, but increasingly vertical, building on our port side,
lumbering towards us in proportions that could easily swamp us.
Sitting on the portside gunwale became increasingly hazardous.
Sometimes the crests broke into froth and splashed us, and once
there was a full-scale dousing when a freak wave toppled over just
as it reached our flanks, showering across the deck. Any higher and
the waves would begin to break onboard. That night I joined Erik
to sleep on the roof of the cabin, lying in among the spare reeds
in full emergency gear and clipping my harness to the guard rope.
I couldn't believe I hadn't tried it sooner. Instead of rolling sideways with each wave, I was rocked backwards and forwards. Gazing
up at the astounding, swinging stars as the warm night wind tousled my hair, I was soon dreaming of flying high above the *Viracocha*,
watching her tiny progress onward.

'We're eighty miles from the island? Shit, that's a big problem.'

I woke in the aching beauty of the dawn to hear Phil talking
worriedly in the cabin below.

'I don't understand, *capitán*.' It was Jorge, by the sound of it.

'If we keep up this speed we'll be arriving at 2 a.m. In the dark. *Muy peligroso.*'

'So we must stop and wait?'

'No, that's just as dangerous. We lose all manoeuvrability against these waves, and risk drifting so far north that we miss the island altogether.'

By Phil's reckoning, we needed to slow our speed down from its current 10 knots to a mere 4 knots in order to time our arrival right. But how? After a bowl of porridge we tried a few experiments. First solution was to lower the mizzen sail, which we did around 11 a.m. An hour later this seemed to have taken our speed down to 8 knots, but it wouldn't delay us beyond the hours of darkness. And the wind was rising even further.

The next trick was to reef the mainsail. By unlacing its bottom third from the yard, a large part of the sail could be folded into itself and secured out of the wind using short ropes called reefing points. I was deeply proud of this, having spent countless hours hammering grommets into the sail at Arica. By the time we had wrestled the canvas down to a fraction of its former size, it looked like it might pay off.

'Can't be exact right now,' said Phil after squinting at the GPS, 'but I'd say we're travelling at about five knots, which should be about right.'

Excitement on board was by this stage approaching the unbearable – half the crew seemed to be up the masts at any one time, scrutinising the horizon, which was barricaded with dark clouds. Stephane, meanwhile, was doing crotch thrusts at the front of the boat, shouting: 'Women of Isla de Pascua, here I come!' and howling like a dog in season.

At 7 p.m. the fevered cry finally went up: '*Tierra allá!*'

It was Carlos who glimpsed it first from the side deck, and Marco who shinned up the mainmast to bellow confirmation.

Then the whole boat erupted in shouts, whoops, high fives and a general scrambling aloft to borrow the binoculars. Not that you really needed them, once Marco had pointed it out. Squatting boxed-in between a scuffed horizon and dirty rainclouds were the low volcanic mounds of a large island.

'It looks like a woman's breasts!' proclaimed Stephane excitedly.

The breasts lit up for a moment as a stray ray of sun broke through the heavy clouds, then blurred and faded from sight as rain moved in.

Phil, I noticed, was looking a little preoccupied. Even Jorge's excited announcement that he had managed to pick up Rapa Nui FM on his transistor won only a strained smile. The problem, it emerged, was that we were already too close for our own good. Still travelling at 5 knots, we were going to arrive at the island in the early hours, well before dawn. The picture worsened when Marco managed to contact the Chilean navy on Easter Island on the VHF radio, and was told that the usual navy launch was out of service. With only small open motorboats available, there was nothing that could be done to help guide us in until morning.

'The sail's already reefed as small as it'll go, right?' said Phil, scratching his beard.

'Right.'

'But we can't afford to take it down altogether because we'll lose steerage.'

'Right.'

'So what we need is some kind of sea anchor . . . Carlos? Jorge? Can you knock something up? Try using one of the empty water flagons.'

It was the most urgent commission so far for our resident inventors, and they lost no time. By 10.30 p.m. they had sewn an empty flagon into a net bag and tied it, opening foremost, to a length of rope, ready for deployment. Securing the rope to the rear of the boat

in yellow torchlight, they pushed the makeshift sea anchor overboard. There was a sudden roaring as the flagon filled in the current,
and presently a squeak of rope as it yanked itself to the end.

'Now all we can do is hope it works,' said Phil.

None of us slept much that night. I lay on the roof again with
Eric, watching clouds rumbling across the sky like tanks, and drifting in and out of consciousness as the radio hissed and coughed
and delivered sporadic warnings and instructions. When I got up
for my watch at 4 a.m. gusts were coming directly over the port
side. 'Has the wind changed direction?' I asked, clambering through
the various bamboo railings of the steering platform. 'No, *we've*
changed,' said Phil. 'The navy can't get to Anakena, so we're aiming
for Hanga Roa instead, just in case we need their help. We're steering two hundred and ten degrees till I say otherwise.'

Hanga Roa was the island's only town, situated on the west
coast. To get there we would have to sail round a rocky peninsular
and a volcanic stack at the southwest corner, then sail due north.

It was a dark night, and difficult to distinguish between the battalions of clouds and anything more solid. But several miles ahead,
a line of white lights indicated the southernmost corner, which
meant the island could already be to starboard. Marco handed
over the helm with the grateful exhaustion one might feel in handing over a handcuffed but violent delinquent. No sooner had I put
my hand to the tiller than it yanked sideways with a gurgling roar
from astern, and I had to use all my force to push it back round.
Jorge, on the second tiller, chuckled in the darkness. 'Feeling energetic?' he said.

Something was wrong with the whole steering platform. It
seemed lower on my side than on his. Lashing the tiller in position
for a moment, I peered over the railings and saw that the structure
beneath us was slowly collapsing. The kitchen wall of woven
bamboo below me was warped and crumpling under the descending

roof. At Jorge's side, the rail had pulled itself loose at one corner leaving a dangerous weakness and a mess of empty rope loops in mid-air. The long rudder shaft on my side seemed looser too, thudding up and down against the rearmost flank with each wave. I noticed its restraining harness was frayed and broken in one place. Little by little, the sea was taking us to pieces.

The darkness was already a little less intense, and the clouds to starboard were beginning to look more solid than clouds should. I peered harder, trying to make out an outline. As the first grey streaks of dawn appeared on the horizon, the island finally revealed itself. We heard it first, a sort of distant hiss – then as a grainy undark insinuated itself across the cratered water, we saw the source of the hiss, and the end of our journey. Huge cliffs rose vertically from a seething ocean. I had imagined a tropical island furred with greenery and palms, but this was more primeval, more barren. Above the cliffs, slopes of sparse, tough-looking vegetation gave the place an oddly Scottish look. It was empty, heath-like, cold. At the crest of one of the cliffs, it was possible to make out a little line of what looked like stone pillars, but what we knew to be our first glimpse of Easter Island's mysterious *moai* statues, tall as tenements, which guard its coasts. For now they remained dark shadows, unlit by the sun. Then as the first rays of weak sun filtered over the horizon, the cold greys warmed to rich browns, the monolithic rock grew shadowy wrinkles.

Erik, lying with his back to it all, was beginning to stir on the cabin roof.

'Hey, *hermano*, take a look over your shoulder.'

Erik looked at me quizzically, still hooded with sleep, saw the direction of my gaze, and rolled over. He propped himself up on one elbow and quietly drank in the sight. I saw his mouth turn up slightly at the corners and a sigh escape.

'I've waited a long time for this moment,' he murmured,

presently. 'I always knew it was possible. Now we are the first in more than a millennium to show how!'

'All we've got to do is get ashore.'

This looked like the hardest part. There was nowhere remotely welcoming for incoming vessels to land. Instead, wherever the cliff met the sea, there was a pulsing line of white where the water was smashing itself into foam on rocks, booming and echoing oddly. We continued sailing more or less parallel to the south coast of the island, perhaps three miles offshore, as the rest of the crew gradually surfaced, struck silent by the enormity of their dreams suddenly made solid, towering dark and volcanic before them. Erik took over the helm and Jorge and Carlos got to work reharnessing the starboard rudder. If we lost steering ability here, or even for some reason lost control of our single sail, the result could be catastrophic. With a strong southeast wind blowing onshore, we would have little time to avoid shipwreck. I thought of the *Kon-Tiki*, ending her voyage crashing on to a reef, unable to steer round it due to her rudimentary sails. Yet perhaps here, equipped with a more adaptable rig, we could demonstrate how the first settlers might have done it.

As the southern coast of Easter Island scrolled past for the next 20 miles, Phil ordered a thorough clean of the boat in preparation for visitors. This was no small task, I realised, looking around me. Imagine your average bachelor pad, then shake it up and down a bit, and you get the general idea. The kitchen, predictably, was the worst. The floor didn't so much need scrubbing as excavating. I had played my own part in the mess, after knocking over our last tin of instant coffee that very morning. Stephane scrubbed like a maniac while I tried to get the bits off the cooker. Even the walls had a kind of pebbledash effect left over from the day the pressure cooker had sprayed Greg's bean hotpot all over him. I did a final batch of washing up, amused at the pathetic inventory of dented pans, orphaned lids, and scuffed plates.

While we worked, Marco switched on Rapa Nui FM and we found ourselves listening to the island's main Catholic Mass, seemingly broadcast live from the church. A passionate yet somehow plaintive hymn rang out, sung in close harmony by what sounded like hundreds of people, and accompanied on a mixture of guitar and accordion, with some drumming in the background.

A-ley-loo! A-ley-loo-yah!

There was a rumbling as the congregation sat down, and a male voice broke in, intoning in that flat, unreal way that clergy always seem to have, whatever their language or culture. Prayers? Notices? It was hard to tell. But suddenly we recognised a name: '*Viracocha*'.

'. . . will be arriving from Chile this afternoon after a long journey. There will be an opportunity to see the boat and welcome her crew over at Anakena beach, where she's expected to arrive at about two p.m. . . . Finally, the elders' meeting will take place as usual . . .'

Phil flicked the radio off and poked his head out of the cabin. 'I don't believe it!'

'What? That they're throwing us a party?'

'No – that they're throwing it in the wrong place! We're not going to Anakena! I told the Navy we were coming to the main town – but the priest has just sent everyone in town to the other side of the island!'

'Marvellous.'

Phil radioed to shore to double-check our intended destination with the navy radio-operator, who confirmed our rendezvous at the south western corner of the island. It was, however, too late to convey this information to the various prominent community members. Phil groaned and signed off.

I clambered up to join Greg on the steering platform. He had a half-smile on his face and a pair of binoculars in his hands. He handed them to me.

'Even the *moai* are looking in the other direction!'

Scouring the clifftops, it was now possible to see that the huge stone men were facing inland.

'Think we should take a hint?' I said.

'No way. Not now.'

He grinned an easy grin and gripped the tiller. I thought how much we had both grown in confidence since those first days afloat.

Phil poked his head out of the cabin. 'Steer two hundred and forty, OK guys?' Then he disappeared. Greg pushed the tiller across, keeping his eye on the compass as he did so. The needle was just hovering over 230 when Marco strode along the sidedeck and yelled officiously: 'Steer two hundred and eighty.'

Greg and I looked at each other quizzically and laughed. Greg kept his previous course.

'Steer two-eighty – quickly!' repeated Marco, agitated.

'But that takes us closer to the island again . . . are you sure?'

Marco's expression darkened.

'Are you saying you don't believe me?'

'Well about thirty seconds ago, Phil told us to steer two-forty. It seems strange . . .'

I watched a sudden fury ignite in Marco's eyes.

'You'll obey Phil, but not me? Is that what you're saying?'

'Well, Phil's the captain. We're just checking that you hadn't made a mistake . . .'

Marco stalked off down the side deck. We heard his raised voice on the foredeck. 'Phil, I've passed on your order, but Nick and Greg are ignoring it.'

Marco had seemed wound up for days, perhaps even weeks. I realised I hadn't heard him crack a bad joke since the storm. He had written 'I love you, Doris' on the underside of the bunk above his head, enabling him to lie there for hours, staring at this graffiti shrine. Clearly he was a man in serious yearning.

Phil appeared again at the cabin door, grinning apologetically.

'Actually, Marco's right, guys – I changed my mind about the course.'

Greg shrugged and shouldered the tiller across. 'No problem.'

I went and apologised to Marco. He accepted, sulkily.

Let's just keep it together a little while longer . . .

The new course was designed to position us for a last crucial manoeuvre. Between us and our intended haven lay a dark and jagged fin of rock, rising from the ocean some 800 metres from the southwestern corner of the island, and 2 interconnected islets another 300 metres further out. We knew these from our reading: Motu Iti and Motu Nui, the focal point for the annual birdman festival. The island's strongest men had climbed down the cliffs from the settlement of Orongo, high above our heads, and swum across to the islands, competing to bring back the year's first egg of the sooty tern, intact. It had been a riotous affair. Once proclaimed the birdman, the winner could send his followers out to ransack the homes of all the other islanders, and competitors were regularly taken by sharks as they battled across the narrow channel with only small reed rafts for buoyancy. Now, nearly 150 years after the last festival, and on a somewhat larger raft, we were to sail through the same strait in a last test of our seamanship.

Which meant we had to change the sail one final time.

'OK at the helm, Dobbers?' asked Phil, as the rest of us congregated on the foredeck.

'Ah, sure,' said Greg, with a shrug.

In theory it was simple enough. We only had the mainsail to worry about, as the mizzen was still furled and lashed to the cabin roof. Fumbling with the reefing knots, however, I began to have my doubts. The wind was both strong and impetuous, blowing in sudden gusts that yanked the furled edge of the sail away from our struggling fingers. Its corner was securely tied with three separate sheets. Now we had to untie all three against the full force of the wind, pass them round the front of the sail, and resecure them on the other side.

Phil was determined this would be a model manoeuvre, the perfected fruit of our past mistakes. He ordered the raising of the *guaras* to avoid splintering them, stationed a man on each of the three sheets, and calculated the new course that would be needed.

'OK Greg, take her stern to wind,' shouted Phil. 'And the rest of you, start untying the mainsheets.'

Marco, Carlos and I each began working on a separate rope. Marco's and Carlos's came undone easily enough, which left mine to take the strain. I untied the slip knot and felt it burn through my fingers. 'Hold them!' yelled Phil, as the sail began to flap and jerk. We each let our own sheet out slowly, leaning our body weight against it. The jerking increased, as if the ballooning sail sensed its chance to escape, and I lost my footing. It was as I put out my hand to steady myself that I inadvertently let go of the rope. Marco yelped angrily as it whipped past his face in the wind, and he too let go, which left only Carlos. '*Ayúdame!* Help me!' he yelled, trying vainly to restrain the sail. I jumped up to try and catch one of the ropes, but they were flailing about like circus whips, each one a potential noose. Carlos's body jerked as he was dragged sideways, until he too was forced to let go. We watched in alarm and shame as the ropes took off, whipped against the thick rope connecting the masthead with the bow, and thrashed themselves into an impenetrable tangle there.

'Dammit! We forgot to loosen the mainstay!' yelled Phil, rushing forward to help.

'What do I do now?' came the voice of Greg, faintly, from the helm.

'Just try and keep us pointing at the channel!'

Our only sail was now a tangled mess, flapping in the wind and providing no manoeuvrability. Phil took an anxious glance at the gap between the cliffs and rocky volcanic stack. Somewhere on the other side awaited our naval escort, with Ali and Eli on board. *Where was it?* Even now, the faint boom and hiss of spray was getting louder as we drifted towards the rocks.

With every jerk of the sail, the ropes became more tightly tangled. Carlos and now Jorge, perched precariously up on the curved prow of the boat, picked and pulled at the knots with their tough fingers, while Marco, Phil and I tried to stop the flapping sail from garrotting them as they worked.

'*Eso!*' gasped Jorge above us, finally managing to drag the three sheets away from the mainstay. Passing them quickly beneath it, we all began shuffling backwards dragging the sail. There were six of us now, hanging on to what had metamorphosed from three strands into one thick dreadlock. The sail filled again and jerked savagely upwards, whipping the rope from the grasp of at least two people. I held on this time, determined not to be the one who let go, and felt my arms lift momentarily in their sockets, sending a shiver of pain through my shoulders. I screamed in anger and agony, but kept my grip.

'Tie the sodding thing off, somebody!'

But the ropes were so looped and matted that they would not reach the nearest tie-off point. Jorge would need to untangle it *before* we could let go. There followed a kind of anarchic tango-for-six as a clump of us stumbled backwards and forwards around the deck, dragged by the angry sail. The wind whistled around our ears, warning that all this was folly, while Jorge's muscled fingers worked furiously in our midst. Marco was growling like a dog

poised behind a garden gate. Stephane, meanwhile, roared and
went crimson. At last, Jorge unplaited a long piece of rope; and we
dragged it far enough back for him to wrap it twice around a
eucalyptus pole, and tie it off.

'*Concha tu madre*,' gasped Stephane. For a few moments several of
us lay panting on the side deck, palms tingling, as the ship regained
steerage.

We watched the cliffs pitch and swell, closing in around us.

'Ship ahoy!' shouted Carlos, from the bow deck.

I scrambled to my feet. Perhaps a mile away, rising and falling,
half-hidden in the troughs of a steely blue sea, a white dot caught
my eye. It could have been anything from this distance – a piece of
polystyrene flotsam, a fishing buoy.

'That's the navy boat?'

Phil shrugged and clambered up to the steering platform. 'I
guess that's the largest they could find.'

I stood and watched the little white dot grow larger. It was a
strange moment, a mixture of excitement and loss, preparing to
resume contact with our loved ones, our lives outside, yet preparing also to give up the life we had all shared on this boat. I felt a
sudden shudder of protectiveness, a sense of what we were about
to lose – this little community, about to dissolve, never to be
recreated, as other relationships impinged. I felt my crewmates
retreating like hermit crabs, back into their own thoughts.

Soon it was possible to make out individual figures in the boat.
It was an open fibreglass motorboat, pitching crazily in the swell,
with about eight people on board. A few photographers, a naval
official, and Ali and Eli, both clad in bright yellow sou'westers and
life jackets. Ali recognised me and started waving, her wide grin
sporadically obscured by her long curly hair blowing across her
face. I blew her a kiss, and she mouthed something rather personal
between cupped hands. We both laughed. The little boat circled us

several times, everyone waving, shouting, a couple of journalists shooting film, Phil proud at the helm of his beloved boat, Eli smiling weakly through her seasickness.

More puzzling was a lanky stranger perched in the bow and waving excitedly at each of us in turn. He had a goatee beard and long, auburn hair, and was wearing bright red waterproof trousers with an olive green army shirt bearing some kind of crimson crescent symbol on its sleeves. Around his neck hung a pendant adorned with what looked like a ram's horn. He seemed a strange hybrid of mystic and marine. Gandalf meets Gadaafi.

'Do you know that guy?' I asked Phil, as the boat passed out of range beyond our bows.

Phil frowned. 'No, but I recognise the shirt he's wearing — it's part of the Mata Rangi crew uniform, which means he's one of Kitin Muñoz's men. Keep an eye on him.'

The mystic marine soon showed his intentions. As the launch made a final circle and pulled alongside, he strapped on a rucksack and prepared to board, still grinning. Ali also stood up, nervously, while Eli shook her head sadly, clearly too ill to do anything. The swell was such that the two boats rose and fell by up to four feet in relation to each other. I hooked one arm round a mast stay and held out the other hand to help Ali, who leaped across just as the little boat reached its highest point, landing in my arms. The wizard man took the same leap, but aimed for the rope ladder a couple of feet further along the boat. He timed it badly. As his hand gripped the rung, the launch fell away beneath him, and his rucksack jerked downwards awkwardly. For a moment it looked as if he might be sucked down beneath the boat, but Jorge and Greg both rushed forward to drag him bodily from the water and helped him up on to the foredeck. The launch pulled away, and sped back off towards the port.

'Hello sailor!' said Ali, pale but happy. 'You made it!' We enjoyed the most precarious kiss of our relationship, still wrapped around the swaying mast stay, then made our way to the bow to find out what had happened to our other visitor. We found him laid out on the deck, with Jorge and Greg standing nervously over him. He had turned a waxy white colour, his eyes were wide with pain, and when he unbuttoned his shirt we could see that his bare shoulder bulged oddly where it emerged from his singlet.

'This is Dany,' said Greg, nervously, trying not to look as if he was standing guard. 'I think he's dislocated his shoulder.'

Evidently it was going to be some minutes before I got the chance to talk to my wife. Instead we spent our first moments together in a protracted search for painkillers. Dany confirmed he was one of the Mata Rangi crew, and had come to welcome us to his island. 'But now I'd like to see a doctor,' he said, panting with the pain. Presently a navy rib inflatable buzzed alongside bearing greetings from the captain of the port. Dany tottered into the rib, and hitched a swift ride back to shore ahead of us.

Carlos sidled over and offered his hand to Ali. 'Welcome to our boat,' he said with a wide grin. I was pleased to see Erik and the others approach too, evidently wishing to draw a veil over their previous aversion to women on the boat. Perhaps they felt any accompanying bad luck had already conveniently descended on Dany. His was the only injury of our voyage.

'So you've done it!' said Ali excitedly. 'The navy here told us you'd most likely get caught in the weather systems and blown back the way you came.' Indeed, the realisation of what we had done was only now creeping over me, warm honey oozing down over my scalp. *We had built our own boat and sailed it to Easter Island!* The implications kept unfolding in my head like some complex piece of origami. Nobody had believed in us, eight unqualified men! *I* hadn't believed in us! Yet here we were, arriving at ancient shores, still successfully making it up as we went along!

Above us, dark volcanic cliffs turned the colour of copper in a sudden burst of sunlight as we passed, and seabirds wheeled overhead, shrieking. Phil stood proud and erect at the helm, the image of a heroic adventurer, smiling and confident.

The fart of our makeshift foghorn aroused me from my daydreaming. It was Marco, as ever, trying to alert some fishermen sitting anchored in fibreglass boats ahead of us. They looked up, startled, as we bore down on them, and quickly pulled themselves out of our way using their anchor lines. I waved cheerily. I'd love to pretend that the smiles we got back were welcoming, congratulatory. But they weren't. They were smirks. In another boat, idling past us, a man began a slow handclap.

'I hate to break it to you,' said Ali, awkwardly. 'But you might want to know that people here have mixed feelings about the expedition — I'm afraid not everybody will be glad to see you.'

I blinked and frowned. 'What do you mean? Why not?'

Ali sighed. 'The people here are passionate about being Polynesian. We've found nobody really wants to talk about possible links with South America. You're going to have to tread carefully.'

I stared at her, then back out at the fisherman, still slow handclapping, his face now a contemptuous scowl.

'How strong is the feeling?'

'Depends who you talk to — some people will welcome you, some aren't bothered either way, but one or two are quite angry. You might want to warn Phil and the guys.'

Suddenly, I was unsure what to expect as we rounded the rocky peninsula. Perhaps it was just as well that the priest had sent most of his flock to the wrong side of the island. I quickly went astern to pass on to Phil what Ali had told me. He seemed annoyed by the news.

'It'll be fine. Nobody's telling these people they're not

Polynesian — we're just suggesting possibilities of additional contacts, earlier on. Don't worry, I'll be tactful.'

A number of fibreglass fishing boats were now buzzing at our
side, their occupants guarded in their welcome, raising a hand
with a quick smile, but businesslike, impatient to secure towlines
on board. Rounding the headland, I began to see why. A few
single-storey houses dotted here and there along the shore indicated that we were about to reach Hanga Roa, but as yet I could
see no sign of a harbour, only jagged lines of volcanic black rock,
on which the waves broke in furious explosions of foam. A few
people stood on isolated rocks, watching us curiously. I was
relieved to see that some of them waved. We lowered the mainsail
for the last time, tied it up, and stowed the whole yard out of the
way along the port side, trusting ourselves to the fishing boat now
towing us.

Almost immediately, its skipper made a turn, dragging us
directly inland towards what looked like a blind alley of jagged
rocks. I twisted round and shot Phil a quizzical glance. He climbed
on to the steering platform, seemingly untroubled. The waves were
increasing in size as the depth decreased, and huge swells passed
diagonally beneath us, causing the straining engine of the fishing
boat to whine angrily with the tugging and slackening of its load.
Where were we going?

When we were perhaps 100 metres offshore and even Stephane
was beginning to twitch nervously, a gap opened up in the jagged
lava. It was a tiny harbour hidden among the rocks, its entrance not
more than twice the width of the boat, and invisible except from
a certain angle. As the boat towed us in, a concrete quay became
visible, populated with a crowd of about 100 people, peering at us
curiously, their brows furrowed with afternoon shadows. They
wore western clothes — cargo pants, shirts, jeans, a few print
dresses — though some of the women wore flowers in their hair.

Were these the ones who *hadn't* gone to meet us on the other side of the island, or had the new plans got round?

We waved nervously at them. In the crowd there was a murmur, punctuated by one or two unintelligible shouts. '*Hola!*' yelled Greg, unabashedly good-natured. A few arms lifted and dropped. People seemed to be squinting rather than smiling exactly. I got the distinct feeling that we were being weighed in the balance. I struggled to remember the magic word of greeting with which Thor Heyerdahl, viewed with similar ambivalence as he approached in 1955, had broken the ice.

'*Iorana!*' shouted Phil from the steering platform.

The atmosphere seemed to change instantly. Hearing themselves addressed by a foreigner in their native Rapa Nui, a few people broke into startled grins, and a chorus of '*Iorana*' spread and grew among the crowd, and among the crew. Somebody began to clap, and the clapping spread until the little harbour echoed with applause. It was a welcome of sorts.

An odd shriek rang out. I turned to see a long-haired man with wild, angry eyes, dancing on a bollard on the opposite side of the little harbour. In his hand he held a wooden spear, which he was thrusting into the air above him. He was a little more like the Easter Islander I had imagined for much of our voyage. I raised my hand to wave in a calming and conciliatory manner, noticing that, save for some bracelets of shell and feather and a few daubs of body paint, he was entirely naked. The man guffawed in a deranged kind of way, and flexed his legs like a frog, making rhythmical 'Ooh-ah!' sounds. Then, quite suddenly, he turned his back to us and stuck out his hairy posterior.

I looked back at the crowd, unsure whether to be offended or amused. Did mooning someone on Easter Island have a different meaning than on a Manchester United supporters' coach? Not everybody had noticed him, but those that did seemed to be laughing heartily. Perhaps here it was an ancient form of welcome? We never did find out. I went to the bow to throw a line to shore, and by the time I'd done it, the man had vanished.

Instead, when the flank of the *Viracocha* nudged the quay with a sigh of rustling reeds, we were engulfed in a glorious pandemonium as excited bystanders jumped aboard. A harassed-looking naval official shouted something about passports, while Stephane leapt triumphantly into the harbour. Eli, now apparently recovered from her seasickness, finally clambered aboard to be reunited with Phil, eagerly filmed by Chilean TV's Easter Island correspondent. The rest of us, hugging and backslapping and soon garlanded with Polynesian flowers, grinned a lot.

A middle-aged woman in a floral print dress, was helped on board cradling a steaming parcel of aluminium foil. I saw Greg eyeing it, presumably thinking the same as me after six weeks at sea: *Please let it be steak.*

'Come and share our traditional Rapa Nui welcome,' announced the lady, opening the parcel. 'Some lovely baked tuna.'

As we scooped chunks of flesh from the foil with greasy fingers, the people seemed to multiply around us, the whole boat now crowded with islanders. They poked at the bundled reeds, sniffed suspiciously behind the curtain of our cluttered cabin, and peered at Pablo the remaining duck, still sitting fractiously in his pen. Eli passed round beakers of Kool Aid, and we all circulated, and shook hands and smiled until our faces ached. Mostly, the people were in awe of the boat, doubtful that we had come so far on it. They nodded approvingly as we told our stories. One older man, however, eyed me from a leathery face lined with scepticism.

'Tell me,' he said, poking me in the chest with his long, bony forefinger. 'Why have you come here?'

The way he held himself – proud, erect, somehow taller than

the mere extent of his elderly frame – made me wonder if he was a chief of some sort, but he did not introduce himself.

'*Buen pregunta, señor*,' I said, stalling for time while I chose my words. 'The idea of the trip is to . . . show the seaworthiness of these reed boats. To show that much older civilisations could have crossed wide oceans without sinking . . .'

The man raised his eyebrows. 'And?'

'Well, from my point of view it's really mainly an adventure – like the *Kon-Tiki*.'

'Like Thor Heyerdahl's expeditions? The same theories?'

Damn. 'Er, more or less.'

'I see.' The man nodded, forced a wry smile, then turned and walked away without another word.

Whatever it was he had been testing us on, it was clear we hadn't passed.

Over by the cabin door, Jorge and Marco were sharing a joke. 'Look at Stephane,' whispered Jorge. I scanned the boat and groaned. Our arch-Casanova was engaged in what looked like an earnest and life-changing conversation with a beautiful young woman wearing a lily in her dark hair. I watched her smooth a stray lock behind her ear, and laugh shyly at something he said.

'Quick work, eh?' said Jorge, shaking his head.

We had been in port for less than quarter of an hour.

Inside the cabin, away from the crowds, Phil was staring angrily at a piece of paper. He handed it to me with a mute shake of the head.

It was a faxed press release informing the people of Easter Island that the *Viracocha* expedition was a shameless fraud, and the arriving ship an insult. The usual stuff from the Kitin Muñoz contingent.

'Where did you get that?'

'The TV journalist showed it to me. Apparently Kitin's been phoning and faxing all his island contacts for days, trying to whip up feeling against us.'

I tried to be angry about it, but could only summon up a ripple of *ennui*. 'Better just to ignore him, Phil. It doesn't seem like anyone's taking much notice.'

This was more true than we realised. At that very moment, outside the cabin, Jorge was chatting animatedly to one of Kitin's own crew members – the second that day.

'This is Hopo,' said Jorge, introducing Phil to a lanky islander. 'I worked with him on the *Mata Rangi II*. He is a good friend.' Hopo was a distinctive-looking young man, probably in his early 30s, whose skinny frame and angular features were topped exuberantly with a 4-inch Afro.

'*Iorana*,' he said, shaking Phil's hand with a grin that displayed a solitary white tooth in his upper jaw. 'Welcome to Rapa Nui.'

Dany, the other *Mata Rangi* crewmate we had met that afternoon, was apparently getting his shoulder 'fixed up' by the local doctor. 'But you'll see him again tonight.'

'Tonight?'

Hopo grinned. 'You're all invited to my mother's house for a party. Eight o'clock.'

After six weeks at sea, there was something miraculous about getting into a taxi. The driver looked sceptically at me as I bounced experimentally on the car seat, reacquainting my backside with a form of padding that wasn't criss-crossed with knobbly rope.

'Where you goin'?' he asked, when Eli, Phil and Ali had climbed in.

'Do you know where Hopo's mother lives?' asked Eli, doubtfully. He grinned. 'La Mama? *Everybody* knows Mama.'

We drove inland in a convoy of taxis, along dirt roads, past fields of sugarcane and occasional views across wind-ravaged grass-land. The sparse beauty of the landscape was unsettling, left you feeling a little too exposed. Phil took it all in with an absent, distant look. He had been reluctant to leave our floating home unattended, but everyone was so eager to go to the party that in the end he had hired a local family to guard her for us for the few hours we were away. I could tell he still wasn't quite ready to trust our hosts, particularly after discovering that Muñoz was looking to stir up trouble for us. On the other hand, a party was a chance to find out where we really stood, perhaps make some firm friends on the island.

We drove into a small, almost suburban-looking paved road lined with simple single-storey homes set in their own gardens of banana trees. Our driver stopped at the largest of these, a box-like modern dwelling the size of a small aircraft hangar. A door opened.

'Good evening,' came a slow, oracular voice. 'Who is the captain?'

Ana Lora Tuki Chavez was a monumental figure who swayed slowly as she walked towards us in a long robe-like dress of blues and violets. She peered at us from behind Sophia Loren-style sun-glasses encrusted with fake diamonds, and propped on her round, almost glowing face.

Phil stepped forward with a slight bow and politely kissed her on both cheeks.

'My son tells me you are a brave man,' she pronounced, smiling benevolently. 'You are very welcome to our island, and to this house.'

We thanked her with profuseness appropriate to royalty, and moved past her in a production line of greetings, each of us in turn being clasped to the voluminous bosom of this frizzy-haired matriarch. Before us, a long table flanked with varnished hard-wood chairs was set for about twenty-five people and lit from above by elaborate chandeliers made of thousands of tiny shells.

'These are my daughters,' said La Mama, indicating some smiling women setting out bowls of fruit and trays of meat on a side table. In fact, our hostess gave whole new dimensions to the role of earth mother. She had 14 children, 58 grandchildren, and was directly related to a staggering 1500 islanders – roughly half its 3000-strong population. It made her a good person to know, even if she had a birthday card list from hell.

Out in the garden, I recognised a familiar figure, with one arm in a sling. With the other, Dany gave me a vigorous hug. I felt a brief pain in my chest, which turned out to be caused by his lucky ram's horn.

'Actually it's a pig's tusk from the Marquesa Islands.'

'Ah. Right.'

'I am sorry I couldn't meet you in the harbour,' he said, grinning ruefully. 'My doctor was putting my shoulder back into its socket.'

'It's OK now?'

'A little bit painful,' he shrugged manfully. 'But I am used to pain.'

I found myself instinctively liking Dany. He had changed his clothes since we met him on the boat, and was now dressed in long black silk trousers, and a robe apparently made from a huge screen print of Bob Marley, tied round his waist like a kung-fu fighter.

'I'm a kind of shaman, you know?' he said, seeing me eying his odd evening wear.

'Great,' I said. He was a bit of a chancer, but an open-hearted one. I felt sorry that we had mistrusted him earlier. 'Phil said you were one of the *Mata Rangi* crew, and we've had a lot of criticism from Kitin. We were a little nervous about you coming on board . . .'

He waved aside the comment.

'Kitin has got the wrong idea. He phoned me this afternoon, said you were out to cause disgrace among us. But when I saw the

Viracocha sailing towards the island, I knew it wasn't true. I broke out in goose bumps – there was such a good vibe about it. I knew I had to be there to welcome you. Hopo too.'

'I'm glad you see it like that. I wish Kitin did too.'

Dany shrugged. 'He'll get over it.'

We went back indoors as the first large drops of rain began to patter on to the banana leaves, and gorged ourselves on platters laden with chicken and haunches of salted ham, garnished with salsa and onion salads. By the time we tucked into the mounds of pineapple, melon, and papaya, a thunderstorm was rattling the metal roofing above our heads, momentarily drowning out conversation.

'The rain is a blessing,' said La Mama, just in case anyone should misinterpret it.

Later, sitting out on the porch beneath the dripping banana trees, Hopo brought out his guitar and various members of La Mama's family began to sing to us. Dany accompanied them on what looked like a horse's jawbone, hitting it so that the teeth rattled in time to the music. As the beer and wine flowed, the singing became ever more forceful and sincere. Heads were clasped in affectionate locks, handshakes criss-crossed the patio. Hopo threw his head back in a full-throated yodelling, bringing to mind a curious hybrid between Jimi Hendrix and Stan Laurel, and as midnight approached, everybody joined in with an improvised jamming session around a simple chorus of *Bienvenido* Viracocha, Welcome *Viracocha!* Phil swigged at his beer, and grinned at La Mama, who patted his hand maternally. Greg slumbered peacefully in a plastic lawn chair, and Marco was so laden with flower garlands you could barely see his Prince T-shirt. Erik, Jorge and Carlos roared with laughter, and as the guitar and banjo strumming rose into a harmonised, alcoholic finale, and collapsed into a chaos of toasting and applause, it was clear we were among friends. Then La

Mama eased herself forward on her chair, and coughed politely until the noise died away and only the chirp of the cicadas could be heard in the sudden poise of the night.

'Now, Phil,' she said, smiling. 'Where will your beautiful boat take you next? Tahiti?'

Phil sat up. 'Actually, this is pretty much the end of the road for this boat, Mama. The *Viracocha* will not last much longer in the water.'

Mama looked a little startled. 'Then what will you do with her?'

It was a good question. None of us was quite prepared for the answer.

13

Things To Do with a
Used Reed Boat

'You want to *burn* my boat?'

It was mid-morning on the Tuesday after our arrival, and Phil was sitting on a municipal sofa in the Mayor's office, trying to keep his voice level. I watched his fingers clench his kneecaps. The mayor gave a dry cough and pushed his chair away from his polished desk.

'It's not what *I* want, believe me,' he said, with a sympathetic shrug. 'But I represent the islanders, and one of the suggestions is that incineration would be the simplest way to dispose of it.'

Jobani Teave was a well-groomed and articulate man, with an immaculately ironed Hawaiian shirt. He had a relaxed, confident air, though he had in fact taken up office only three days earlier, after his predecessor had resigned suddenly following allegations of favouritism in the judging of a local beauty pageant.

'Perhaps there's been a misunderstanding,' said Phil. 'When I said I wanted to leave the *Viracocha* to the islanders, I meant as a gift – I thought perhaps a local institution might want to keep it as a permanent monument, maybe an open-air museum . . .'

The mayor pressed his fingertips together, stared intently at them for a moment, choosing his words.

'It's a nice gesture, Mr Buck, and no doubt one we will consider. Nobody can deny it is a beautiful boat. But my understanding is that the people are afraid of contamination.'

'*Contamination?*'

'Yes. As you may know, some years ago another adventurer called Kitin Muñoz attempted to build a reed boat on the island itself. The expedition failed, but what is less well known to those outside the island community is that we have been troubled ever since that time, by a new species of biting mosquito. No doubt you already have some experience of it . . .'

I scratched involuntarily at the previous night's collection of red welts on my leg.

'We never had biting mosquitoes before that. So, rightly or wrongly many people believe Kitin unwittingly brought them over with him in materials imported from South America. I'm sure you can appreciate that the people are anxious that no more foreign insects invade our island.'

Phil stared at the floor for a moment, trying to process this improbable new angle on the man who had dogged our expedition so effectively from start to finish.

'I can see how annoying that must have been for you all,' he said finally. 'But may I ask if Kitin has any closer involvement in this decision? I had heard that he had been phoning and faxing people here telling them that the *Virachocha* was an insult . . .'

The mayor waved away the rest of the sentence. 'Mr Buck, the disputes of rival adventurers are of no real interest to me. My job is simply to welcome you here, assist you in your stay . . . and to address the concerns of the islanders.'

Phil nodded in embarrassment. He tried another tack.

'Wouldn't it be possible to fumigate the ship with insecticide?'

The mayor looked at his watch, and got up from his chair.

'Mr Buck, I assure you I will do everything in my power to find an alternative solution. If it is possible to decontaminate it, and if you can find a private individual who wishes to put the boat on his land . . . who knows? But I regret that if we are no further forward when you are due to leave, we'll have no choice . . .'

He smiled briefly, extended his hand, and opened the door.

'Thank you sir,' said Phil. 'I certainly appreciate that. I'll get to work right away.'

It was out of the question. We could no more contemplate burning her than the Lone Ranger would have contemplated selling Silver to the glue factory.

'It's an insult to Erik's family!' said Greg, as agitated as I had ever seen him. 'You can't just send all that work up in smoke! It makes us all into a joke! Surely somebody would like to winch her into a garden, do her up nice, charge tourists to look round her . . .'

'Not if Kitin can help it,' speculated Erik, his brow darkly furrowed. 'Anybody can make whatever claim they want once the boat is burned – because we'll have destroyed the only evidence that proves we were telling the truth!'

In common with most of the other conspiracy theories that flourished like exotic flowers in the hothouse of the *Viracocha* that afternoon, this made sense only up to a point. We had heard our Spanish rival had been actively canvassing against us before our arrival. For all we knew he might be on the phone to the mayor at this very moment. But the theory fell apart on the insect element. Why would Kitin use or encourage such a potentially self-damaging story to bring about our downfall? And if the people really held him responsible for the spread of a new strain of mosquito, why would they now take instructions from him on who they should or shouldn't welcome to their island? None of it seemed to add up.

Phil and I took a taxi back to the guesthouse where Eli and Ali had stayed since their arrival. *El capitán* seemed far away, staring out over the fields to the ocean.

'This ought to be the best week of my life,' he said, suddenly, with anger. 'This is the thing I dreamed of doing since I was eleven years old. We've just sailed two and a half thousand miles in a reed boat, against all the odds – we ought to be celebrating now. Instead it's all we can do to prevent the whole thing going up in flames!'

That afternoon two new hopes arose in the form of phone calls (made from a callbox, as the Iridium phone had rather punctually given up the ghost that morning). Our friends in Arica had heard the news of our arrival and were so scandalised when Phil told them of the *Viracocha*'s possible fate, that they pledged there and then, with typical Latin passion, to bring her back to their own city, to form a permanent monument. The only obstacles were: a) finding a way to transport a sodden boat 2500 miles back across the Pacific; b) raising the estimated $40,000 it would cost to do so by cargo vessel; and c) doing so within our two-week deadline before the incinerators moved in. The Aricans assured us they would look into these minor issues and get back to us within a few days. Meanwhile, Dany and La Mama, both dismayed to hear of the mayor's plans, promised to do some sums of their own and see if they could find a way to fund the large sheltering structure that would be needed to keep the *Viracocha* on Easter Island.

*

I decided to do a little discreet groundwork. We only had the mayor's word that the majority of his people wished to see our boat burned – I wanted to hear it from the people themselves. After all, if our new friends were behind us, perhaps other islanders might be persuaded. It didn't take much effort to bring the subject up in conversation: the *Viracocha* already seemed to be the talk of the town.

'So, you're going to burn the boat?' said my taxi driver, on the way back down to the harbour.

'Seems like we were the last to find out,' I said.

'Shame – she's a beautiful boat,' said the driver, looking at the *Viracocha* as we approached her on the quayside.

'The mayor told us about your insect problem. I guess people feel it's better not to risk it again,' I said, doing my best to be conciliatory.

This time the driver laughed. 'Is that what he told you? Listen, even if Kitin brought the insects here, burning your boat is not going to make them go away.'

I was puzzled, and he saw it in my face as he took my fare. He lowered his voice. 'Believe me, friend, this is not about insects. It's about politics.'

He winked and drove off.

Carlos and I had been co-opted as tour guides and watchmen that afternoon while the rest of the crew went to play football with a local five-a-side team. I pondered the taxi driver's remark as I sat on the quayside. What exactly had he meant by 'politics'?

First to arrive at the boat was a long crocodile of children, flanked by a bespectacled and polite schoolmarm. I greeted the teacher warmly as she lined up the children on the quay. I noticed that among them was a noticeable mixture of different skin shades, ranging from dark, treacly brown to almost white.

'I'm intrigued,' I ventured after the usual pleasantries. 'What do you teach the children about the theories of their origins?'

The teacher frowned and looked nervous. 'Excuse me?'

'I mean, where this island was originally populated from. Do they see themselves as Polynesian, or . . .'

'Polynesian, of course. It's common knowledge.'

'Right, right.' I was beginning to feel a little nervous myself. 'But, um, what's the general view of the *old* legends of the very first settlers, the ones who may have come from—'

'We're here to see the duck.'

'Pardon?'

'We heard you had a duck on board?'

'Er, yes, we do – Pablo.'

'Can the children go and look? They've never seen a duck before.'

You only had to look at the history books to see why South American ancestry was such a taboo topic. From that direction had come one of the most devastating events in the island's tangled history: the Peruvian slave raid of 1862, in which a thousand islanders, including the last island king and almost all dignitaries and community elders, were tricked, captured and carried off to work in plantations on the Peruvian mainland. Bishop Tepano Jaussen of Tahiti brought diplomatic pressure to bear on the Peruvian government for their repatriation, but by the time a return voyage was agreed, 900 – including the royal line – had already died of disease and overwork. Of the 100 who made the trip, smallpox claimed all but 15 on the voyage, and the remainder spread the epidemic across their homeland. As a result, the total population of the island was soon reduced to 111 people. Annexation by Chile in 1888 had done little to heal the resentment.

In fact, when you thought about it like that – which I hadn't, much, up to this point – a reed boat full of foreigners arriving from the South American continent claiming to be retracing the path of ancient, pale-skinned, bearded settlers who predated the Polynesians on this shore looked suspiciously like cultural imperialism. It could be argued that our expedition was about as politically correct as driving into a Native American reservation in a reproduction Wells Fargo coach claiming to represent the 'original' cowboy settlers.

I would have disowned all connection to Heyerdahl's theory there and then had it not been for a nagging point of principle. It was important to ask, 'Is this offensive?' But that could not be allowed to overshadow the fundamental question: 'Is this true?' Were the original long ears – the ruling tribe who hung weights from their lobes – from South America or not? I still had no firm conviction one way or the other. But as a journalist I was determined not to stop asking the questions, even if I had to whisper them.

My next opportunity came the following day when I accompanied Nicolas the French photographer to commission a few souvenirs from a local stone carver. José Tuki Pakarati, one of Mama's 1500 relations, was sitting at a little wooden table in his garden, chipping away at a piece of volcanic stone.

'You want to know about Thor Heyerdahl?' he said. He wore only a sarong, flip-flops and a headband of fern, which gave him a puckish look. 'First of all, Thor has done a lot for tourism. His books have gone round the world, and without him we would have no economy. But there is one thing we don't like here: he said that we aborigines came from Peru. Now, I'm glad the *Viracocha* has arrived – good, fine, perfect – so you've proved you can go from there to here. But so what? Our use of language is very Polynesian.'

'But what about the two tribes? The short ears and the long ears?'

José put down his pick, sat back, put his hands on his knees, and prepared a history lesson for the evidently hard-of-thinking.

'OK: we have a very traditional legend which says that the long ears were exterminated by the short ears. We therefore hail from the short ears. The long ears were very fat, not tall like us, and they didn't do much work. The short ears did all the work, and were very intelligent. For this reason the short ears said to the long ears: If you're not going to work . . .'

He drew a finger across his throat. 'Only one long ear survived – he was called Ororoina. He married a short ear and had children. For us, this is the truth. So we're of Polynesian origin, like the short ears.'

'I don't think anyone would argue with that,' I said, diplomatically. 'All that our voyage is trying to demonstrate, is that the long ears – the race that were wiped out – *might* have been an early wave of settlers who came from South America.'

'Maybe they were,' shrugged Jose, amiably. 'But we killed them all, so . . . who cares?' He chuckled.

Clearly the long ears were of no further relevance, wherever they came from.

And unless we could persuade the people otherwise, neither was the *Viracocha*.

'Anybody see what happened to *Viracocha*'s other thunderbolt?'

Phil was standing frowning on the dockside, staring at the figurehead on the front of the boat. In one hand the great creator and storm god still held his fearsome staff of lightning. The other was missing, a wooden stump in its place.

Jorge sighed sadly. 'It fell off, *capitán* – into the harbour.'

'Nobody managed to get it back?'

A general shrug passed round the boat like a palsied Mexican wave. Marco munched something hungrily. From the cabin came the sound of snoring.

In truth, a week in harbour had done what six at sea could not. Our once proud vessel was looking old. Her bow had grown grizzled and whiskery from constant butting on the concrete dock, and the drag on her anchor line had prised apart the twin stern like the prongs of a bent pitchfork. Little columns of flies were dancing above the brown patches of dried fishblood. Bits of the cabin, oddments of rope, were missing.

And it wasn't only the boat that was falling apart. It was getting harder to assemble the crew. Since we had taken all valuable or personal equipment to Phil and Eli's room at the guest house, the *Viracocha* had lost her sense of homeliness. Greg, Carlos and Erik were the last to sleep on board, and they soon found a room with new friends. Marco and Jorge were living in a store cupboard at the guest house, and nobody had seen much of Stephane since he had discovered the local disco.

Visitors too, had grown more scarce. Even Pablo the duck was not drawing the crowds like he used to, after one fateful afternoon on which the boat had worn through her moorings and swung suddenly out into the harbour bearing a squealing party of primary schoolchildren. Carlos, the lone crew member on board at the time, had averted near-disaster by diving into the harbour with a climbing rope between his teeth and swimming ashore, enabling us to pull them back to safety. The children left white-faced, and didn't come back.

Today we had been called out by an angry naval officer, who had seen the now empty hull break free again, swing dangerously from her anchor. We had pulled her back to the quay with heavy hearts.

'It's like she wants to go back to sea,' said Greg now, patting her razzled old flanks with sad affection. 'Like she knows what's coming.'

'I don't suppose *you* have any bright ideas?'

The Wise One did not surprise me. He continued to peer at me down his long, stone nose. Around us on the hillside, dozens of other stone *moai* reared from the scratchy, windswept grass, uniformly indifferent, mysterious, inscrutable, and tall as houses. Others lay half-formed, still attached to the quarry wall when the ancient stonemasons for some reason had dropped their tools and left for ever. By that time there were already 600 of them, between six and ten metres tall, and somehow transported to every part of the island. Here alone fifty stood where they had been left, as if walking out of the hillside, on their way somewhere.

The Wise One was different from the others. He was my favourite. Somehow, he'd fallen aslant so that his head was cocked quizzically to one side, as if he was actually listening. He listened in the way that wise people often did, wordlessly, seeming to see through all your frantic gabbling until you slowed down, talked yourself to a standstill. He'd been there for centuries of course, calm and all-seeing, listening with those long ears of his.

But even he hadn't seen the first voyagers arrive; he couldn't tell us where his long-eared creators had come from; and he couldn't intervene to save the *Viracocha*.

'Weird place, huh?' said Greg, wading through the rippling sea of long grass behind me. 'Like we're being watched.'

We were in our final days on the island. Phil had called us all together for a crew outing, a day of island exploration, a last-ditch attempt to resurrect the solidarity and spirit that had brought us across the sea together. Looking across the hillside of the quarry of the *moai*, Ranu Raraku, I could see everyone except Carlos, who was cradling some huge and unspecified grudge elsewhere. We'd spent the day touring the island with help from Dany, who seemed to materialise unnervingly at each destination like a spirit guide. From Anakena beach, an unspoilt horseshoe of white sand where King Hotu Matua – and possibly the original *Viracocha* – had landed, we'd found a rougher-hewn *moai* dating back only to 1956.

It had been carved and erected as an experiment under Thor Heyerdahl's leadership by a team of the last remaining descendants of the long ears – now dead. Later, we had hiked up to the rim of the vast Rano Kau crater, surveyed its weird and mottled patchwork of ponds and reedbeds. Nearby, on the cliffs at the deserted ceremonial 'birdman' village of Orongo, we had stood and looked out over Motu Kao Kao, the jagged rock we had narrowly avoided on our approach.

Our arrival seemed a long time ago now. In two days we'd all separate, get on planes, it would be the end. We had a day to save the *Viracocha*, but it wasn't looking good. The people of Arica had stalled, unsure how to get a 25-tonne, waterlogged reed hull back to mainland Chile. Dany, still desperate to preserve her, had found a suitable patch of ground on which to build a shelter, but neither he nor La Mama was able to prevail against the will of their people. And it seemed a solid will. I had asked the island priest for advice. 'Burn her,' he said, kindly but firmly. 'She has served her purpose now.'

So here we were, out among the ruins of an ancient civilisation, steeling ourselves for our own day of reckoning, rekindling our team spirit, and catching up on a bit of gossip.

'How is your new girlfriend?' I asked Stephane, winking. I hadn't seen him for days.

'Never try anything with an island girl, that's my advice,' he said, wincing at some undisclosed memory. 'You've got to deal with her whole family. Far too complicated!'

'So what happened to settling down?' I teased.

He grinned and slapped my shoulder. 'Soon, *hermano*, soon!'

Behind us, Phil and Erik were deep in conversation about *totora* reeds, while up ahead, Dany was pointing out the belly of a *moai*, on which was carved what looked suspiciously like a reed boat with three masts.

We were standing on the outer southern slope of the crater, looking seaward at the drama of an approaching rainstorm. Silhouetted cliffs sliced into the ocean like saw blades, spray curled up around the point, while the last antenna-like shafts of sunlight probed the foamy surface. Everywhere was windswept grass, black rocks, the light like overexposed slide film, the clouds vague and undecided.

'Basically, the mayor has already made his decision,' said Phil, sadly, as we stared out over the sea. 'We can go down fighting, or we can accept it, make something of it, go out in a dignified way. I'm beginning to think it's time to say goodbye. Move on. What does anyone else think?'

We all looked at Erik.

'Burn her,' he said quietly. 'But with dignity.'

First thing on the morning before Good Friday, the crane began its work. We watched it groan and scream as the steel hawsers cut into the rotting reeds, dragged the rear end of the hull above the sea in a torrent of greenish water and organic stenches.

'I'm not sure I can watch this,' said Phil, hiding behind his video camera. The boat was too heavy to lift from the water in one go, and had to be dragged instead, sluglike over the edge of the quay, breaking open like bread.

'Wait!' shouted Phil suddenly, as the crane dragged the fractured shape to a standstill. He climbed up on to the twisted bow, got out his pocket knife and began cutting feverishly at the reeds, binding foot-long swathes of them together with left-over string. 'I've got to keep something.'

The drivers broke for lunch. 'We'll continue this afternoon,' said the mayor, without making eye contact.

'I don't think I can bear to see her burned,' said Phil.

Dany walked up flustered. We had asked him to prepare a

simple ritual for the moment of her burning – something traditional, fitting.

'Phil, everything's ready for the ceremony, but there wasn't
enough money to buy a chicken.'

'A chicken?' said Phil.

'In Rapa Nui, we sometimes sacrifice a chicken on this sort of
occasion. But it's not essential.'

Phil gave a sad, dark smile and put his arm round Dany's shoulder.

'Don't worry about the chicken.'

We went back to the guest house for a last lunch together, but
found that Carlos was still missing. Phil shrugged. 'I don't know
what's wrong with that guy. It's like he's totally disconnected now.
I can't reach him. I don't even know where he is.'

We set out for the ceremony at 2 p.m. in brilliant sunshine. It
was a perfect afternoon, the sea leaping and thrashing exultantly as
we wove along the coast road, its spray magnesium-white. Above
us, ranks of heaped cumulus clouds moved slowly across the sky
like stately galleons. The only oddity was a single dark cloud,
which seemed to hang directly ahead of us.

'That ain't cloud,' said Greg suddenly. 'That's smoke.'

It was unmistakable: from just beyond the next hill, plumes of
dirty yellowish smoke writhing skywards. Phil shook his head in
mute disbelief.

'They wouldn't start burning her without us,' said Eli.

Yet they had. We crested the last hill, and drove down into the
harbour to find the boat already well ablaze. Council officials,
under the order of the mayor, were tossing buckets of petrol on the
blackened hull, many of them with lit cigarettes in their mouths,
and the Chilean TV cameraman was filming. He looked somewhat
sheepish as we approached, incredulously. A few islanders, standing in a rowdy huddle with beer cans, went quiet too.

'You started already?' said Phil, keeping his voice level.

The cameraman shrugged. 'The mayor said you didn't want to see it.'

I noticed Carlos was among those already watching, dressed in a black shirt and garlanded with white flowers. 'I saw the smoke,' he said. He was lodging up the road. 'So I came to see what was happening.'

Phil was still shaking his head, when an elderly man in khaki shorts, stepped forward, carrying what looked like a Brownie box camera round his neck. Like a colonial hunter stranded in the wrong decade, he lacked only a pith helmet and handlebar moustache. He was crying.

'You are the captain?' he said to Phil, wiping his eyes. 'This is your ship?'

'*Was*,' said Phil, still in shock.

'My name is Germán Carrasco,' he said. 'I sailed with Thor Heyerdahl aboard *Tigris* in 1978.'

An astonished smile of recognition broke on to Phil's face. *Tigris* had sailed through the Persian Gulf and Indian Ocean for five months before finding its onward journey blocked by warmongering nations around Djibouti.

'We burned *Tigris* too, as a kind of protest against inhumanity,' continued the old man, clasping Phil's hand, looking into the flames. 'It was one of the most emotional moments of my life. This brings it all back as if it was yesterday. Your boat is – *was* – just like her.'

Phil looked wondrously confused. 'That's incredible *señor*. But. . . So you came here especially to see . . . ?'

'No! It's pure coincidence! I had never heard of your expedition until I saw your boat this week. I am here visiting my old friend Juan Haoa,' said Germán. 'He is an island elder, and a great friend of Thor.'

Beside him stood a wizened islander, who nodded solemnly.

His eyes were like deep pools. 'This is a great shame,' he said, pointing at what was left of the ship. 'She was a beautiful vessel, and should have been accorded more respect. I am sorry for what has happened.'

Phil nodded and smiled sadly. 'We would be very honoured if you would join us in our ceremony,' he said, gesturing all onlookers to group themselves upwind of the smoke. There was nothing for it but to begin, salvage our dignity. The mayor and his men disappeared like all good undertakers. Dany, dressed in his strange robes, stepped forward carrying a stick with feathers on the end, and shook it at the smouldering black heap, muttering strange incantations which nobody could decipher. He continued for five minutes, then bowed his head for a few seconds, then turned round.

'It is done,' he said to Phil. At that moment there was a cough from the little crowd that had gathered. A woman stepped forward, wearing a wreath of plaited fern on her head.

'My name is Sophia, the school music teacher,' she said, unfolding a piece of paper. 'I would like to sing a small tribute to your brave journey.'

'Sure,' said Phil.

Her voice was thin and clear against the crackling of the burning reeds behind us. It soared plaintively, full of hope yet laden with grief, an Aymara hymn whose words seemed to imitate the beating of wings: *raphaphaphashan.*

> *Oh condor, Spirit of heights*
> *Brothers, listen to its vibrating flight*
> *Feel the gentle breeze of its trail.*
> *Who could this messenger be?*
> *Could it be father Viracocha ?*
> *Listen, welcome,*
> *And spread the good news.*

A few feet away, the fire roared furiously, and a piece of rope burned through and dropped its load of blackened reeds, sending burning stubble and ash dancing upwards into the afternoon sky.

Sophia stopped singing, smiled shyly, nodded and stepped back into the crowd. Then a familiar bush of black hair appeared behind her. Hopo, guitar in hand, began strumming a familiar set of chords, bidding us all join in: *Bien-ven-i-do, Vi-ra-co-cha!* Welcome *Viracocha!*

Even Phil couldn't help but smile at the irony. One by one, we all joined in, voices comic and quavery with emotion, none of us able to look the others in the eye, our arms wrapped across one another's shoulders, united one final time: Phil, Erik, Jorge, Marco, Greg, Stephane, Nick, and, finally, Carlos, as lost as the rest of us.

Thrown together by chance and shared longing, we now stared at the blazing remnants of what we had in common.

Phil poked at the smouldering remains of the *Viracocha* with his toe. 'Well,' he said. 'I guess that's it.'

Erik was transfixed by the flames, his face an emotionless mask, giving nothing away except his refusal to show weakness, to compromise his family's honour. Watching him standing dignified amid the smoke, I thought suddenly of his nightmare.

I dreamt that the Viracocha *was on fire . . . and however hard we tried we couldn't put it out . . .*

These things are usually only symbols.

But not this time.

The next morning, a taxi, bound for the airport, pulled up alongside the black and still smoking pyre at Hanga Piko docks, and a man got out. He stood for a moment, looking at what lay before him, then pulled something from his coat pocket — a small, brightly coloured clay pot. Bending down, he emptied its contents on to the ashes and stared for some time, his eyes hidden by sunglasses.

Then he got back into the car, and was gone.

Epilogue

Thor Revisited

The tyres of the hire care yelped as we swung round another hair-pin, climbing steadily into the mountains of Tenerife. Phil gripped the wheel and grinned.

'This is it, Nickers,' he said. 'It's actually going to happen.'

It was a flawless December morning on the Spanish island. Far below us, depleted ranks of winter sun-worshippers were under-going ritual anointings with Factor 8, as jet-skis buzzed at the margins of a shimmering Mediterranean.

'Have you practised your opening line?' I asked, as we barrelled up narrow streets frothed with bougainvillea.

'You bet,' said Phil. 'It's an honour and a privilege to meet you, sir.' Not a flicker of irony disturbed the edges of his neatly clipped beard.

Getting off the plane the previous day with all the beach tourists laden with inflatable lilos and already smelling of suntan oil, I'd felt a twinge of disappointment that the world's most famous explorer had ended up living in this capital of European package holidays. It seemed somehow inappropriate, like meeting Egon Ronay in the queue at McDonalds.

But up here in the mountains, away from the beaches and time-shares, the gravity and importance of our pilgrimage was quietly closing in around me, like the sandstone cliffs which loomed as we wound further up the valley. It was like driving up Mount Olympus to meet the gods – or more accurately, the *god*.

Thor.

Eight months had passed since we had watched the *Viracocha* burn.

News from the rest of the crew had filtered back sporadically, via email, but few of us had remained in regular contact. Greg had returned home to his tree surgery in Texas, and was considering whether to take on Jorge, who was having the usual problems finding permanent work in a Chile now hit by recession.

In the mean time, Jorge had dramatically severed all contact with Carlos, who he claimed had declared on local Arican radio that he had been taken in by a captainless ship of fools. We had apparently reached dry land only through a combination of luck, providence and his own sound judgement. I felt sad to hear of him ostracising himself like this. He was, after all, partly right.

Erik was busy catching up on his lost semester at college in La Paz, and desperately trying not to become lured on to another expedition – though the last thing I had heard was that he was busy building a new reed boat for the British explorer Colonel John Blashford Snell. Marco, meanwhile, had returned to his wife and children in Santiago and (ignoring his most obvious calling as a game-show host) shortly afterwards had landed a promotion as manager in a jewellery business.

Pablo the Duck, more or less accustomed to a lifestyle as a minor celebrity, had gone to live with La Mama.

Stephane had stayed a further month on Easter Island, before working a free passage as a night watchman on a supply ship back to Valparaiso. He had spent several weeks wandering slowly up mainland Chile in an increasingly joyless hedonistic haze until he reached Lima, Peru. There, quite suddenly, he met his destined *mujer tranquila*. She was a pretty Peruvian called Nena, an old friend seen with new eyes. They went back to France together, promptly got married, and were now trying for their first baby.

I had to read that particular email several times.

My own return home to Edinburgh had involved somewhat less jolting changes, though my experiences had left an odd confection of after-effects. After a year and a half out of the office, I preferred not to contemplate a staff newspaper job, and had instead decided to freelance indefinitely, travelling on short commissions to Oman and Zanzibar that autumn. In another sense I felt more rooted in Scotland than ever before. I volunteered as a youth leader and enrolled in a rowing squad, trying, perhaps, to recreate the closeness of the floating family I had lost. I even joined a church.

At the same time, I was intrigued to learn just how risky ordinary life seemed to have become in my absence. The newspapers were full of it: food poisoning was on the increase; supermarket shoppers risked being assaulted due to 'trolley rage'; farmyard animals were going crazy; children were maiming themselves on little metallic scooters. A new series called '999' showed terrifying reconstructions of people accidentally impaled on park railings or being electrocuted by their own hedge-clippers. It was enough to reduce you to permanent whimpering stasis in a darkened room — and even there you risked deep-vein thrombosis.

Had we always been this obsessed with our personal safety? Or had I just not noticed it before? In such a climate, mention of my journey on the *Viracocha* elicited a surprisingly broad range of responses. There were some people, usually with children and hefty mortgages, who said I was mad, by which they meant irresponsible (which was apparently much worse). Others, usually young men or those having mid-life crises, were stricken with envious yearning. But most simply lit up and said: 'You mean like *Kon-Tiki?*'

Thor Heyerdahl, I was discovering, was still very much a popular hero, despite – or perhaps because of – the inexorable march of the safety inspectors. An older family friend recalled with untrammelled nostalgia how she had spent an hour showing the explorer round an Ulster museum in the 1960s: 'I remember his eyes – deep blue, very intense – he always seemed to be looking for something in the distance.'

My first real opportunity for library research into the Norwegian revealed a less flattering picture, however. Yes, he was a friend of presidents and monarchs, showered with plaudits and honorary degrees, a consummate showman with a documentary Oscar to his name. But across wide swathes of the scientific community he seemed to be considered deeply batty.

'His efforts in the Pacific greatly resemble the muddling attentions of, say, the hack writer of detective stories when faced with an actual crime scene,' the writer Paul Theroux had claimed, after interviewing a number of archaeologists for his book *The Happy Isles of Oceania*. 'In a lifetime of nutty theorizing, Heyerdahl's single success was his proof, in *Kon-Tiki*, that six middle-class Scandinavians could successfully crash-land their raft on a coral atoll in the middle of nowhere.'

He had 'painted himself into a corner' claimed two critics Paul Bahn and John Flenley, his Easter Island theory 'a tottering edifice precariously based on preconceptions, extreme subjectivity,

distortions and very little hard evidence.' What new evidence there
was certainly didn't seem to be helping him much. Pollen from the
reeds he believed to have been brought from South America by
pre-Inca boatmen had been genetically tested and found to be
30,000 years old; the long ears were now widely believed to have
arrived from a Polynesian island to the west, probably the
Marquesas.

It was difficult to resist the thought that in trying to strengthen
Heyerdahl's theory, we had backed the wrong horse.

And yet I couldn't let it go. Nobody had yet given a convincing
explanation for the presence of the South American sweet potato.
And I sensed the irritation of Heyerdahl's critics seemed to run
much deeper than mere scientific debate. His recent autobiography
seemed modest in its claims, compared to the bitchy, dismissive
verdicts of specialists. It was as if they were railing less against
what he had said than what he represented, still, after sixty years of
study: an interloper, a perpetual straddler of disciplines, popular-
ising science, taking it out of the laboratory into the world.

All the same, I couldn't help thinking it was a little ironic that
we had been branded 'unscientific' by a man who had himself
been dismissed as a crank by scientists for much of his adult life.
Shouldn't us cranks stick together? It continued to rankle with me,
however much I told myself it didn't matter. Which was why,
when Phil emailed me one day to say he'd arranged a meeting, I
bought a plane ticket the same afternoon.

Phil had been keeping himself busy since the trip, guiding on
mountains, giving slide presentations, and writing conciliatory
faxes to his great mentor. Still equipped with a seemingly inde-
structible optimism and his plan to circumnavigate the globe (not
to mention his Iridium phone, unexpectedly resurrected after its
doomed satellites passed to a new company, thanks party to intervention from a disgruntled customer known as the Pentagon), he

intended to build another reed boat, *Viracocha II*, on Easter Island and sail it to Australia in 2003. This time around he was determined to do it with the blessing of Heyerdahl. Germán Carrasco, the *Tigris* crewmember we had met on Easter Island, had done a lot of good groundwork, having flown over to visit his old friend and argue our case for us. Now, with a meeting set up, Phil was hoping to clear the air, receive his long-awaited benediction.

My own agenda was a little different, I realised, my pilgrimage more agnostic.

I wanted to meet the great Thor to find out, finally, if I believed in him or not.

Phil pulled the car into a roadside repair shop, wound down the window, beckoned to a mechanic. We were lost.

'Excuse me, do you know the place where Thor Heyerdahl works?' asked Phil. The man, stubble-headed, twenty-something, looked blank, wiped his hands slowly on his overalls.

'Is he a mechanic?'

Phil looked exasperated. 'He's an explorer – pretty famous actually. He's got a museum somewhere in Guimar – that's this village, right?'

The man frowned. 'Yeah – but I've never heard of any explorer.'

Phil peered over his shades.

'I think he's been excavating some pyramids . . .'

The man's face brightened. 'Back down the road, take a left . . .'

The Pyramids of Guimar were what had first attracted Thor Heyerdahl to live in Tenerife – that, and a chance meeting with the woman who was to become his third wife. In 1991, local archaeologists had unearthed what they thought were agricultural terraces. But Heyerdahl, flying in on a strong hunch after reading a newspaper article, argued that they were ceremonial platforms aligned for summer and winter solstices.

Now that they had been restored, you could see what he meant. Before us on the hillside were six flat-topped rectangular pyramids in rust-coloured volcanic stone, fronted by a smart low-roofed visitor centre and museum. With half an hour to spare before our noon appointment, we checked in with a receptionist and wandered among the pyramids in a silence broken only by cicadas. We were, according to the press blurb, in an 'ethnographic park'. The pyramids that towered above us, it was argued, were startlingly similar to those found in Egypt, Mexico, Mesopotamia and Peru, adding a further layer to Heyerdahl's underpinning 'big idea' that diverse ancient civilisations across the world were somehow spawned from a common source.

Diffusionism, as this idea is generally known, was rather out of fashion among scientists these days, according to my research. The opposing isolationists scoffed at Heyerdahl's drawing of parallels between, say, pyramids and sun worship in Egypt and Latin America. Even a child with building blocks would eventually come up with a pyramid, they argued, and the sun was an obvious focus for worship — wasn't it more likely that two primitive civilisations separated by a vast ocean simply came up with them independently?

Yet in the museum adjoining the pyramids, Heyerdahl had displayed scores of closer parallels — suspicious likenesses in intricate pottery and carving, matching statues from disparate civilisations, reed boats carved on pyramids and *moai* — while leaving the visitor to make up his own mind. Given what we now knew personally about the reliability of reed boats over large distances, surely it wasn't such a cranky hypothesis to suggest that they may have emerged from a common source? I was grudgingly impressed.

Further down the hillside, shaded under an enormous marquee, stood replicas of all Heyerdahl's various watercraft — *Kon-Tiki, Ra II, Tigris* — and two by Kitín Muñoz. Phil eyed them silently. 'Maybe one day there'll be a replica *Viracocha* in here?' I suggested.

Phil looked at his watch, and started walking back up the path. 'That all depends,' he said, 'on what happens now.'

The first thing that struck me about Dr Thor Heyerdahl was his age. It wasn't that he wore his eighty-six years heavily – quite the opposite. In fact he looked about seventy-five as he rounded the corner of the museum, his snowy white hair almost hidden under a Lacoste baseball cap. But it was a shock, none the less. I had spent the last few months reading books from which he grinned like a young, Nordic Kirk Douglas, and nobody expects great explorers to get old.

'It is *more* than a great honour to meet you,' said Phil, improvising slightly in his excitement as we all shook hands. 'Thank you so much for agreeing to see us.'

Heyerdahl looked awkward, his watery eyes flicking downwards involuntarily. At his side was his French wife Jacqueline, a glamorous former actress some decades younger, who smiled sympathetically as she took our hands in turn. Clearly, nobody was under any illusion why we were there.

'I am sorry about the criticism your expedition received,' said Heyerdahl carefully, cutting through the pleasantries. His voice was papery, restrained, his English strongly accented.

'It wasn't your fault,' said Phil, with a good-natured smile.

'No,' said Heyerdahl. He turned towards the exit. 'But let us go and have lunch by the ocean and see if we can resolve things.'

In the car on the way back down the winding road he listened, nodding gravely like a high court judge, as Phil made his case for the defence, passing photos, documents and brochures to him in the passenger seat.

'What about the flotation devices, the nails in the mast?' asked Heyerdahl.

'All lies,' said Phil. 'Our only non-authentic material was a small amount of plastic string on the innermost bundles.'

There was a silence as Heyerdahl scrutinised a colour photo of the *Viracocha*. I could tell he was impressed. 'So the string had no effect on buoyancy or direction,' he mused presently. 'The only real effect was that it gave people something to criticise . . .'

By the time we had finished our fish course at the little café on the seafront, things were looking very good indeed. 'I think the scientific result of this reed ship voyage is very important and very positive, I think we must admit this,' said Heyerdahl, unprompted. 'It's the first primitive vessel that has shown that it is possible to navigate directly from South America to Easter Island.'

He promised to try and clear up the 'misunderstanding' with his friend Kitin Muñoz, and everybody steered politely around what he himself had said about us. Instead, Phil, glowing from his benediction, engaged him in an increasingly animated discussion involving molluscs, use of *guaras*, the best time for cutting reeds, and the importance of certain knots on lateral ropes.

Jacqueline, sipping at a glass of white wine, smiled as her husband's eyes grew bright and wistful. 'You're lucky to catch us in Tenerife,' she told me. 'We're rarely at home – in fact we're going down the Nile the day after tomorrow.' It was, incredibly, their seventy-first trip that year, she said, and Thor showed no signs of slowing down. He was working on three different book manuscripts even now, trying to set down his life's work, and digging feverishly in his vegetable patch each afternoon to keep his mind and body agile.

But for this afternoon, at least, he was allowing himself a few hours of leisure to talk shop with a fellow explorer.

'And tell me,' he said, leaning closer to Phil across the table, the two generations almost invisible between them. 'Did you feel a special kind of security in a reed boat?'

'Absolutely,' smiled Phil. 'I never had any doubts about the boat.'

Heyerdahl nodded nostalgically. 'Correctly built, they are the safest form of maritime transport.'

He absolutely meant it too. I had been amused to read that he had once been terrified of water, until falling into a river on some tropical island, when he realised that 'the water buoyed me up instead of sucking me down'. Clearly I was in the company of two incurable optimists. What, I wondered, would Thor have made of Carlos's strange premonition, or Erik's dream? Had he ever found himself out of his depth, definitively non-self-sufficient, praying for outside help? I hazarded a carefully worded question. Thor eyed me with interest for the first time.

'I definitely think that if you really believe, you can do a lot of things you cannot explain,' he said, thoughtfully. 'I myself have often had contact with . . . something – I don't think it's up in the sky above the clouds or down in the ground – but there is something inside myself, when I have managed to get in contact with it, which has helped me through a lot of difficult situations. Without it, I would have been dead twenty times over. I don't think we can get away from the fact that there is a creative power, whether we call it God or the forces of evolution. We must not believe that the human brain is born out of nothing.'

I nodded back, thinking of nights under the wide heavens, of fish flashing silently along glassy waves, of strange shivers of knowing at the creaking helm. But when I thought of the human brain, I still saw wrestling matches in squeaking rubber canoes, the almost daily splintering of *guaras*, or furious six-man tangos with delinquent sails.

'How did you choose your crews, Dr Heyerdahl?' I asked suddenly, biting the bullet. 'Was it important to have people who knew exactly what they were doing?'

Phil eyed me with a slight frown, seeing a critical cloud looming over an otherwise perfect meeting.

But Heyerdahl sat back and smiled. He knew what I was getting at.

'What the critics need to understand about these voyages is that it's not the crew that is fantastic, but the reed boat they're sitting on. When I set off on *Kon-Tiki*, I had no form of training in maritime affairs. Yet I came back and I was applauded by admiralties for my seamanship! It was the most ridiculous experience in my life!'

He burst into guffaws, his eyes suddenly branching crow's feet, and we all laughed with him.

'No, my friends,' he said, pushing back his chair to get up. 'Experience is not as important as a good sense of humour.'

Appendix A
The Easter Island Enigma

Anyone hoping for a detailed scientific defence of Thor Heyerdahl's theories of Polynesian migration may by now have realised that this book isn't it. In practice it's difficult to find a total defence of such multifaceted ideas outside the work of the man himself. Nevertheless, even a layman perusing recent academic debate over Easter Island can see that the case against Heyerdahl's central propositions isn't quite as firmly closed as his critics would like us to believe.

'There is no "mystery" to Rapanui,' asserts philologist Steven Roger Fischer in the first sentence of the introduction to the 1993 volume *Easter Island Studies*, clearly with Heyerdahl in mind. 'After its very early settlement by one canoeful of East Polynesians possibly from the Marquesas Islands, it seems likely that Rapanui remained culturally isolated for over a millennium and a half.'

This is certainly the majority view. If an entirely different Amerindian race arrived from the other direction, say Heyerdahl's critics, where is the evidence? So far, all skeletal remains point the other way – even indicating origins in Polynesia's Gambier Islands according to one recent study. Likewise gene mapping in the Pacific region has so far revealed no Amerindian influence. 'Population genetics,' claims British geneticist Steve Jones, 'has sunk the *Kon-Tiki*.'

And yet mysteries *do* remain. Part of the problem is that a lack of evidence is itself consistent with Heyerdahl's theory. If, as he suggests, the entire 'long-ear' tribe was systematically exterminated and then incinerated by warring opponents, it's perhaps not surprising that nobody's yet stumbled on their bone or DNA samples. That legend – the same one we heard during our stay – holds that the long ears were pushed, en masse, on to a pyre of their own making after being surprised from behind at the edge of their own defensive ditch. Iko's Trench, named after the vanquished chief, has been dismissed as a natural feature by those who are sceptical about the legend. Nevertheless, excavations by an archaeologist on Heyerdahl's team did uncover a thick layer of ash and charcoal there, indicative of a fierce fire which burned for some time.

None of this proves the existence, far less the identity, of any massacred tribe; but neither does the absence of evidence *disprove* it. And if, as the legend has it, only one long ear survived among thousands of short ears, genetic proof either way is likely to remain elusive.

Which leaves the *Kon-Tiki* not so much sunk as irritatingly adrift.

It is certainly true that the raft of Heyerdahl's original argument has been through some stormy seas since he first outraged the scientific establishment with the idea of long-distance Amerindian voyagers.

Research by John Flenley has shown, for example, that the island's *totora* was not grown from the seeds of pre-Inca reed boats, as Heyerdahl proposed – carbon dating on its pollen indicated that it had been present for 30,000 years. (This does not prove that the South Americans did not come, of course – only that it wasn't they who planted the *totora*.) His identification of a number of distinct architectural periods marking different waves of settlers has also been widely dismissed in favour of an unbroken progression suggesting only one race, as Fischer states above.

Yet even if parts of his original raft of theories have apparently washed away, others seem resolutely buoyant. Heyerdahl contests that nobody in the scientific community has adequately explained the similarity between the superb façade of closely fitting blocks on one of the *ahu* (ceremonial platforms) of the *moai*, and Inca walls in Cusco, Peru.

And the most enduring thorn in the side of his critics remains the early presence of the sweet potato on Easter Island. There is broad agreement that both the plant and its Rapa Nui name, *kumara*, originate in South America. So how did it come to be here, well before Europeans 'discovered' the island?

Some have conceded that contact with America is a possibility, though many prefer to believe that it was the Rapa Nui who travelled to the Americas and then brought the sweet potato back with them. An experimental voyage in a replica double-hulled Polynesian voyaging canoe, *Hokule'a*, in 1999 successfully reached Easter Island from Hawaii via Mangareva, using Heyerdahl's pioneering methodology to try and strengthen this opposing point. But of course, Heyerdahl has never denied that Polynesians were good navigators and settled most of Polynesia in that way — only that they were necessarily the first to reach Easter Island.

Interestingly, only one of the dozens of experimental raft expeditions that have followed the *Kon-Tiki* has ever attempted to make the trip *against* the prevailing winds and currents from Polynesia to South America. Frenchman Eric de Bisschop was determined to prove it was possible in 1957, but had to be rescued by the Chilean Navy 1000 miles from his destination.

Few now question, as they did in 1947, the ideal winds and current for east—west voyaging, or indeed the basic seagoing ability of the pre-Inca civilisations of South America — particularly after Heyerdahl's undisputed 1952 discovery of pottery on the Galapagos Islands. It is true that there remains an uncomfortable lack of such pottery on Easter Island — though as some of Heyerdahl's sympathisers have pointed out, such weighty artefacts would be the first to be thrown overboard if a long-distance reed boat sank too low in the water. Their destination also lacked the raw materials from which to fashion new ones — assuming the potters even survived the journey.

In any case, if the critics want convincing evidence of cultural exports between South America and Easter Island, they need look no further than one of Heyerdahl's most startling recent discoveries at the huge 140-acre excavation of Túcume, Peru, over the past decade or so. Here, in a small temple mount among 700-metre long adobe step pyramids, archaeologists uncovered well preserved reliefs showing two large sea-going reed boats and 'birdmen' that are suspiciously similar to those found on Easter Island. The indications are that the Peruvian motif is the earlier — if so, it would suggest that the birdman cult was brought to Easter Island from Peru.

Unfortunately, many critics have proved unwilling to engage with any of this new evidence. The most revealing comment was that of American researcher Jo Anne Van Tilberg, who on hearing that Heyerdahl was beginning excavations there, remarked: 'My personal condolences to colleagues in Peruvian studies.' It would seem that Heyerdahl's detractors have long since made up their minds to ignore him regardless of what he turns up.

Indeed, this cliquey and overkilling attitude is more puzzling to the lay onlooker than anything in Heyerdahl's theories – and arguably does more harm to the reputation of science. He has been accused of being a racial supremacist (on the basis that the man-god Viracocha was reputed to have white skin) and a buffoon, patronised as 'the swashbuckling Señor Kon-Tiki' and most outrageously classified by Theroux as 'a nuisance, an obstruction and a pest'.

So what, exactly, has been his crime? As far as one can tell, to have entranced a generation of ordinary readers with the possibilities of Polynesian migration, by daring to take science beyond the laboratory and on to the sea.

If, in the unifying melting pot of his mind, he has occasionally stirred in a little too much imagination and conjecture, Heyerdahl's critics still have him to thank for the enormous expansion of interest, funding and research in the field that resulted from his outlandish experiment. Many, whether they admit it or not, will have been attracted to that field in the first place by reading his books.

'Those who look down on Heyerdahl's work,' points out the anthropologist P. J. Capelotti in his recent book *Sea Drift*, 'do so from a convenient perch atop his broad Viking shoulders.' Capelotti, a lecturer at Penn State University, Pennsylvania, is one of an increasing number of mainstream scientists who are now standing up to defend Heyerdahl against what they perceive as a long-standing pattern of misinformation over his theories. Donald P. Ryan, an archaeologist at the Pacific Lutheran University in

Washington, US, is another convinced that the subject of Amerindian influences in Polynesia remains 'sufficiently provocative and viable to keep the door open'. In particular the Túcume discoveries 'seem to confirm that the extent of ancient Peruvian maritime culture may have been hitherto woefully underestimated and several findings might provide a link to Easter Island'.

Like many of his peers, Ryan had grown up admiring the Norwegian explorer, fascinated by his experiments, and only later heard the rather less flattering assessment by the science community. When he finally met him a few years ago, he 'was pleasantly relieved to find in Heyerdahl an authentic and well-balanced modern Renaissance man – a dedicated, joyful, and unselfish man with an abiding curiosity about this planet's past and a sincere concern about its present and future'.

Ryan was so impressed by Heyerdahl's professionalism and scientific pedigree, that he is now working with him on a revised update of *American Indians in the Pacific* – the Norwegian explorer's definitive, and perhaps final, attempt to draw together the threads of a lifetime's research and persuade the sceptics to keep open minds.

It's unclear whether he will succeed. What is certain is that for the vast majority of Heyerdahl's admirers across the globe, the views of his critics are largely irrelevant. They know him as one of the last great role-models, an ambassador for international understanding, a campaigner against pollution and environmental damage long before it became a fashionable cause, and a man determined to share his passion for knowledge of humanity's epic migration stories.

Appendix B

How to Build a
Reed Boat

by Phil Buck

The *Viracocha* Reed Ship was 64 feet in length with a 16-foot beam (or width). The 1.5 million reeds and 5000 feet of 1-inch and ¾-inch diameter sisal rope that made up the hull weighed 16 tons. The superstructure included two masts, cabin, steering platform and deck and weighed in at an additional 4 tons, and the total rose to an estimated 25 tons once the boat was fully loaded with drinking water, food, equipment and crew (see diagram on p. 299).

The *totora* reeds *(Scirpus Riparius)* were harvested in November of 1998, from the shores of the Peruvian/Bolivian Lake Titicaca, where they grow in abundance. Each reed used was around 1 inch in diameter at the base and 6 feet in length. They were cut 2 feet below the water surface using specially designed sickle-like tools on long poles, and brought ashore in small rowboats. Here they were loosely tied into *amaros* or bundles each containing roughly 500 green reeds. They were stood on end and dried for up to four weeks in the sun, until they were a golden brown colour.

Once dried, the reeds were assembled into at least thirty cylinders or *chorizos* 1.5 feet in diameter and 60 feet in length and bound with synthetic string at 2-foot intervals. The string was used to hold the cylinders together for positioning in the main hull later, and had no strengthening function. The curve of the bow and stern were to be built up later.

Two *ballenas* or whale-like structures were then made by bundling together a number of *chorizos*, resulting in bundles 2 feet deep and 7 feet wide and around 60 feet long. Each *ballena* was designed to act as a 'boat inside a boat', adding rigidity and strength to the vessel.

The jig or cradle was built next, following a crescent shape at its elevated ends to ensure a correct curve to the bow and stern. We used horizontal eucalyptus poles spaced 3 feet apart, supported by vertical poles, the ends of which were buried in the ground. The entire boat was then built a few feet off the ground upon this foundation, which was later reconstructed in Arica.

The first layer to be placed on the cradle was the *estera*, a kind of encircling outer 'skin', which could later be wrapped around what we placed on top of it, to hold everything together and give the ship an outwardly pleasing appearance. We used the best stock of reeds for this skin, weaving them first into several mats and then into two skins each wide enough to wrap around half of the boat. The 'whales' were then lifted on to the skins, side by side, and approximately 3 feet apart. Next the long *chorizos* of reeds were placed directly on top of each 'whale', and loose reeds used to smooth out furrows between cylinders. Finally, each skin was wrapped around and over the top of each result-ing bundle, forming what would eventually be the two parts of the main hull, each roughly 8 feet thick and 64 feet long, lying side by side.

Between them we placed the *corazon* or heart of the vessel, consisting of three long cylinders stacked on top of one another. Alongside this heart we positioned two open-ended wooden boxes – one close to the bow, the other close to the stern – forming slots that would eventually allow the removable centreboards to pass through the hull.

Next came the remarkable process of joining the two main bodies of the hull. We used two unbroken strands of 1-inch sisal rope, each 2250 feet in length. Each spiralled around one large bundle and the *corazon* in revolutions spaced 1 foot apart from bow to stern. Neither rope ever encircled more than one side of the boat – indeed, the separate ropes crossed each other only twice, at the bow and stern – but the two sides were held together by the common core (see diagrams on p. 300).

Then came the laborious task of tightening the ropes, starting at the bow and working towards the stern, using a double pulley system anchored several feet away from the side of vessel. Between five and fifteen people were required to lend a hand in this rigorous procedure, as tight ropes are the key to a reed boat's strength. The ropes were tightened thirty times on each side, drawing the two main bundles together until the heart was compressed and disappeared between them, forming an ingenious, stable, almost double-hulled vessel.

The next phase was to build up the bow and stern. Tapering cones of reeds were jammed into the ragged ends of the main reed bundles, and encircled with rope to form a solid bow and double stern each some 8 feet above the main deck of the ship. The double stern – two separate but adjoining cones of *totora* – added more stability and carrying capacity to the ship while at sea. The design was borrowed from an ancient South American

Moche ceramic depicting a double-stern reed ship on a long voyage.

The final step was the attachment of the two continuous 2-foot bundles that formed the gunwales or *sawi*. A ¾-inch rope was wound around each gunwale, passed through each main bundle along the length of the ship (see diagram on p. 301) and was pulled tight several times. The strength and durability of the gunwales was important, as mast stays and other rigging were to be attached directly to them.

After the boat was transported to Chile in December of 1999, the ropes were retightened once again. Two eucalyptus bipod masts were positioned at either end of a bamboo cabin. The masts were held in place by hardwood *zapatos* or 'shoes' roped into the reed bundles. Two rudder oars — eucalyptus shafts with almond wood blades — were lashed to a steering platform at the rear of the cabin. The ship was rigged with 1-inch natural-fibre sisal rope, the same type of rope that encircled her all-important reed bundles. Two removable oak centreboards were placed in the slide boxes fore and aft of the cabin to aid in tacking into the wind. Three eucalyptus fixing points were installed along each side of the boat to enable removable cedar leeboards or *guaras* to be installed on whichever side was downwind at any given time. Two cotton triangular lateen sails were sewn from a design passed on by Cameron McPherson Smith, anthropologist of the Mantena expedition, for which we were very grateful. Full instructions can be found at: www.sfu.ca/~csmith/genstuff/manteno/report99/report.html. The main sail or front sail was painted with two *moai* observing sun rise, while the mizzen or rear sail was displayed the birdman symbol common to both Easter Island and Peru.

Finally, after constructing fore and aft decks and internal bunks and tables from pine planking, we installed a wooden *Viracocha* figurehead on the bow of the completed ship.

For further information consider visiting The Catari Family Hostel 'Inti Karka', a reed boat museum offering lake tours in at Huatajata, Lake Titicaca, Bolivia. Tel: +591 8 115058. Also please feel free to contact Xplora International, of which I am co-Director, at 20 Brown Road, Rowe, Massachusets, MA 01367, USA, buck@incaproject.com, website: www.xplorainterna-tional.com

VIRACOCHA

REEFING POINTS

MAIN SAIL

BIPOD FORE MAST
(EUCALYPTUS, ROPE AND DOWELLING)

VHF RADIO AERIAL

YARD

MIZZEN SAIL

YARD

FORE MAST STAY

BIPOD MIZZEN MAST
(EUCALYPTUS, ROPE
AND DOWELLING)

SPLASH BOARDS

BOW

GUNWALE

BICYCOCHA
GENERATOR
BIKE

ZAPATA -
MAST SHOE

MAST STAYS

CABIN

STEERING
PLATFORM

SIDE DECK

LIFERAFT

FOOD STORAGE

GUARA / LEEBOARD

GALLEY

TOWLINE

FLIP-UP LINE

DOUBLE STERN

GUARA / CENTREBOARD

SAFETY LINE AND BUOY

RUDDER OAR
(EUCALYPTUS POLE)

RUDDER OAR
(EUCALYPTUS POLE)

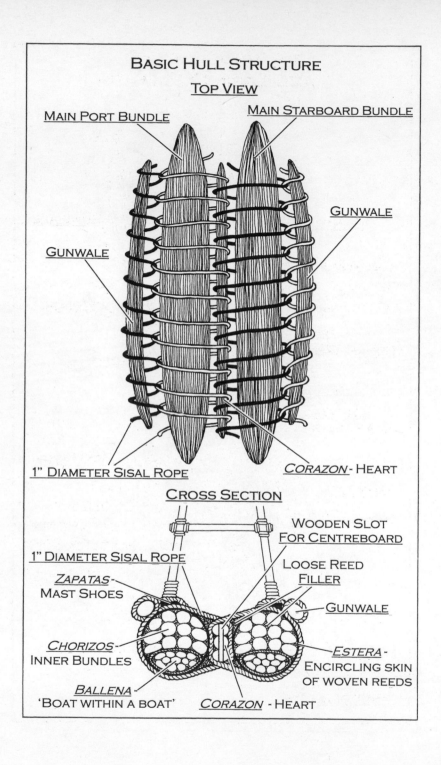

Basic Hull Structure

Top View

Main Port Bundle

Main Starboard Bundle

Gunwale

Gunwale

1" Diameter Sisal Rope

Corazon - Heart

Cross Section

Wooden Slot For Centreboard

1" Diameter Sisal Rope

Loose Reed Filler

Zapatas - Mast Shoes

Gunwale

Chorizos - Inner Bundles

Estera - Encircling skin of woven reeds

Ballena - 'Boat within a boat'

Corazon - Heart

TOP VIEW OF DECK
AND CABIN ELEMENTS

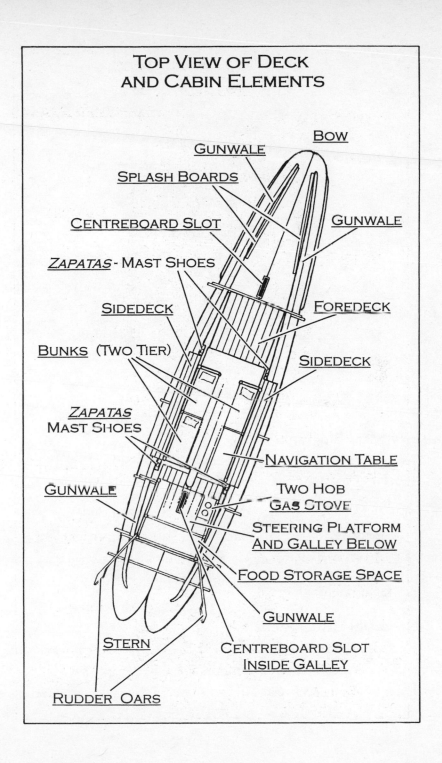

BOW

GUNWALE

SPLASH BOARDS

CENTREBOARD SLOT

ZAPATAS - MAST SHOES

GUNWALE

SIDEDECK

FOREDECK

BUNKS (TWO TIER)

SIDEDECK

ZAPATAS
MAST SHOES

NAVIGATION TABLE

GUNWALE

TWO HOB
GAS STOVE

STEERING PLATFORM
AND GALLEY BELOW

FOOD STORAGE SPACE

GUNWALE

STERN

CENTREBOARD SLOT
INSIDE GALLEY

RUDDER OARS

Bibliography

Heyerdahl Biographies

The Kon-Tiki Man, Christopher Ralling (BBC Books, 1990)
A useful (if uncritical) biography and overview of Heyerdahl's life and
expeditions.

In the Footsteps of Adam, Thor Heyerdahl (Little, Brown, 2000)
Not so much an autobiography as an eccentric ramble through the years.

Heyerdahl Explorations

The Kon-Tiki Expedition, Thor Heyerdahl (Allen & Unwin, London,
1950); reissued Flamingo, London, 1993
The classic voyage reissued with new modern day epilogue answering
critics and catching up with members of the crew.

American Indians in the Pacific, Thor Heyerdahl (Allen & Unwin, London, 1952)
An impressive tome setting out the academic evidence behind the *Kon-Tiki* and Easter Island theories.

Aku Aku: The Secret of Easter Island, Thor Heyerdahl (Allen & Unwin, London, 1958)
The best-selling story of Heyerdahl's 1955–6 archaeological trip to Easter Island.

The Ra Expeditions, Thor Heyerdahl (Allen & Unwin, London, 1971)
Heyerdahl takes to the Atlantic in an adventure even more exciting than *Kon-Tiki*.

The Tigris Expedition, Thor Heyerdahl (Allen & Unwin, London, 1981)
Heyerdahl's most recent reed boat expedition, this time in the Persian Gulf.

Easter Island: The Mystery Solved, Thor Heyerdahl (Souvenir Press, London, 1989)
Recent restatement of Heyerdahl's arguments regarding Easter Island, and a good guide to its history.

Pyramids of Tucumé, Thor Heyerdahl, Daniel H. Sandweiss & Alfredo Narvarez (Thames & Hudson, 1995).
Details of new archaeological discoveries apparently linking Peru with Easter Island.

For a more complete listing of the huge number of books and scientific papers written by Heyerdahl, consult the following website: www.plu.edu/~ryandp/thor.html.
For further information contact The *Kon-Tiki* Museum,

Bygdøynesveien 36, N-0286 Oslo, Norway, Tel: +47 23 08 67
67, Fax: +47 23 08 67 60, Email: kon-tiki@online.no
Website: www.media.uio.no/Kon-Tiki/Museum

Easter Island Anthropology

Easter Island, Earth Island: A message from our past for the future of our planet,
Paul Bahn and John Flenley (Thames & Hudson, London, 1992)
Cambridge Encyclopaedia of Human Evolution, Steve Jones (ed.)
(Cambridge, 1992)
Sea Drift: Rafting Adventures in the Wake of Kon-Tiki, P.J. Capelotti
(Rutgers University Press, 2001)
*Easter Island Studies: Contributions to the History of Rapanui in Memory of
William T. Mulloy*, Steven Roger Fischer (ed.) (Oxbow Books, 1993)
The Happy Isles of Oceania, Paul Theroux (Penguin, 1993)
*Pacific 2000 – Proceedings of the Fifth International Conference on Easter
Island and the Pacific*, Christopher M. Stevenson, Georgia Lee and F.J.
Morin (eds), Easter Island Foundation (2001)

Internet: For a multitude of links to websites and research
covering all sides of the ongoing debate, log on to:
www.netaxs.com/~trance/rapanui.htm

Acknowledgements

An astonishing array of people worked to make the *Viracocha's* voyage possible – many of them involved long before I got off that bus in Huatajata. It's my pleasure, therefore, to pass on the heartfelt thanks of Phil Buck, echoed strongly with my own, to all of those who dared to believe in this improbable dream:

The Expedition: For hospitality, kindness and friendship in Bolivia and Chile (in alphabetical order): Carlos Aguilera, Eduardo Alvarez, Ruben Alvarez, Victor Burgos, the Catari family, Steve Carter, Roberto Cisterna, Anne Cronin, Patricio Delgado, Ines Henriquez, Manuel Herrera, Craig Homan, Ellen Homan, Nicolas Le Corre, the Limache family, Patricia Mckenna, Nirma Montenegro, Diego Nuñez, Jorge Paez, Patricio Palma, Karen Pampaloni, Lorena Plaza, Gustavo Rivas, Arnoldo Rocco,

Fernanda Rodríguez, Ernesto Romero, Guillermina 'Gloria' Salas (for those huge portions!), Richards 'Steiny' Steinbock, Miriam Valladares, Pablo Zepeda, Juan the electrician, Pablo the dozer-driver, Arica Police Department, and all the kind people of Arica who turned up, time after time, to give us encouragement and some much-needed shoving.

On Easter Island: Sophia Abarca, Hector Arevena, Elsa Calderon, Germán Carrasco, Patricio Carrasco, Dany Huke, José Tuki-Pakarati, Juan Haoa, Mara Horo Rapu Tuki, Karlo Huke Atán, Jean-Marc the friendly Frenchman, Rod McCurdy, Pedro Gonzalo Nahoe, Stefanie Pauly, Anny Reyes Huke, Carlos Sierra, Jobani Teave, Hopo Rapu Tuki, Marcos Tuki, and of course the wonderful Ana Lora 'La Mama' Tuki Chavez.

From the US/Europe: Norman Baker, Beyon Buck, Dr Michael Coe, Fred Contrada, Dr Thor Heyerdahl, Rod McCurdy, Andrea Meyer, Cameron McPherson Smith (and others from the Manteño Expedition), Jeff Olmsted, Susan Silvester.

The expedition sponsors: Continental Airlines, PowerBar (including free lessons on human nature), Cascade Designs, Soar Inflatables, Best American Duffels, Stratos Communications, Uni-Solar, Trimble, Northern Airborne Technology, Pelican Cases, Uco Corporation, Fiorentino Para Anchors, Gregory Packs, Swiss Army Brands, Javanet, Teva, Black Bart Paddles, Kelty, Nalgene, Hotel Bahia Chinchorro, Luchetti, Transporte Alanoca, Compania Electrica Arica, Empresa Portuaria Arica, Agua Arica, Icil-Icafal, Crillon Tours, Supermercados Santa Isabel, Gruas Alvarez, Chilean Navy.

And particular thanks from Phil Buck to: Charles Buck, Elizabeth Rodriguez, the reed boat builders, the crew of the *Viracocha*.

The Book: Writing a first book is itself a kind of adventure. I'd like to thank the following for their invaluable navigational help.

For constructive criticism on various drafts: Ali McBride, Mark and Graham Thorpe, Robin Connelly, Lisa Clark; my agent Giles Gordon and my editors Tim Whiting and Stephen Morrow for their boundless enthusiasm and timely tweaks. Many thanks to Steiny for his elegant drawings; and to Nicolas le Corre and Joel Donnet at Gamma for allowing us free access to Nicolas's excellent photos. For writerly encouragement along the way: Jeremy Seal, Philip Marsden (and others at the Arvon Foundation), Cole Moreton, Kathryn Heyman, Ron Ferguson and Michael Riddell; Alan Ruddock, Alan Taylor, Tim Luckhurst, Richard Neville and Jenny Hjul, all at the *Scotsman*, for letting me off the leash in the first place (and Dave Montgomery for making that phone call!). And to the many people who have helped with research: Phil Buck and Eli Rodriguez who gave full access to expedition notes, maps, documents and photographs, and put in many months of work to ensure I had the information I needed; Dr Donald Ryan, P. J. Capelotti, Georgia Lee and George Gill for advice on Rapa Nui; Ken Croswell for astronomical know-how; Kimberly Bland for fruit fly expertise; Heather Walker and RSPB Northern Ireland for tips on duck identification; Dr Colin Graham; and our Bolivian friends José and Dula Pareja.

Finally, to those people without whom this book simply wouldn't exist: to Ali, whose open-handed love has kept me going from the start; to my supportive family, Graham, Jan, Mark, Dan and Han Thorpe, and Desmond and Maralyn McBride, for agreeing not to panic (much); to my long-suffering crewmates aboard the *Viracocha* — Erik, Carlos, Greg, Jorge, Marco and Stephane — whose open hearts and amiable eccentricities taught me so much about community (and so little about cooking).

And above all thanks to Phil Buck, a generous and tolerant leader and now also a good friend, who from the outset has supported and encouraged me in writing a starkly honest account of our voyage. I am deeply grateful both for access to his tireless research and for his willingness to see even our least enlightened moments in print – knowing, perhaps, that air-brushed adventurers are rarely as interesting as ordinary humans who find themselves in deep water . . .

Nick Thorpe
Edinburgh, UK